Buying Wine
in France

Buying Wine in France

THE TRAVELLER'S GUIDE TO CHATEAUX AND VINEYARDS

HILARY WRIGHT

RESEARCH, MAPS AND INSPIRATION:
IAN WRIGHT

MITCHELL BEAZLEY

First published in this edition in 1995
Some of the material first published as *Buying French Wine
from the Château and Vineyard* in 1994
by Mandarin Paperbacks
an imprint of Reed Consumer Books Limited,
Michelin House, 81 Fulham Road
London SW3 6RB
and Auckland, Melbourne, Singapore and Toronto

© 1994, 1995 Reed International Books Limited

Text copyright © Hilary Wright, 1994, 1995
Maps © Reed International Books Limited, 1994, 1995

ISBN 0–85732–707–1

The author and publishers will be grateful for any information
that will assist them in keeping future editions up to date. Although
all reasonable care has been taken in the preparation of this book, neither the
author nor the publishers can accept liability for any consequences
arising from the information contained herein, or
from the use thereof.

A CIP catalogue record for this book is available
from the British Library

Executive Editor: Anne Ryland
Art Director: Jacqui Small
Editor: Stephanie Horner
Design: Bryan Dunn, Richard Johnson
Index: Ann Barrett
Map artwork: Bob Reed
Production: Juliette Butler

Cover photograph: SCOPE/Jacques Guillard

Printed and bound in Finland
Typeset in Monotype Bembo, Gill Sans and Palatino

Contents

How to Use this Book	7
Introduction	9
Why buy wine in France?	9
When to go	11
Planning the route	13
Where to stay and how to book	16
How to buy direct:	18
How to taste	20
A note on winemaking	23
To buy or not to buy	25
Bringing it all back home	27
Getting around, getting along	30
Wine rules and regulations	32
The Regions:	
Alsace	36
Champagne	62
Burgundy	84
The Mâconnais	118

Beaujolais	132
The Northern Rhône	150
The Loire Valley	175
The Pays Nantais	177
Anjou-Saumur	184
Touraine	194
The Golden Triangle	207
The Aube	208
Chablis	214
Sancerre and Pouilly-sur-Loire	221
Bordeaux and Bergerac	229
The Médoc	241
Entre-deux-Mers	255
Bergerac	260
The Côtes de Castillon and Côtes de Francs	267
St-Emilion	269
Pomerol	272
Fronsac	273
Bourg and Blaye	274
Ferry Factfile	281
Further Exploration DIY visits	286
Index	289
Acknowledgments	300

Maps

ALSACE 43
CHAMPAGNE 74
BURGUNDY 94
THE MACONNAIS 121
BEAUJOLAIS 136
THE NORTHERN RHONE 156–7
  Die 168

THE LOIRE VALLEY
  Pays Nantais 181
  Anjou-Saumur 186
  Touraine 197, 199
THE GOLDEN TRIANGLE
  The Aube 208
  Chablis 217
  Sancerre and Pouilly-sur-Loire 222
BORDEAUX AND BERGERAC 240–1

Abbreviations and Symbols

ha	hectares	M	millions
	(1 hectare = 2.47 acres)	FF	French francs
hl	hectolitres	*H*	Hotel
cl	centilitres	*R*	Restaurant
km	kilometres	♥	Wine producer
kg	kilograms		

A Note on Producers, Prices and Opening Hours

All prices and opening times quoted in this guide are based on information supplied in 1993–5 and are correct at the time of going to press. Do bear in mind, however, that the information may change before the date of your visit and telephoning ahead to confirm details and, if necessary, that English-speaking staff will be present, will avoid inconvenience. If you decide to travel with a party of friends, remember that the details of visits to producers apply only to small numbers of visitors, and many estates require an appointment to cater for a group.

What this Book is and How to Use It

This is the book I wish I'd had with me ten years ago when I first went to France. Back then, I didn't know what to expect. I was unsure what to do and rather shy, but even so I enjoyed myself in France's wine country so much that I kept going back, exploring further and further afield. Now that decade of experience is here at your disposal. If you've never been to France's vineyards before, here's all the help you need: advice, encouragement, warnings, and masses of practical tips. More experienced direct winebuyers will also, I hope, find much to deepen their knowledge and expand their horizons. Here, too, are some of the mistakes I made, so that you won't have to make them too!

The Introduction tells you all you need to know to help plan the journey and book accommodation, what to expect when you visit a winemaker, how to taste the wine and discover which ones you most enjoy. I explain the winemaking processes in a simple way, and show you how what you see in a wine producer's cellar will make a difference to what you get in your glass. Finally, there's guidance on how to get it home safely – without destroying your axles.

Each subsequent chapter covers one wine region in detail, starting with what kinds of wine are sold, how the wines are labelled and which might offer best value. I look at the various routes to the wine region and describe a scenic wine route to follow once you're there. I suggest producers to visit, and places to eat and stay; and when there's an interesting wine museum or exhibition nearby you'll find that mentioned too. I also suggest how you can link the various routes together for a longer stay; those in a hurry can explore the Golden Triangle, which actually allows you to visit parts of three different wine regions in a single long weekend.

Each wine route is illustrated by a map, showing H for hotels, R for restaurants and ♥ for producers. And at the end of

each chapter you'll find complete listings of all the establishments mentioned, complete with producer opening hours and
hotel and restaurant prices.

The Ferry Factfile is an unbiased evaluation of the different
ways of crossing the channel, and finally there's advice on
making further wine country explorations on your own. The
whole book offers you a key which unlocks the pleasures of
saving money buying direct from the producers, while enjoying good food and a good time.

Bon voyage!

Introduction

WHY BUY WINE IN FRANCE?

I think everyone's heard by now about the amazing cheapness of wine bought in French supermarkets. Bargains can be had by anyone prepared to cross the Channel for the morning. This stupendous offer is brought to you courtesy of the British government, which has denied British wine merchants the chance to compete on equal terms with the French. Our duty laws impose over £1 in tax on each bottle we buy (the exact amount varies from budget to budget); the French pay about tuppence.

So we cross the Channel in droves, depriving the UK wine trade of millions of pounds in turnover and the Chancellor of vast sums in Excise and VAT revenue. Obviously the sum is not sufficiently vast to make him change his mind, so it's up to us to go and buy yet more wine in France, to make the revenue lost so enormous that he has no option but to 'harmonize' duty rates.

And even then I'd still buy wine in France. It would still be cheaper. Maybe not in the supermarket, but I don't buy wine there anyway. French supermarket wine isn't a patch on what we have available to us in the UK high street. We have teams of hideously well-qualified wine buyers in every supermarket and off-licence chain, dedicated to sniffing out wines from every producing country in the world. In France they have no need of this. Why seek out wines from all around the world when you consider its products inferior to your own? The French are notoriously parochial about the wines they drink, and frankly if I lived there I would be too. If you've got the best wine in the world on your doorstep, they argue, why look further afield?

You won't find the great wines of France in their super-markets because people tend to buy direct from growers. They'll go to a wine region for the weekend and buy a few cases or arrange for a year's supply to be delivered. They make contact with a grower and build up a personal relationship. Dinner party conversations centre around 'my' winegrower – much more fun than drinking an impersonal bottle from a supermarket shelf.

Wouldn't it be wonderful to be able to turn up at a vineyard and arrange for 20 cases to be sent home to you? And at vine-yard prices? There are UK haulage firms which would be happy to transport your wine to your door for as little as £3 a case or less. Unfortunately our friends the UK Customs and Excise take the view that this is a commercial transaction as you are not accompanying the goods, and will levy the full £1-plus duty per bottle. You must import the wine yourself.

So let's do as the French do: visit châteaux and vineyards, make direct contact with winemakers and buy wine at astonish-ing prices. For this is where the real bargains are to be had. My rule of thumb is that you can buy a bottle in the vineyard for about half what you'd pay in the UK high street. This applies just as much to bottles costing £3 as to those at £6; whatever you like to spend on average on a bottle of wine you'll find a bargain in your price range. Only over £10 or so a bottle does the price differential level out. Unless you're in Bordeaux, where the high prices make most of the wines less of a bargain.

Now I know that in order to enjoy these prices you have to spend money – on ferries, petrol, hotels and restaurants. But here again, events are moving in our favour. The opening of the Channel Tunnel has prompted a flurry of price cuts among the ferry companies. They're particularly keen to encourage us to cross to France more frequently, and their new tariffs reflect this. Not that I need any encouragement.

Nostalgia isn't what it was, and neither are French hotel prices, but they still seem reasonable to those of us used to the high cost of British hotels. Then there's the enjoyment of trav-elling in France. Compared to our overcrowded roads, driving in France can be a pleasure. Motorways in particular are quiet (except around Paris, except in rush hour, except in the peak holiday season), largely because you have to pay tolls for the privilege of using them.

Eating in France is also a real pleasure. Sometimes I like to worship in temples of gastronomy, but more often I prefer the simpler cooking of small places with regional dishes and local customers. The value you can find in French restaurants, especially on the fixed-price menus, still amazes me. And the chance to experience a completely different rhythm of life for a few days entices me back again and again.

So although you can certainly argue that you don't save money on the trip as a whole, I'd argue that the experience as a whole knocks buying wine at Sainsbury's into a cocked hat.

WHEN TO GO

Next week. Next month. As soon as possible and as often as possible. Me, I don't need an excuse. But I do have certain rules of thumb: principally, never go to France in August. The French don't believe in off-season holidays. Their *vacances* run from mid-July to the end of August, and woe betide you if you travel on 'black Saturday', the day *le tout Paris* gets into its car and heads to all points south and/or coastal. Families tied to school holidays have no choice; but this book isn't about family holidays, it's about having fun (sorry).

September and October are without doubt the best times to travel to wine regions, to see the harvest. The excitement is almost palpable as tractors steam firmly down the middle of the road, trailers overflowing with grapes. Teams of pickers trudge between rows of vines, their caravans snaked around the edges of fields like wagon trains. Walking through villages, the heady smell of fermentation is everywhere. The two or three weeks of harvest are the culmination of a whole year's work; mistakes now, or bad weather, can severely reduce the year's income. No wonder it's a fraught, hectic time. I adore it.

It's the best of times and the worst of times. The best because you can see all the machinery in operation: conveyor belts loading grapes into the press, juice pouring out of the press as it turns, open fermentation vats frothing away. Suddenly all the theory of how wine is made makes sense, it all comes together. The downside, of course, is that the wine-makers are much too busy actually making the stuff to talk to you about it.

Many small-scale growers don't accept visitors at all during the harvest, or if they do they have much-reduced time to talk

to you. Some larger firms, on the other hand, positively welcome you at this time and will proudly show you all the
processes in detail. It really pays to contact growers in advance
if you plan to visit during the harvest. You won't waste time
trying to see people who are too busy to help you, and you'll
learn a lot from those who <u>are</u> geared up to receive you – especially if you're expected.

Late autumn and winter, when the harvest is safely gathered
in and bubbling away in the cellars, is a good time to go.
Winemakers have more time for you (any excuse to put off
pruning the vines in biting winds and sub-zero temperatures).
Note, though, that many hotels close for a month or more in
winter: January can be a lean month for accommodation.
Spring and early summer, as the buds break on the vine and the
flowers develop, also have their attractions, not least the better
weather.

It makes sense to travel light if you're going to buy wine.
Excess luggage reduces your payload. So do excess passengers.
Although it may be fun to travel in a foursome, you won't have
much room in a family saloon to bring back much wine. In
particular, children with all their paraphernalia take up a great
deal of precious space. Also, children have a different agenda,
and trudging round estates, watching you taste something
they probably don't like is unlikely to feature highly on it. So
this seems like the best possible excuse to leave the children
with the grandparents, or indeed anyone who'll have them, and
take off on your own, otherwise you may find your
loyalties split. I heard a story in Chablis about a prominent
British newsreader who packed his two children off home by
train in order to free their seats for extra cases of wine in the
back of his Volvo.

How long you go for is of course determined by both time
and financial constraints. The visits to most of the wine regions
I describe in the following chapters can be made in a long
weekend, reckoned as five days, taking advantage of the ferry
companies' five-day return ticket. Bordeaux and the Rhône
will easily occupy a week or more, and it's simple to extend the
itineraries if you have more time as there are plenty of estates to
visit and sights to see. The routes are also modular, so that if you
have more time you can join one or two wine regions together
and stay for as long as you can manage.

The decision on where to go can be determined by the kind of wine you prefer, your desire to explore, or your fondness or otherwise for encountering your fellow countrymen and countrywomen while abroad. The Loire valley and Champagne are certainly the most popular regions with Brits, and a fair number get down to Burgundy, but Alsace sees relatively few British cars (Germany and Scandinavia make up for this). Bordeaux is full of tourists of all nationalities.

PLANNING THE ROUTE

There are three elements to consider: getting to the Channel port, choice of Channel transport, route to wine territory. The second element is likely to be determined by where you live. I'm fortunate to be living in Kent, which puts the majority of Channel transport on my doorstep; but when I first travelled to France I lived in Cumbria, and the journey to any Channel port from there is not undertaken lightly. Nor is the M25, and in particular the queue for the Dartford Tunnel, for the faint-hearted, although I believe that if I only travel on the M25 outside rush hour I'll never get caught in snarl-ups, and this has indeed been the case. (This is a very useful belief to have.)

For the north and Scotland, the Hull ferry to Zeebrugge is more useful than is at first apparent. To reach Alsace, Burgundy and the Rhône, the route via Brussels and Luxembourg down to Metz is, if anything, slightly shorter than travelling via Calais; and for Champagne, dropping south at Brussels to Reims is very straightforward. For southerners, Calais is the obvious port for these three regions. Portsmouth to Le Havre avoids London for people in Wales and the west of England but unfortunately you then have to contend with Paris. Portsmouth to St Malo on the other hand, is the most direct route for Muscadet and Bordeaux.

To reach the Loire valley, the situation is rather different. The western Channel crossings are an attractive option, especially if you want to take what airlines so inelegantly call an 'open-jaw' route, out on one crossing and back on another – perfectly permissible if you travel with the same company on both legs. This is a particularly good idea when exploring along the meandering Loire. From Calais, the Loire is a long slog. (Further details are in the Ferry Factfile.)

Once in France, three types of road are at your disposal. Motorways are called 'A' roads (for Autoroute) and offer a useful network, although heavily biased to routing you via Paris. These are toll roads, except on urban stretches. Expect to pay about FF200 one way from Calais to Strasbourg – it's not cheap.

A slower but more comprehensive network is provided by the 'N' roads: Routes Nationales. No tolls, but lots of heavy wagons. The Routes Nationales are the main arterial roads, and personally I don't like using them. I prefer to get where I'm going on the motorway, then switch to 'D' roads for meandering once I'm there.

The 'D' is for Départementale, for roads administered by each separate county (*département*). Each county has its own numbering system, so expect to see many different D1s. These are strictly local roads, often surprisingly wide and quiet, which allow you to devise very attractive routes bypassing towns.

There are many touring maps of France available, but there's only one I give car room to, the Michelin. Published every January, it's a bang-up-to-date, accurate atlas. Make sure you travel with the latest edition, as France is still expanding its motorway network and building bypasses that could make quite a difference to your choice of route.

A new map should help you avoid what happened the first time I tried Continental navigation. Mainland Europe now designates some of its motorways as long-distance Euroroutes, signified by E numbers. Attempting to navigate around Brussels, things went disastrously wrong until I realized that all the E roads had been renumbered. It caused severe marital disharmony until we bought a new map.

I prefer to buy the complete atlas, so that I can fantasize about visiting bits of France I haven't yet been to; others prefer to buy the maps as individual fold-out sheets as they're less cumbersome on your lap. (You can ensure the sheet maps are up-to-date by checking the year of printing, shown in tiny numbers on a corner of the cover.)

The other advantage of using Michelin is that the maps cross-refer with the guidebooks. I do think it's worth obtaining the red Michelin guide to French hotels and restaurants. I find its recommendations reliable and it contains masses of information not possible to include in this guide, such as when a hotel closes, because it changes each year. It can also help if you need an extra stopover en route. If you want to navigate in towns, Michelin red guides are particularly helpful. In the atlas, a red box is drawn around major towns. The area covered by the box is mapped in detail in the red guide.

Other purchases to make before you leave include personal and car insurance – and pick up a reciprocal health treatment E111 form from the Post Office. Many insurance companies offer a free green card as part of the package, which is well worth having. Car recovery and personal insurance are vital, in my opinion, and it's worth shopping around on price. If you intend to make several trips in a year it'll pay you to take out an annual policy, such as that offered by Europ Assistance. The RAC offers vehicle recovery throughout Europe as an add-on to its usual package, but you still have to arrange personal cover. I found last year that this arrangement didn't work out as competitive as a full annual policy.

Another preparation you must make is to adjust the beam on your headlights. This usually involves blanking off a small part of the headlight lens using a rather pricey kit with various adhesive black plastic shapes. You can see the area to be covered up clearly outlined on the headlamp. The Wright Patent Gaffer-Tape Method (also known as the oh-drat-I-forgot-to-buy-that-blanking-out-kit technique) involves cutting a piece of gaffer tape to fit the outline and sticking it on. This can also work with black electrical tape. Make sure the surface is dry first. A more sophisticated solution is provided by clear plastic reflectors, which cost about £5 from the AA. These deflect your beam, rather than masking it, and if you intend to do a lot of night or winter driving will give you much better light. Earlier versions of these reflectors weren't terribly well-made (or not well-glued), but they seem to have got their act together and the latest ones I bought worked very efficiently (and stayed put).

Check with your insurance company what other equipment you need to take, such as spare bulbs, a red reflective warning triangle and fire extinguishers, as the legal requirements change from time to time.

A final note: petrol is dearer in France than in Britain, so cross the Channel with a full tank. Petrol is cheapest in Luxembourg, however, so contrive to fill up there if you can. French credit card machines occasionally refuse to read UK credit cards (French cards now contain a microchip). On the one occasion this happened to me, a slip was made out manually. Ask the shop to swipe the magnetic band rather than read the chip. Teething problems were caused by French banks not explaining to their clients that UK cards were different, but happily they've now spread the word and problems are few.

WHERE TO STAY AND HOW TO BOOK

There's a great deal to be said for spur-of-the-moment, go-as-you-please trips, where you potter idly along until you find somewhere you'd care to rest for the night. Great idea, and a lot of fun, but I wouldn't recommend it when going to buy wine. Especially if you have to travel at weekends. Chablis, for instance, is only a couple of hours' drive from Paris and not much further from Brussels. Parisiens take just the same pleasure in buying direct as we do, so ensure your accommodation is booked well in advance. At weekends and after 8pm, economy telephone rates prevail; and it doesn't take a long call to say: 'Have you got a room with a bath on the 25th?' Here's a cautionary tale: A reader reported last year that, having spent a delightful afternoon *chez* Drappier, they headed off on spec to the local recommended hotel, the Relais des Gouverneurs in Bar-sur-Aube – only to find it had burnt down. It was late evening before they found somewhere else to stay. Do phone ahead!

That applies to producers too – people retire, move, get divorced. Or even get out of bed on the wrong side. Another reader reported turning up at Clos de Vougeot in Burgundy and asking, as this book suggests, for the English-language tour. 'Impossible', came the response. 'We don't do tours in English.' The reader notes that the guide was standing directly beneath a sign saying 'English tours available' at the time.

I've never confirmed by letter, and I've never had a mix-up with bookings, although that doesn't mean it doesn't happen. These days I often confirm with a short fax – but I never book that way as many French hoteliers don't regard faxes as things they need to respond to. I feel far safer sorting out everything on the phone first, using paper only to confirm what's already been agreed. Sometimes I book the first night or two from the UK, the rest on the road. (Many French phone boxes use phonecards, *télécartes*, available from tobacconists, petrol stations etc. They're also useful for phoning ahead to producers.)

There are several hotel chains and associations in France. Some chains, such as Novotel and Campanile, are handily situated near main routes on the edge of towns, all based on exactly the same design and offering a good level of comfort, if rather functional. Then there are groupings of independent hotels. The most widespread of these is Logis de France, made up of small- to medium-sized family-run concerns. These are often furnished in 'traditional' style, featuring heavy furniture and loud floral wallpaper on every available surface including furniture panels and ceilings. Plumbing may be idiosyncratic, which all adds to the fun – no two hotels are alike. The association encourages regional cooking among its members, and organizes an annual competition to seek out the best. The Logis guide is published annually (not free, alas, it costs about £8 from bookshops or the French Tourist Office).

At the other end of the scale is the Relais et Châteaux group. Its brochures come complete with a colour photo of each establishment, and members are often firmly in the luxury class. Some are temples of gastronomy, others merely pretentious (although not, of course, those listed in this book). In between lies Relais du Silence which, as you might imagine, concentrates on tranquil locations. Prices are closer to those of Logis than those of Relais et Châteaux.

One important difference between French and British hotels is that in France it's quite common to have a weekly closing day. I recall attempting to explain this to an American colleague and being met with a look of blank disbelief. Restaurants frequently close on Sunday night, after serving a blow-out Sunday lunch, and may not reopen until Tuesday. Hotels may do the same. Monday night accounts for a disproportionately high number of closures, so if your trip includes one, plan well ahead.

When booking, note that the price quoted is per room, not per person, and doesn't include breakfast. This is usually brought to your room on a tray on demand, but you're under no obligation to order it. Sometimes you can be charged FF50 for little more than coffee, bread and jam. If you're in a town, there's nothing to stop you nipping out for breakfast in a local café or bistro. It's half the price, and you get to see the world going by.

When you arrive at a hotel it's normal practice to inspect the room before accepting it, and it's perfectly OK to ask to see something bigger or better if you wish. I still remember the buzz I got after doing this for the first time – the second room I was offered was superb. Hoteliers often hold back their best rooms, so don't be afraid to ask.

HOW TO BUY DIRECT

You *Can* Survive a Tasting

It can be very easy: walk in, taste a couple of bottles, flash the plastic, walk out with a couple of cases. Put at its simplest, that's all you do. But it can be much more involved, with visits to the cellar or out into the vineyards, and an explanation of the winemaker's philosophy and the styles of wine available in the region which could run into an hour or two. For me, that's what makes it fun, and that's how I learned about the wines of France. There is absolutely nothing like being in the region and visiting the growers to enable you to understand the wines. In fact, I'd go so far as to say it's the only way to make a wine region truly come alive.

Naturally, if you walk into someone's cellar, the selection on offer will be limited to what the winemaker produces. In particular, it's important to realize that not all the wines on sale will necessarily be ready to drink. A generalization: the dearer the wine, the longer you need to keep it. Like all generalizations, this isn't true in every case; wines made from Sauvignon Blanc, for instance, need to be drunk young, which is handy to know when buying in Sancerre. But in Alsace, the finest Rieslings will benefit from several years in bottle, whereas the cheaper ones are designed to be drunk more or less straight away. The French way of buying is to lay in sufficient quantities to enable you to keep the wine until it's ready to drink, opening a bottle every now and again to check on progress.

Who will you meet? In smaller properties, usually the wine-grower himself (in most cases, but not always, it's a man) or his spouse. Often husband and wife teams will split the work so that he's outside with the grapes and she's inside with the paperwork and visitors. You set the pace. If all you want to do is quietly taste a couple of bottles, they'll let you get on with it.

If you want to know more, they'll gladly answer your questions. The pride people take in their wines quickly becomes evident, so it's important to treat the samples you're offered with proper respect.

You may be received in a large, commercial tasting-room or in what feels like the front parlour. You may be invited to sit at a table, or there may simply be a long counter to stand round and be served at. Usually you're handed a price list, but there may be a noticeboard showing the range and prices. When you're asked what you want to taste, it may be easy, as there may only be a few wines on sale. If there's a big range, such as in Alsace, you can choose. You may want a selection from the range, which takes in all the grape varieties, or you may prefer to concentrate on a particular variety. You may be shopping for cheap wines or for dear wines.

The basic principle is to taste white before red, young before old, and dry before sweet. In practice the principle is also to taste cheap before dear; the more complex, expensive wines will, the theory goes, completely overwhelm your palate with their superior taste and intensity so that you can't then taste their more ordinary, cheaper cousins. It's helpful therefore to give an idea at the outset of what you want to taste, so that the pourer can offer the wines in the best order.

If you don't know what you'd like to try, feel free to say so. Most growers won't mind that you know nothing about their wines, or the wines of the region, and will be happy to take it from the top. (A few winemakers prefer not to do this, and want you to have some experience with wine. Where this is the case among the producers listed in this guide, I've made that plain in the write-up, so that you can pitch your visit with confidence.) All the growers I list welcome visitors; you won't find yourself being haughtily assessed by some chic château proprietor, nor do you have to turn up in a suit and tie, though you may find you get a better reception in Bordeaux if you do. (And if anyone mentioned here should give you an unfriendly welcome, I'd like to know about it.)

HOW TO TASTE

So you've got the first wine in the glass. A tasting sample is small, enough for one or two mouthfuls. You don't need more any more than this to tell what the wine is like, and a small amount gives you plenty of room to swirl it about in the glass without risk of spillage.

But first, contemplation. Look intently at the wine. Tilt it away from you against something white if the light is good enough, because that will give you the best idea of its colour and clarity. This is a good way to indicate your respect for the wine you're about to taste. What are you looking for? Colour can tell you about age and condition. To generalize again: in whites, the darker the wine the older and/or richer and sweeter it is. A wine that has been exposed to oak will be a little darker than one that hasn't. A young Muscadet will be very pale in colour, a mature oaky burgundy much richer and deeper. Late-harvest Alsace wines will be golden and almost viscous in texture. However, if air has leaked into the bottle via a faulty cork, it will have oxidized the wine and turned it gold before its time through premature ageing. Your nose will confirm this diagnosis by picking up 'off', dusty, fusty smells. The colour of red wines move from purply-red when young to browny-red when mature. The lighter a red wine looks, the lighter-bodied it will be.

Once you've paid your visual respects, sniff the wine briefly to check it's in good condition. (If it's faulty, as described above, you won't want to inhale more of the pong than absolutely necessary.) Then swirl the glass vigorously. This brings air into contact with the wine, encouraging it to release its aromas. If the wine is too cold – often the case with reds straight from the cellar – warm it by cupping your hand around the base of the glass. Then stick your nose right into the glass and breathe in deeply. I often close my eyes at this point. Closing down vision releases the brain to concentrate on other senses – my nose needs all the help it can get. What does it smell like?

This is where wine-tasting gets very personal. What the smell reminds you of may mean little or nothing to anyone else, but that doesn't matter. It's a subjective art, which happily means you can never be wrong if what you're doing is deciding on the right wine for you to buy. There is a useful check-list, however, of smells and tastes that many people have attached to particular grapes, which is handy for identification purposes.

The most commonly identified scents and flavours are:

Riesling (mature) oily, petrolly, often minerally
Gewürztraminer lychees, elderflower, turkish delight
Sauvignon Blanc gooseberries, cat's pee
Chenin Blanc wet wool
Pinot Noir manure
Cabernet Sauvignon blackcurrants
Cabernet Franc blackcurrants (but less intense); stalky, and minty
Chardonnay (oaky) butter, vanilla, toast

You may find you disagree entirely with this list, and that's fine, because nobody knows what someone else's nose is telling them. What is helpful is to build up pictures or associations in your own mind about what particular varieties smell and taste like, as your own points of reference.

Finally, taste. Take a good mouthful and do with it all the things mother told you not to: draw in air over it, make gurgly noises, chew the wine, rub it over your gums. Do whatever you have to do to draw more air into the wine, encouraging it to release its taste, and then spread that taste all over your mouth to where the different taste receptors are. Then spit it out. Yes, really, not just the person who's driving. If you want to taste more than a handful of wines, the mouthfuls you swallow will blunt your tastebuds for the wines yet to come. You won't experience more of the wine if you swallow, the swirl and chew has alerted all the parts of you which can taste.

That's my rule, and I admit I break it all the time, especially in Champagne where nobody appears to spit, ever. And sometimes, at the end of a tasting when really classy wines are being poured, I can't resist swallowing them. Some growers deem it a real waste to spit out their lovely wine. If you see no spittoons, ask for one (*un crachoir*); they'll probably give you an ice bucket.

When tasting I prefer to avoid eye contact and I certainly don't want anyone talking in my ear, or I become completely distracted and forget what I thought about the wine. Turning away helps. Finally, having spat, I write down what I thought. This last is not essential, but it can be very useful if you're tasting lots of wines in various places, or you simply want a record to look back on – or you happen to be writing a book.

It also gives you time to think if you're not sure how you feel about the wine.

Now you need to give some response to what you've tasted. In a large tasting-room, with many customers and pourers, there isn't much pressure to respond. When someone's giving you their personal attention, though, it's different. If they're looking at you expectantly an appreciative nod is always a good start. You may feel you don't have sufficient vocabulary to convey your opinion; don't let that put you off. It's said that 93% of what we communicate to others is non-verbal. By this reckoning, if you don't speak a word of French that puts you only 7% behind the native speakers.

If you can establish a rapport with the grower you'll find communication remarkably easy. If they're shy (and many small-scale growers are) there's no need to say much. If they're voluble and expressive, waving your arms about in similar fashion will help things along nicely. I know it sounds daft, but I've tried it and it works.

Most of us studied French at school and think we can't speak it; but with a little practice it's surprising how much can come back and find a useful purpose. We British have a dreadful reputation as linguists, and I could perhaps be accused of pandering to this by emphasizing those producers who speak English. But I believe it's a matter of confidence. I recommend producers who speak English as a starting-point for exploration. After a while it becomes easier to visit producers who don't speak English, and to branch out on your own. Rapport will help enormously.

If you have struck up a successful rapport you may even find yourself invited into the cellar to taste the wines still in cask. Don't pass up the chance. This is a great compliment to your interest in the grower's wines, to your knowledge and to your tasting ability, as you are being invited to assess wines still in development. The grower will extract wine from the cask through a tap at the bottom of the barrel or with a pipette. Definitely spit this after tasting – in a cellar it's normal practice to spit on the floor. Watch what the grower does with the untasted remains in the glass. Some will pour that on the ground too, others will carefully pour it back into the cask. If the latter is done, hand your glass back so that yours can be poured back into the vat as well.

A NOTE ON WINEMAKING

If you're taken on a tour of the cellars, you can learn a great deal about the winemaker's approach. Any cellar should be spotlessly clean, but some will be packed with shiny stainless steel towers and others full of dank wood, complete with black mould on the ceiling. Can this really be a hygienic place to produce wine?

The truth is that the black mould is a very good sign. It only grows when temperature (low) and humidity (high) are the optimum for maturing wine. Dank cellars are just what wine needs. But what about vinification itself – the process whereby grapes are made into wine? The producer has many options at each stage, beginning with the choice of press. Pneumatic ones, using pressure from an inflatable air-bag, are held to be the gentlest, but they're also the dearest. The gentler the pressure, the clearer the resultant grape juice or must. Now, let the must settle for 24–48 hours (*débourbage*) or filter it straight away? And can we design a cellar so that the must flows from one tank to another (the best method), or do we have to pump it?

Where will the must ferment? In stainless steel or wood? In small oak barrels or in larger, old wood vats? Stainless steel is very popular as a fermentation vessel because it enables you to control the wine's temperature. This can be done simply by pouring cold water down the outside of a tank to cool down a too-vigorous fermentation, or with sophisticated coils within the vat that can cool or heat the wine as required, all wired up to electronic control desks. Cool fermentation of white wine, at about 18–20°C (65–68°F), has caused a revolution in wine-making and is responsible for all those crisp, fresh, dry, neutral wines we buy in the UK for about £3-4.

You can't mess about with heating coils and electronic con-trol panels that look like something out of Star Trek when you ferment your wine in a wooden vat (or not unless you're a horribly rich Bordeaux château). Nor are the post-Second World War vessels you'll see – glass fibre things or tiled con-crete chambers – any use with the high-tech approach. Winemakers using older or more traditional equipment may have less control over proceedings but they may like it that way, preferring to let the wine develop as Nature intended rather than intervening too much.

Some producers swear that barrel-fermentation makes a more elegant, structured wine. Wood is also prized for maturing wine in because it's slightly porous, allowing a small amount of air through to the wine as it matures. New barrels also add a woody taste, currently very fashionable in whites as well as reds. After a few years in use, say four or five, a barrel has given up all its 'woody' flavours, so wine placed in it to mature is not going to taste of wood, but simply benefit from controlled exposure to air. The downside of maturing wine in wood is that it evaporates. Producers lose money through having to top up the vats (you can't leave a gap above the wine, as this would allow too much exposure to air and the wine would oxidize). That's why many producers mature their wine in stainless steel.

What will be used to start fermentation? The natural yeasts found in the 'bloom' on the grapes, or specially-made cultured yeasts? The latter give you more control, the former, it's argued, bring out the genuine taste of the grape, the vintage and the location.

What temperature do you want to ferment at? For red wines, the higher the temperature, the more colour and tannin you'll extract. For both whites and reds, the lower the temperature, the better the aromas, freshness and fruitiness. Too low, however, and the yeasts become dormant; the fermentation process then stops and is difficult to restart. Too high a temperature and the yeasts are killed off, with dire consequences. Light, aromatic whites are best fermented below 18°C (65°F), while heavier ones such as white burgundy and many of the Alsace whites may be better at 18–20°C (65–68°F). Red wines ferment at higher temperatures, say 25–30°C (77–86°F), so you'll probably want to keep them somewhere else during this stage.

Once the wine has finished fermenting, do you leave it on its lees – the spent yeast cells – to gain more flavour (as with Muscadet)? Or do you rack the wine, ie transfer it to a clean barrel, leaving any sediment behin)? Do you 'do the malo', a further, malolactic fermentation which converts sharp, appley malic acid into softer lactic acid? Do you leave it to mature – in which case for how long? Do you fine it (clarify it) or filter it?

The presence of other equipment, particularly a great deal of filtration apparatus, indicates an interventionist attitude.

Filtration is a sad thing to inflict on a wine. You're removing tiny particles in suspension in the wine, and that's bound to detract, in however small a way, from the wine's taste. Unfortunately we consumers are partly responsible for this. We object to seeing 'bits' in a wine and think it's faulty, whereas usually the reverse is the case. In white wines, for instance, white tartrate crystals often appear. This is actually a sign of un-mucked-about-with wine, but so many people complain about it that many producers nearly freeze the wine after fermentation in order to precipitate the crystals before bottling, to stop us taking the bottles back. Let's start a campaign for unfiltered wine – 'bits in bottles now!'

A very few producers avoid filtration altogether. Others filter 'as gently as possible'. It's one of the questions you can ask which will tell you a great deal about winemakers' attitudes to their wines. Modern winemaking technology is extremely expensive, all that stainless steel and control equipment, for instance. Often it's only the larger estates which can afford it. Often, too, they're the ones which go for filtration in a major way. But take a good look round. What does the equipment you see tell you about the sort of wine that's made? Is it all tightly controlled and regulated, or is the attitude more laid-back, with the wine allowed to 'do its own thing', to follow a natural course? One thing's for sure – even the tiniest, oldest cellar should be scrupulously clean, with nowhere for harmful bacteria to lurk that could interfere with the wine.

Another invitation you may receive is to go into the vineyards. I always accept with alacrity; there's usually something to learn, and if you're lucky the view will be terrific. Here you can see at first hand what the soil is like, how the vines are grown, and where the site is located. (For more information about vineyard activities, see pages 32–5.)

TO BUY OR NOT TO BUY

So you've tasted the wines, you've seen the cellar perhaps or been out into the vineyards. It comes to the crunch – what are you going to buy? If you've paid for the tasting, then that was a commercial transaction which leaves you with no further obligation. You can say thank you and goodbye without a backward glance. But usually the producer has spent time with you explaining the wines and offering you several free glasses to taste. Although the producers listed in this book enjoy receiving visitors and explaining the regions and their wines, selling wine is their livelihood. It's only courteous to buy a couple of bottles at least, in acknowledgment of the time they've given you.

If you like the wine, and it's something you'd enjoy drinking at home, then buy it in sufficient quantity to give you pleasure. I'd recommend that six bottles was the minimum to allow you to enjoy the wine on different occasions, served with different foods, and to experience the changes in taste as the wine matures over months or years. One of the mistakes I made when I first started buying in France was to bring home just two or three bottles of a wine I liked. Even with six, I found that because I'd bought the wine before it was ready and started drinking it too soon, only the last bottle gave me any idea of what it really had to offer. And by then, of course, it was too late.

Wine-buying Brits used to be known as 'one-bottles'. I blame the dreadful old import laws, where we had to ration ourselves tightly to keep within the 12-bottle limit. Now, only our axles hold us back, and the pleasure of buying by the case direct from the people who make the wine is finally within our grasp. Grab it with both hands.

A growing number of estates do now accept Access and Visa (although very few take American Express), mainly because they know we buy more if we can use plastic. This information is given in the producer listings. The majority of estates, however, still don't accept credit cards so be prepared with Eurocheques, French franc traveller's cheques or ready money.

Once you've bought your wine you'll be given an invoice, a *facture*, showing details of the wine and the price paid. It will also make clear that you've paid the VAT. Do hang on to this paperwork until you're back in the UK, just in case a marauding Excise inspector wants proof of what you've been up to. These invoices are required by French law of all wine that's on the move, and it's particularly important if you buy wine in containers other than labelled bottles. The invoice proves that what you've got in that plastic barrel is legitimate AC burgundy, say, and not something shady from over the border for surreptitious blending with the indigenous stuff.

Another way of discovering local wines is to check out your hotel's wine list. The establishment may very well make its own wine, and if it doesn't it will certainly have links with several local producers. Ask your waiter for a recommendation, and if you enjoy what you've been served, don't hesitate to ask for the producer's address. The hotel may even make an appointment for you to see the winemaker, which should ensure a warm welcome. This is a great way to discover your own personal hot tip: it may be a rising star the wine press hasn't yet pounced on, or someone making wine in a very small way, part-time or as a hobby.

BRINGING IT ALL BACK HOME

How much will the car hold? Tricky question, this. You can make all the experiments you like, fitting suitcases and boxes into the boot, but real life will be different. Your vehicle manufacturer may be able to help, although none of the ones I phoned could offer much advice. For guidance, here are some approximate weights:

Still wine 12 x 75cl bottles: 15kg
Champagne or Crémant 12 x (heavier) 75cl bottles: 20kg
Pack of beer 24 x 33cl bottles: 13kg (cans are lighter)
Spirits 1 litre: 2kg

If your wine is in wooden boxes, you should allow an extra kilogram per case.

So if you add it all up, assuming you've bought your full champagne allowance, but that it isn't packed in wooden boxes, the total weighs around a staggering 370kg. I found that in a Rover a dozen cases of wine in the boot and the luggage on the back seat is just about as much as I could manage. In one of those big Volvo estates it's another matter. These are now the biggest load-carrying cars in Europe, and I gather the unofficial record in a 940 is 400 bottles plus two people and even the odd piece of luggage. This would certainly be my vehicle of choice: driving back in one from the Rhône with 200 bottles, baggage, and then stopping to buy half the produce on sale in Mâcon market, it just flew along. If you're in any doubt, add to the load a couple of cases at a time. The driver should soon notice when things are getting heavy. Don't forget to pump up the tyres as the load grows.

A word of warning: be extremely careful where you leave the car once you've reached the stage of storing suitcases on the back seat. To any passing thief, luggage left on seats means that the boot is probably full, too, and this is easily verifiable by pushing down on the back of the car.

If you want to bring back as much alcohol as is physically possible, buying wine 'from the pump' can be advantageous. This is known as buying *en vrac*, in bulk, and it involves you bringing over a large plastic container which is filled at the cellar by a device looking exactly like a petrol pump. And you buy it by the litre. The finest wines won't be sold like this, of course, it's much too undignified, but often it isn't just cheap plonk either; I've seen many AC wines sold this way. Apart from price – it's always cheaper than the equivalent wine in bottle – the main advantage is weight. You're not carting all that glass home.

Some people bottle the wine when they get back, which is fine if you know how to sterilize your bottles (get a home-brew buff to help). If you leave it in the container, though, beware. It's not under vacuum in one of these, and as the wine is drunk the air that takes its place will slowly turn what's left to vinegar. Best drink it all at once (just the excuse I need). If you'd like to experiment with this method, most estates which sell *en vrac* will also sell you a 5-litre plastic cubitainer, or 'cubi', for a few francs.

Even using this method, I doubt whether the average family car, holding two passengers and their luggage, will be able to exceed the new import limits. Let's be precise: it's not a limit, but simply the level below which you don't have to justify yourself. Above that, and you have to prove the wine is for your personal consumption. If you've borrowed a friend's transit van, with its larger payload, this suddenly becomes more of a problem, so make sure you've got a good reason for purchase all prepared.

UK Customs were full of promises that if you say the wine is for a family wedding they'll want to see an invitation. Perhaps they will. If in doubt, invite them. They certainly still try to look as intimidating as possible when you drive past their Customs shed (oh, how liberating it is not to see those red and green channels any more!). If you've been buying wine direct from growers, it's quite possible that you will have bought wine in two categories: for drinking now or over the next few months, and for laying down to drink in a year or two. The indicative levels are meant to be a gauge of how much wine you personally are likely to drink in a year. It's a moot point – which year are we talking about?

This guide is based on the idea that the best bargains, in both taste and price, are to be found in the château and vineyard. That doesn't mean I ignore French supermarkets on my trips, however. On the contrary. Although you won't catch me buying wine there, beer is another matter. It's amazingly cheap, and you can bring 110 litres home with you. Spirits, too, are available at the price you'll pay on the boat, so you can legally import them in far larger quantities, if your liver can stand it – 10 litres instead of just 2 on the boat.

I'll also be buying up fruit and vegetables, especially those wonderful, waxy potatoes such as Ratte, Belle de Fontenay or Charlotte; salted or smoked pork called *poitrine*, not unlike bacon, sold either chopped or in a piece, and used for flavouring casseroles; tins of *cassoulet* (thick haricot bean stew with sausage, pork, goose or duck, depending on the source), goose fat (nothing like it for fried potatoes), preserved duck *confit*; even, if I get really carried away, tins of *haricots verts* (because the British equivalents just don't taste the same).

If I discover a market going on just before I leave, I'll do the shopping there, but don't underestimate the quality of the fresh produce available in the hypermarkets. We entertain all sorts of romantic notions about how the French only shop at markets or in tiny specialist stores, but who do you think keeps the hypermarkets in business? It's not just down to beer-hungry Brits, the French use them as a matter of course. And demand good-quality produce, too. And get it, which is more than we often do.

A final word: let your wine rest once you've got it home. Wine is a living thing; and if you're exhausted after being bounced about in a car for 800km, so is the wine. If you open a bottle the night of your return, you're in danger of thinking you've made a major mistake. There's a good chance the wine simply won't taste right because it's all shook up. Wait three to four weeks before tasting it again.

GETTING AROUND, GETTING ALONG

Driving in France

On the right, of course. Easy to say, easy to forget. Every time you start the engine, the navigator should remind the driver. You can pull off a petrol station forecourt onto a deserted road, and without thinking take the wrong side.

The main difference when driving in France is the rule of giving way to traffic joining the road from the right, *priorité à droite*. Unfortunately this is rather muddled, as the rule applies in some circumstances and not in others. Generally, if you have priority along a stretch of road you'll see a large yellow diamond with a white border. The same sign with a grey diagonal bar across it says you've lost it.

Recently the French have discovered roundabouts. Again and again you'll come across newly laid out circles indicating the local engineer has been to roundabout school and is bursting to perfect the art. You'll see them in the strangest places. French drivers are deeply mistrustful of this new-fangled idea, and approach them with extreme caution.

Almost always, traffic on the roundabout has priority, but occasionally you'll be on one and discover the hard way that joining traffic has right of way. It's just to keep you on your toes. Your Michelin atlas contains guidance on French rules of the road, including speed limits and the symbols to tell you when you have priority on the road.

Just a couple of extra points: don't exceed the speed limit. Don't. French traffic police can extract large fines from you on the spot. They don't take plastic, and they carry guns. It can really put a damper on your holiday. If you want to stop on the open road, pull right off the highway – don't park on the side of the road. And be aware that speed limits drop by an average of 10km per hour when it's raining (in other words, when your wipers are going).

The French way of life

The French way of life differs from ours in several respects which are important to the prospective wine buyer. First of all, France treats its lunch break with proper respect. It generally lasts for two hours and is used to consume a properly-cooked three-course meal. Most properties close from 12 to 2pm, and the owners take a dim view of the British habit of turning up at 11.55 and looking expectantly at the tasting-table. If there's one message French winegrowers want to give their esteemed British customers, it's this: have a proper lunch! We have a dreadful reputation for not respecting food, and our attitude to lunch-time compounds it. Florent Baumard of Rochefort-sur-Loire spoke for many when he said: 'We really hate to answer the phone at lunch-time, or to hear "sorry, we got lost on the way" at 1pm.'

There are a few estates which don't mind you turning up over lunch, and I've noted these in the producer listings. I do ask you to respect the opening hours given. Take the opportunity to have a decent lunch, or lay in a good stock of picnic material. Alternatively, lunch-time is a perfect time to be on the road, taking advantage of the absence of traffic. (The corollaries to this are the need to beware the maniacs driving at great speed at 12.30 because they're late for lunch, and the erratic driving at 2.30 of those whose lunch has been too liquid.)

Picnickers are well catered for in France, with plenty of well laid out picnic areas on the wine routes, or simply with lay-bys offering stunning views (Michelin maps have a symbol for viewpoints, and there's usually somewhere to park). An alfresco lunch is also a great excuse to inspect some of the splendid shops selling picnic food. Ask for the regional or house specialities. Note that food shops will close somewhere between 12 and 1pm, so plan your picnic early.

The other major cultural difference to look out for is the French system of formal politeness, *la politesse*. It is essential to greet people in shops with a quiet *bonjour, messieurs-dames* and say *au revoir* when you leave. Watch what the French do. They'll acknowledge each other when entering and leaving a restaurant, for instance; it's charming, but we never do it and are thought cold and impolite as a result. Whenever anyone turns their back on you, to open a door or lead the way, they'll excuse themselves with *pardon* or tell you they're going in front of you; do likewise. Saying hello to other guests as you approach the hotel pool, for instance, acknowledges their existence and makes peaceful co-use of facilities much easier than does a stone-faced pretence that there's no-one else there.

WINE RULES AND REGULATIONS

French winemaking is very heavily regulated. The contents of your glass are a product of the soil structure and microclimate (known collectively as the *terroir*), the grape variety grown, how the vine is pruned and trained, the yield (the number of litres produced per hectare of land), how and when the grapes are harvested, how the wine is made, and how long it must mature before it's released for sale. All these factors are regulated, with different rules applying in each of the wine regions you'll visit. Compare this series of regulations to the laid-back approach in the New World: there's a whole world of difference. The rules can have quite an effect upon what you might find in the cellar, so I'll describe them in some detail.

Quality levels French wine divides into three quality types. The most basic is *vin de table*, ordinary table wine, plonk. This is sold for FF5–10 a litre in plastic bottles in the hypermarket; you won't find much of it at the properties featured here. Occasionally, however, very good wine is labelled *vin de table* – usually because a wilful young winemaker has experimented with a technique not permitted in that region.

Second come the *vins de pays*. Country wines are the success story of southwest France but are less common in the north. They're a halfway house, with some regulations applying. In the Loire, 'Vin de Pays du Jardin de la France' covers wine made in the whole of the Loire valley, and most of it is also labelled by grape variety. The term *vin de pays* is slowly replacing 'VDQS', which stood for wines from a delimited area of a superior quality. Sauvignon de St-Bris, made in Burgundy, is an eminently respectable wine which can only be called VDQS because it's not made from the white grape variety of AC burgundy, Chardonnay.

The highest category is AC or *appellation contrôlée* wine. With a few rebellious exceptions, this title covers all the best wines of France, and these are the most heavily regulated. Controlled appellation wines are in increasing demand in France, where the trend has been away from plonk to higher quality wine: people are drinking less, but better. In Eurospeak, these are QWPSR, quality wines produced in a specified region. The regulations aren't set in stone, but change (slowly)

according to circumstances. Further ACs are still being introduced; new names are appearing around Chablis, for instance.

In practice, what does this hierarchy mean for the vineyard
visitor? At the most basic buying level it's irrelevant, but if you
develop an interest and get taken round by a friendly winemaker, his or her attitudes to some of these topics will tell you
a lot about the wines being made.

Terroir New World winemakers used to insist that the soil a
vine grew in, or the local climate, made no difference to the
quality or taste of the finished product. This may largely be the
case in Australia, but I certainly don't believe it's true in France.
There are any number of producers who will offer you proof in
the glass of the different tastes that can come from vines growing in different parts of the vineyard.

Aspect, in this cold northern climate, is also vitally important. The most favoured vineyards face south or southwest, to
take maximum advantage of the available sun. (By contrast,
look at the practice of some winemakers in Provence who
plant on northern slopes to avoid overcooked grapes.) Slopes
are more prized than flat land; even position on the slope matters, as you can discover in Burgundy where the best vineyard
sites are marked out in meticulous detail.

Grape variety With AC wines, the grape variety (or varieties)
is always specified, in the regulations if not on the label, yet
there is a certain amount of flexibility in their use. Some producers grow little-known local varieties which they're allowed
to blend in to give a wine more colour, say, or body.

Then there's cloning, a process whereby selection is made in
the vineyard of a few vines with outstanding characteristics
from which plenty of cuttings are taken. Prolific vines are very
popular, as you might imagine, and can improve the yield of a
vineyard no end, but critics point to dangers: less biological
diversity can mean, for example, that your chosen clone is particularly susceptible to a certain viral disease. Whereas with a
whole vineyard of different plants only a few would die if
attacked, with clones you stand the risk of losing the lot. The
argument also runs that diversity makes a richer wine; more
prolific vines aren't necessarily (or even probably) high in taste.
Each different vine has something to offer.

Pruning and training You'll notice in the vineyard that there are many alternative ways of training vines, varying from region to region. Vines are pruned each winter, and this is when the major decision is taken on how many bunches of grapes you'll allow to grow. If you miscalculate, and too many bunches develop, you may have to go round the vineyard in June and cut some of them off. This is known as the green harvest, or *vendange verte*. These treatments have a significant bearing on the quality of the wine.

Yield In other words, how much wine is produced from a certain patch of vines, expressed as so many hectolitres per hectare ('hecto-' means 'hundred'). Very good growing conditions give higher yields. The maximum amount of wine you can produce per hectare is determined by law in each region. Better producers aim for low yields; the more juice a vine produces the more dilute it's likely to be, and the lower the yield the higher the concentration of flavour in each bunch of grapes.

Some varieties are more prolific than others, and young vines produce more than old ones. Grapes are first harvested from a vine four years after planting, but a vine needs a few more years to become mature. After that it's in its prime, until things start to go downhill around 40 (so unlike life). What an old vine lacks in vigour, however, it makes up for in quality, so although old vines won't give you a high yield they'll give you a rich one. Some producers grub up old vines the minute the decline sets in, others will cherish them and proudly put *vieilles vignes* on the label to mark out the quality. Unfortunately there's no legal definition of what constitutes old; one man's ancient could be another woman's middle age. Rémy Gresser (qv), in Alsace, reckons he's got one vineyard that was planted by his great-grandfather after the First World War, in 1919.

Harvesting and vintage In many regions – Champagne, for example – the date on which the harvest may commence is decided by committee. You can't start work before the *ban de vendange*, but you can start later. There are two methods of harvesting: by machine and by hand. Harvesting machines are great big blue things that pass up the rows of vines and vibrate each individual grape off the cluster; pickers cut each bunch off whole with secateurs. This is an important difference, as hand-picked grapes have a better chance of getting to the cellar with their skins unbroken. Broken skin means the air can get to the grape flesh, and too much exposure oxidizes the juice – not what's wanted at all. Some red wines need the stalks for extra tannin, so their grapes can't be harvested by machine. And in certain regions, again such as Champagne, harvesting must be done by hand. Where both methods are permissible, their relative merits are hotly debated. During the rainy 1993 harvest, for instance, growers who were harvesting by machine were far more sanguine about being rained off for a few days than those who had to pay teams of pickers to hang around waiting.

The weather conditions throughout the year will always have an effect on what goes into the bottle. In 1993, what looked like being a brilliant year was reduced to being merely good in many places by rain during the harvest. In April 1991, frost in the Loire reduced the subsequent harvest to 20% or less of the norm. Ask growers about the latest harvest, and compare what different people tell you. It can reveal fascinating contrasts in attitude and approach.

Alsace

Alsace was the first French wine region I ever visited and it remains one of my favourites. The scenery is heartstopping, the hospitality warm and unforced, the wines as inviting as the people. Stuck away in the northeastern corner of France, it receives few British visitors, yet it's perfect territory for buying direct from the grower.

Alsace's recent history has been marked by war and upheaval: annexed by Germany after the Franco-Prussian war, in 1870, it was returned to France after the First World War only to be occupied by the Nazis in 1940.

Under the Germans both the French language and the local dialect, known as Elsässisch or Alsacien, were banned. Relations are now happily more cordial, as the number of German weekend tourists shows. (You'd be advised to book weekend accommodation about a fortnight in advance.) Alsace is also a popular destination for Scandinavian wine buyers, suffering as they do from wine taxation laws of an idiocy comparable to our own.

Both the architecture and the cuisine are marked by similarities to the other side of the Rhine, but the Germanic ingredients are tempered by the elegance and finesse of French culinary tradition. The wines, too, use some grape varieties thought of as German, such as Riesling, but the winemaking style has a definite French accent.

Geographically Alsace forms a long, thin north–south strip, with the winemaking area sandwiched to the west by the Vosges mountains and to the east by the fertile agricultural plain alongside the Rhine. The Vosges trap most of the rainfall that plagues the rest of northern France. Alsace receives just a quarter of the rain which falls on land west of the hills, making

Colmar the second driest town in the country. Add good sunshine, especially in late summer and autumn, and you get potentially excellent conditions both for grape harvesting and for tourism.

The explorer in Alsace will discover one of the prettiest wine regions imaginable. The heart of the wine route takes you through a succession of villages all competing with each other for one of the 'village in bloom' awards, geraniums cascading out of window-boxes at every turn, tubs of flowers in the village square. The houses are often brightly coloured, clashing with the flowers. Except for those villages bombed to bits during the Second World War, the narrow streets and ancient buildings are intact and well cared for. There are several tourist honeypots that are truly attractive – and popular – but there are many more which, while not being quite so chocolate-box, have much charm with the added bonus of being places where peo-ple can actually live and work without feeling on daily display.

In many parts of the region the local dialect is still widely spoken. This has strong links with the German dialects still heard on the other side of the river Rhine, and as a German speaker I can just about make sense of it, although it's absorbing more and more French words. A generation ago it was the first language children spoke. The local English teacher in Itterswiller, now 54, told me he didn't learn a word of French until he went to school at the age of seven. Sadly, like many local languages, it is fading out because children no longer learn it at home.

When to visit? All year round, of course, but I've found Alsace a particularly comforting place to be in the autumn and winter. The foliage is beautiful as it turns gold, the air is full of the smell of wood-smoke, the geraniums flower well into November. (It can get very cold, though, so do bring your thermals.) In the weeks leading up to Christmas there are mar-kets in several villages, notably Kaysersberg, where traditional decorations, wooden toys and craftwork are on sale, and the festive illuminations look magical at dusk. The light across the mountains at this time of year can be stunning. Occasionally there's fog, but if this descends while you're there, take a road into the mountains and, at perhaps 600m, the air will suddenly clear and you'll emerge into brilliant sunshine while all below you is miserable.

HOW THE WINES ARE CLASSIFIED

Basic Alsace wine law is simple, although over the last decade or so several steps have been taken to make it more complicated. At the root of it all is the grape variety. Alsace used varietal labelling long before it became fashionable, and the grapes are still the key to understanding the wines. There are eight grape names you'll encounter: Riesling, Tokay Pinot Gris, Gewurztraminer, Muscat, Pinot Blanc, Pinot Noir, Sylvaner and Chasselas. The situation does get a little hazy with the Pinots: Pinot Blanc wine can also be made from the Pinot Auxerrois grape (although one or two winemakers swear these two taste quite different and are happy to demonstrate this to you in the glass). It can even be made from Pinot Noir vinified white, or from Pinot Gris (goodness knows why).

So far, so reasonably simple. But some vineyard sites are better than others and so a system of naming Grand Cru vineyards was instigated in the 1980s. There are now 50 and, as you can imagine, much politicking surrounds which vineyards are 'in' and which 'out'.

Grand Cru wines have more stringent regulations all round. For ordinary AC Alsace, a minimum of just 8.5% alcohol is required and a hectare of vines is allowed to produce a maximum of 100hl of juice. This permitted yield is much lower for Grand Cru wines and the minimum level of alcohol is higher. Only certain noble grape varieties can become Grand Cru wine in the first place (Riesling, Gewurztraminer, Pinot Gris, Pinot Noir and Muscat) but not all of these are necessarily permitted in a particular Grand Cru vineyard. Other varieties may also be planted on these sites but you can't say on the label that they've been grown in a Grand Cru vineyard. There are, however, various ingenious ways of getting round this, such as putting the initial of the Grand Cru site on the label.

Top of the range of Alsace wines are Vendange Tardive, from late-harvested grapes, and Sélection des Grains Nobles, from individually selected grapes affected by noble rot (see page 188). You can find these made from Riesling, Gewurztraminer, Pinot Gris and Muscat. They have high potential alcohol and are the finest and dearest of Alsace's wines.

In addition to these official designations, individual producers, as elsewhere in France, have ways of letting you know which of their wines they consider better (and therefore charge more for). They may call them Réserve or Cuvée Spéciale, or give them special brand names. It's also permissible to name certain vineyards on the label even if they're not official Grand Cru sites. The Kaefferkopf vineyard in Ammerschwihr is a well-known example of these *lieux-dits*, or 'named places' (and I gather there was some serious politicking about its status going on recently). Most price lists will show a clear progression from the basic AC Alsace wine, identified only by grape variety, through some fancy names, up to Grand Cru sites, perhaps with a Vendange Tardive to finish off the list.

Alsace shows how wine laws haven't existed immutably for centuries but are constantly evolving. The regulations here were only initiated after 1945 and are still being revised. There's even a call for a level of Premier Cru to sit somewhere between the generic wines and the Grands Crus. There's nothing like making a situation even more complicated, is there?

Alsace winemakers usually offer most of the permitted grape varieties, at several quality levels and often from several vintages. The cheaper, generic wines are best drunk while young and fresh (the wines, that is), within a year or two of the vintage. Dearer wines and Grands Crus can often be drunk young, or after a gap of a few years of dumb adolescence during which they're not worth touching. Producers are only too happy to suggest how long a wine will take to mature.

WHAT YOU'LL SEE IN THE CELLAR

Grapes are the key to understanding Alsace's wines, so a brief description of each of the main varieties and their wines seems to be in order.

Riesling This is a high acidity wine. In youth fruity and refreshing, with age it acquires an oily smell of petrol, is often minerally and is very rich and elegant in the mouth. Sometimes when you taste a young Grand Cru Riesling it will hit you with its lush fruit straightaway; sometimes it can seem rather thin and insignificant, and you will wonder what all the fuss (and price) is about. The Grands Crus can age for a decade or more and often need several years' patience before they start to show you what they've got.

Tokay Pinot Gris Locally, Pinot Gris has long been known as Tokay, but Eurocrats have tried to ban the name, arguing that the consumer could confuse it with Hungarian Tokay. Alsace winemakers have had no truck with this regulation, nor with the compromise suggestion that the wine should be called Tokay Pinot Gris d'Alsace. Expect any variation of the above names, in any order. The wine is a little lower in acidity than Riesling, with a spicy nose when well made and a rich, full-bodied taste. Alsaciens like it with food. It's not widely grown, accounting for only about 5% of plantings, but is becoming popular with Parisiens, which explains the increase in price.

Gewurztraminer 'Gewürz' means 'spice' in German (the umlaut is dropped in Alsace), but the smell of this grape is more like ripe exotic fruit, such as lychees, highly perfumed flowers, like overblown roses or elderflowers, or even turkish delight. It can have high alcohol content with low acidity, and although it has a blowsy, sweet nose it is fermented dry (except for some exceptional Sélection des Grains Nobles). As you move along the wine route you may be struck by the variation in styles of Gewurztraminer, from blowsy, fat opulent wines to restrained, more subtle examples. These are created partly by the difference in soils and partly by the varying attitudes of the winemakers.

Muscat This wine will surprise anyone who knows the sweet Muscats of southern France and elsewhere since, like all Alsace wines, it is dry. The nose is aromatic, grapey and floral, and seems sweet, but the wine is dry and fruity in the mouth and makes a wonderful aperitif.

Pinot Blanc, Pinot Auxerrois, Clevner/Klevner Pinot Auxerrois is related to Pinot Blanc, slightly spicier in taste but often blended anonymously with its cousin. Some producers, such as Rolly Gassmann (qv), make separate wines from both; advanced students might enjoy comparing the two. Clevner/Klevner is a term specific to Alsace and refers to a wine made from a Pinot variety. It's definitely for drinking young. Klevner de Heiligenstein, however, isn't a Pinot at all but a form of the Savagnin grape, related to Gewurztraminer. It's grown around Heiligenstein in small quantities only. Taste it at Klipfel (qv). Both Klevner and Pinot Blanc are fresh, fruity and fairly neutral.

Pinot Noir The great red grape of Burgundy generally meta-morphoses into a rosé wine in Alsace. So far north, it's difficult to get the grapes ripe enough to extract sufficient colour and tannin to make a decent red. But there are exceptions, notably at Zind-Humbrecht (qv), where they can offer an elegant red wine of great finesse and character (at a price). Most places, however, will offer you a deep pink wine, with an attractive smell and taste of creamy, ripe fruit and good acidity, which goes surprisingly well with red meats.

Sylvaner Not a complex wine: light and fruity, not much of a nose, best drunk young. Some producers lavish TLC on it to produce something more complex and interesting, but such wines are rare. It has low alcohol and refreshing acidity, making it a popular café 'quaffing' wine. It tends to be grown in the less favoured sites, particularly in the north, and is in decline (although still accounting for nearly 20% of plantings).

Edelzwicker This is a blend of noble and less noble varieties, in most cases Sylvaner, Pinot Blanc, Auxerrois and Chasselas (a rather dull grape not usually sold as a varietal wine and declining rapidly in planted area). It's cheap and cheerful and to be drunk as young as possible.

Crémant d'Alsace The region's sparkling-wine appellation is made by the champagne – sorry, traditional – method, involving second fermentation in bottle and a minimum of nine months on the lees (although look out for better wines, which are left on their lees for longer; 12–24 months' contact with the spent yeasts imparts more flavour to the wine, which is helpful when it's made from a neutral grape variety such as Pinot Blanc). Crémant d'Alsace has been an AC wine only since 1976, but the rules for its production are nearly as stringent as those for champagne itself. It has grown hugely in popularity, now selling over 10 million bottles a year, and some of it is very good indeed – a creditable alternative to champagne at under half the price. Don't be put off by the fizzy, one-dimensional examples that find their way into many wine shops in Britain. When you've discovered a producer you're happy with, try his or her Crémant – you may find a real bargain.

Where the grapes are grown is particularly significant, too. I doubt if there's anywhere else in France where so many soil types occur in such a small area – the result of the same volcanic activity that created the Alps. Each grape variety responds differently to these soils and some growers love to study the effect this has on the taste of their wines. If you don't think the *terroir* can influence the taste, come to Alsace. There are winemakers here who will delight in spending several hours explaining the intricacies to you, illustrated with tasting-samples.

PLANNING THE ROUTE

The most straightforward route is via the Calais ferries or the Channel Tunnel; direct on the motorway, and with a very early crossing and an iron will, you can be in Strasbourg by teatime. (Calais to Strasbourg is 630km.) Lesser mortals may prefer to break the journey in Champagne, which is reachable from Calais in under three hours (see Champagne, pages 82–3, for hotels near the motorway). The motorway toll from Calais to Reims is FF88, and from Reims to Strasbourg about FF115.

One way of avoiding the tolls, especially for those based north of Watford, is to take a ferry from Hull or Felixstowe, landing at Zeebrugge, and to take the A10 to Brussels and Luxembourg, dropping down via the A4 and A31 to join the A26 at Metz. This is a very practical route, slightly shorter than going via Calais, and brings the northern French wine areas within realistic striking distance of the north of England and Scotland. Travelling via Luxembourg also has the advantage of taking you to the cheapest petrol in northern Europe.

If you live close to the 'Loire' crossings via Portsmouth or Southampton then you may prefer to exchange one dire capital orbital motorway for another and to drive from Le Havre via Paris. From the Newhaven–Dieppe crossing there's a cross-country route to Alsace via Amiens and Reims, which is time-consuming but worth considering if time is not of the essence.

EXPLORING ALSACE

The Alsace wine road is about 200km long, zigzagging from north of Strasbourg down to Thann near Mulhouse. As with all wine roads, the choice of route is dictated by local politics and

---

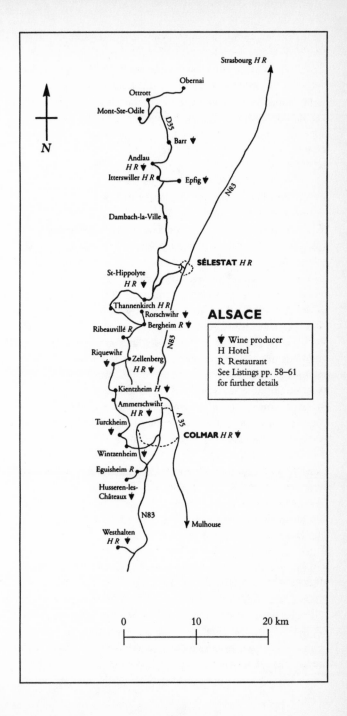

N

Strasbourg *H R*

Obernai

Ottrott

Mont-Ste-Odile

Barr ♦

Andlau *H R* ♦

Itterswiller *H R*   Epfig ♦

Dambach-la-Ville

SÉLESTAT *H R*

St-Hippolyte *H R* ♦

Thannenkirch *H R*
Rorschwihr ♦
Ribeauvillé *R*   Bergheim *R* ♦

Riquewihr   Zellenberg *H R*

Kientzheim *H* ♦
Ammerschwihr *H R* ♦
Turckheim

COLMAR *H R* ♦

Wintzenheim ♦
Eguisheim *R*
Husseren-les-Châteaux ♦

Mulhouse

Westhalten *H R* ♦

ALSACE

♦ Wine producer
H Hotel
R Restaurant
See Listings pp. 58–61
for further details

| 0 | 10 | 20 km |

just because a village is on the wine route doesn't mean it's worth stopping there. To my mind, the central section of the route is most worthy of your attention. When you get to the end, all you can reasonably do is turn around and come back again, but it won't seem repetitive; the scenery looks completely different from the other direction. Also, you can divert from the wine route to follow one of the other waymarked routes, such as the Route des Crêtes, which leads you up into stunning hairpin-bend hills and great views. Incidentally, Alsace is pretty hot on fancy routes; latest additions include the Route of the Fried Pike-Perch and the Route of Fermented Cabbage. In any case, this is a badly signposted route and if my experience is anything to go by you'll find yourself off course with depressing ease. This route doesn't believe in anything so useful as signposts at junctions or roundabouts; all it will do, most of the time, is put up little signs beneath the ones you see at the entry to a village, confirming in irritatingly small print that you are indeed still on the right road – very helpful. Happily the route's zigzag nature means that when you get lost, probably all you've done is missed out a dog-leg and arrived at the next town but one, so when you turn around and head north you can pick up any places you inadvertently missed going south. Most of the time my suggested route follows the official one but there are some points where the route disappears or is simply uninteresting, and in these cases I've offered alternatives.

Although we think of Alsace as one region, politically it is two, with Bas-Rhin in the north and Haut-Rhin in the south. Once upon a time the regions ignored each other to such an extent that they didn't even produce a joint map of the entire area; luckily the two tourist boards do now speak to each other.

The southerly region accounts for nearly all the best wine. The Bas-Rhin has coarser soil and flatter vineyards, the Haut-Rhin has the classic sloping sites and correspondingly more beautiful scenery. As you head south, you can follow the development of wine styles, although of course you can't simply say that the wine improves as you move south; there are too many dedicated producers north of Sélestat just dying to contradict this theory, some of whom are mentioned below.

In a region where over 65% of winemakers own less than a hectare and treat winemaking as a weekend hobby, you'll see forests of *vente directe* signs that signal properties that are simply too small to register in most guidebooks. If a property takes your fancy, check it out. Meanwhile, those producers recommended here make good wines, are happy to receive visitors and in most cases speak English.

Two obvious places to head for as a first-night stop are **Strasbourg** and La Petite-Pierre. Your choice depends to a certain extent on how you feel about navigating in towns. Strasbourg is certainly not for the faint-hearted, particularly since it has dug up most of its city centre to lay tramlines.

The hotel I would currently suggest there, the Sofitel, is large and corporate, but it's relatively easy to find without getting caught up in the roadworks and you can reach the major tourist attractions from it on foot. I've also enjoyed staying at the Hôtel des Rohan, opposite the cathedral (an austere and beautiful building with an amazingly complex astronomical clock which goes into action at 12.30pm every day; be there by 12.15 or they won't let you in). Petite-France, a pedestrianized area of ancient, half-timbered buildings including the Tanners' Quarter, offers attractive walks.

There are several highly-rated restaurants, but I prefer to eat at one of the *winstubs* or at Maison Kammerzell. *Winstubs* offer you good-value, authentic Alsace specialities in traditional surroundings, and I like them immensely. Try Zum Strissel (stained-glass windows, chicken and chips, Baeckeoffe at weekends and Riesling by the pitcher) or s'Klostertuewel. There are several excellent butchers/*charcuteries* where you can stock up on picnic goods – notably Frick-Lutz on Rue des Orfèvres, Kirn on Rue du 22-novembre, and Klein on Boulevard d'Anvers – and the homesick can buy BLT sandwiches from Marks et Spencer.

The countryside option is a stopover at **La Petite-Pierre**, near the Sarre-Union junction of the A4. This is a pretty mountain village with wonderful views. It's very much a tourist honeypot, so you will be sharing your mountain idyll with half of Europe, but it's popular for a reason. There are several good tourist hotels in the centre, such as the Trois Roses, and one, the Auberge d'Imsthal, outside the village on the D178.

If you've stayed one night in Champagne en route, you might consider a lunch-time stop on your second day at La Grange du Paysan at **Hinsingen** (take the Sarreguemines exit off the A4 from Reims). But I should mention that if you eat here, the food comes in such enormous portions that you would be wise to avoid Strasbourg's finest in the evening.

This was one of the first restaurants I visited in France and it remains a benchmark for honest, unpretentious regional cooking, brilliantly done. When I lived in Frankfurt it was somewhere to go for Sunday lunch, when they serve whole roast suckling pig. Before being carved it's paraded around the dining-room on a platter, to a round of applause. I can also warmly recommend their *pot-au-feu* (inadequately translated as 'stew'). Between the starter and the main course they serve *flammekueche*, a bacon, onion and cream-cheese tart on a wafer-thin dough base. Each table has a whole tart and you are given every encouragement to finish it.

The route proper starts at Marlenheim, but I'd recommend skipping the outer section and suggest you pick it up at **Ottrott** or **Obernai**. Almost at once you can deviate from it and climb to Mont-Ste-Odile, for ancient religious monuments and exceptional views (unless like me you visit when it's misty). Back on the road, **Barr** is the first stop for a producer and we begin on the nursery slopes.

DOMAINE KLIPFEL is right on the wine route, in the town, and an easy place to visit. There's always someone on hand to welcome you in English, tasting is free and there's even an introductory slide show with English voice-over. And yes, there are drawbacks. The estate is heavily geared up for group visits and focuses on these rather than individual customers. Groups are served meals, for instance, which aren't available to individuals. You can visit the cellars and winemaking museum, a few streets away, but only during the week – it's parties only at the weekend. The chances are that you won't make direct contact with the winemaker here, but it's a straightforward place to visit, to ease you in perhaps, and the welcome is genuine. The wines are of a good standard and this is one of the few places to offer the local speciality, Klevner de Heiligenstein.

Nearby, reached via Mittelbergheim, is **Andlau**, a pretty village surrounded by steep slopes. Its abbey is currently under-going extensive renovation. In the crypt is an ancient fertility symbol; local legend has it that if women sit on the back of the statue of the she-bear they will be pregnant within a year. Me, I wouldn't go near it.

The family that runs **DOMAINE GRESSER** has been living in the same house since 1667 and the present incumbent, 36-year-old Rémy Gresser, is a firm believer in passing on the land to future generations in as good a condition as he received it from his father. To this end he is a keen advocate of organic methods in the vineyard and has recently had great success in pest control using parasitic wasps. He welcomes visitors in a small, rustic-style tasting-room but is currently renovating a larger room which will offer more facilities. He's very committed to supporting Andlau and helps to organize two- or three-day visits for people who want to explore this underrated area in more depth.

A full range of wines is offered; I was particularly impressed by the Rieslings, ranging from '92 generic at FF26 to various Grands Crus at FF56–70. Rémy Gresser owns several parcels of land on different soils and can take you through the effects of the *terroirs* on the taste of his wines. He's a first-class, dedicated producer, highly recommended.

The place to stay in the village is the Zinck-Hôtel. This is a design victim's dream. The hotel has been converted from an old mill and the workings can still be seen in the breakfast-room. Each room is individually designed, some on traditional lines, others decidedly eccentric. The most popular of these are called Jazzy, Branchée (switched-on) and Baroque. This last has emerald-green walls, a canopied bed covered in red brocade, and a sofa with claw feet that look like they're made from giant blue pipecleaners. It almost seems a shame to open your suit-case and spoil the designer lines by littering your underwear about. This place is a lot of fun. There's no restaurant, but the owner's brother runs a lively *winstub* in the village, Le Relais de la Poste. For grander meals try Au Boeuf Rouge. M Zinck is fascinating on local history; between him and Rémy Gresser you can really get information.

Leaving Andlau, heading south, the road climbs to give spectacular views. It passes through **Itterswiller**, a large, floral, touristy village well served with hotels and restaurants along the long main street. Fans of more traditional places to stay will prefer the rustic style of Hôtel Arnold. Some rooms have balconies and good views across the vineyards, and meals are served in a *winstub* close by. The ceiling in its panelled dining-room appears to be held up by giant winepress screws.

One table in the restaurant was occupied by a session of the local council on the night I was there. Debates were held in Elsässisch, the minutes written in French. The food has a heavy regional emphasis and is very good indeed: melting, unctuous *baeckeoffe* (a hearty stew), excellent *foie gras*, and chicken with *spaetzle* (noodles). House wines are made by their own domaine and are on sale in a boutique next door. This also offers regional craft-work and tableware, attractively presented, as well as the home-made jam the hotel serves at breakfast.

Advanced students would be advised to deviate slightly from the wine road here and head to **Epfig**. **DOMAINE OSTERTAG** is run by André Ostertag and his sister. He identifies 70 distinct areas within his 10ha of vines and produces about 15 wines reflecting the effect of different soils on a number of grape varieties. If exploring this question in depth appeals to you then he's your man, and will give generously of his time, but he's not keen on starting from scratch.

He concentrates on Riesling, Pinot Gris and Gewurztraminer, and makes two ranges. One, in green bottles with green-lettered labels, emphasizes the taste of the grape; the other, with brown bottles and labels, emphasizes the effect of the soil. 'Wine for us is a reflection of our soil and our soul', he says. M Ostertag studied in Burgundy and this influences his technique: he makes Pinot Blanc in oak and uses *bâtonnage* (stirs up the lees) every few days.

This is very personal winemaking. He hates the blowsy, overblown character many winemakers give Gewurztraminer and battles to restrain the grape's natural tendencies: 'I always fight against the grape. It's too exuberant. It's not the way I think you have to be in life.' Certainly he is himself restrained yet intense, lean and wiry; here is a classic example of the wine being an expression of the man. If you usually don't like Gewurztraminer, try his. You could be on to something.

The walled village of Dambach-la-Ville is worth exploring en route to **St-Hippolyte** (continue along the D35 and then join the D1B). St-Hippolyte is the first village of note in the Haut-Rhin and home to the estate of **KLEIN AUX VIEUX REMPARTS**. Françoise Klein and her husband farm 7ha of vines. She's particularly interested in the marriage of food and wine, and receives you in a pretty tasting-room where you can compare different vintages and the effect of her three vineyard soils: sand, limestone and granite. They specialize in Riesling Schlossreben, Gewurztraminer Schlossreben and Tokay Geisberg. (These aren't Grands Crus but named sites, *lieux-dits*.)

Unusually, the Kleins can offer vintages dating back to the mid-1980s, in their Vendanges Tardives. At over FF100 a bottle, these are not cheap but the opportunity to taste such wines is rare. At the other end of the scale, their basic varietal range starts at just FF22. Also try the local speciality, Rouge de St-Hippolyte, aged in wood. Mme Klein is very warm and a fund of knowledge, as you might guess from the way she describes herself as 'winemaker-oenologist'. If you already have some experience of Alsace wines, she'll be particularly illuminating.

There are various options for an overnight stay. In St-Hippolyte itself is the Ducs de Lorraine, a classic Logis with a large dining-room with firmly-starched linen, candelabra, and traditional dishes, some more successful than others. Madame keeps a close eye on all stages of the meal and is most concerned that all should be well. Bedrooms are a mixture of classic and rustic in style. Many have balconies with good views across the village and up to the Haut-Koenigsberg which towers above it. Two rival churches chime the quarters right through the night. It's a British tour operator's base hotel; their clients have voted it the company's most welcoming.

Sélestat (signposted off the D201) is a medium-sized town nearby with one of Alsace's most beautiful Romanesque churches, the Eglise St-Foy, and the remarkable Humanist Library. For a little luxury, stay at the Hostellerie de l'Abbaye La Pommeraie, a recently-restored abbey in the town centre. Rooms are large and dramatically decorated, some Empire, all chandeliers and gilt, others Alsacien, with light wood panelling and imaginative upholstery. Sumptuous breakfasts provide enough for two meals. I think the restaurant is overreaching itself at present and the brasserie, offering simpler regional dishes, is probably a better bet. There's a warm, unstuffy welcome and a parting gift of *kugelhopf* cake.

If you'd like to move off the wine route and into the mountains, head for Auberge La Meunière in **Thannenkirch**. This village has an Alpine feel, with wonderful valley views. The rustic, panelled dining-room shares these views and offers good cooking: pork medallions in beer, beef with marrow and pickled shallots. Here for the first time I was offered bleeding chunks of meat as an *amuse-gueule* (like a mini-kebab, complete with sliver of green pepper). Rooms are modest and heavily-furnished; the most favoured have that view.

From the St-Hippolyte–Thannenkirch road it's just a few kilometres to Haut-Koenigsbourg, a splendid mountain view-point with a château to visit. Then descend from Thannenkirch to **Bergheim**. There's an excellent restaurant here, the Wistub du Sommelier. This is where I first tackled *choucroute* (sauerkraut) and it's also an ideal place to try other classic Alsace dishes at very reasonable prices. It has a good wine list.

Fortified, head back up the wine route a kilometre or so to **Rorschwihr** and **ROLLY GASSMANN**. No English is spoken here; it's a perfect example of how far you can get with smiles, nods and goodwill, and whatever you can manage in French or German. Louis and Marie-Thérèse (whose maiden name was Rolly) come from winemaking families dating back to 1676. These people are relaxed and happy, and so are their wines.

Even the most humble of varieties, Sylvaner, is full and round with surprising concentration for just FF25. You can also taste the difference between Pinot Blanc and Auxerrois. This is user-friendly winemaking, where the philosophy is simplicity: 'The less you touch the grape, the better the wine will be.' I tasted their entire range on sale, 30 wines, and there wasn't one I wouldn't happily have bought – good stuff!

Return to Bergheim for a complete contrast, at **MARCEL DEISS**. If the Rolly Gassmanns and their wines are big and open-hearted, M & Mme Deiss are nervy and intense. And, unsurprisingly, so are their wines. Jean-Michel is in charge of the vineyards, his wife Clarisse is in charge of sales.

Mme Deiss has elevated direct-to-customer sales into an art, establishing early on what style of wine you prefer by assessing your response to two vintages of Muscat, and pitching her explanation of the estate according to how much you know about the wines and how much you want to spend. This is very helpful as the tasting is closely tailored to your require-ments, and she'll give you all the time you need. Sometimes Mme Deiss may appear rather didactic but it's only her passion for the wines getting the better of her. And they are very good indeed – not cheap, but of excellent quality because of the low yields. There's real commitment here, both to the wines and to the region as a whole.

The wine route now leads past **Ribeauvillé**. Here we enter honeypot territory, the villages most popular with tourists. Ribeauvillé centre is pedestrianized and worth a stroll, perhaps stopping at the restaurant Zum Pfifferhüs, which offers regional specialities in a building classed as a historic monument. Then, if you take the right turn at the traffic lights just after the village centre, you'll come to a pottery on the left after about 200m. Alsace is famous for its traditional ceramics – distinctive floral patterns on a blue or brown background – and there's an excellent selection here, reasonably priced, including *kugelhopf* moulds and casseroles for *baeckeoffe*. There's also a range of wine coolers and jugs, some festooned with bunches of grapes.

Next, turn left off the wine route for **Zellenberg**. Here I saw my first Alsace storks. Actually this is where most of France saw its first Alsace storks – the nesting, birth and development of a stork family was filmed from Zellenberg's church tower by French television last year, with regular updates. I gather it did wonders for local tourism.

JEAN BECKER and **GASTON BECK**, based in the village, are the same firm, now run by the 13th generation. Martine Becker-Beck is Sales Manager, and if she's not on one of her sales trips she'll be on duty in the company's large, rustic tasting-room. Martine is extremely knowledgeable about local wines and history. The estate offers a range from generic to Grand Cru, all bearing the stamp of good winemaking. Even the Sylvaner is lively, clean and refreshing. For grapes grown in their Grand Cru vineyard, Froehn, which are not allowed to be designated as Grand Cru wine, they've put the letter 'F' on the label. Martine is equally at home taking you through the basic differences in taste between the Alsace grape varieties as she is in dissecting finer points of oenology with experts. There's a good range of *eaux-de-vie*, from wild raspberry to holly, of all things, and a worthwhile cellar tour. She may even stay open at lunch-time.

The Schlossberg hotel offers a friendly welcome and a cosy dining-room with honest regional cooking, popular with locals. The owners often exchange customers with Maximilien, the village's Michelin-starred restaurant, so you can eat one night at each. They're very informative about local history and can offer a brochure (in French only) describing a 'historical circuit' of the village. Pricey rooms, in rustic style with sombre, dark wood, are housed separately across the road. Some have terraces with views across to the medieval town of Riquewihr.

Riquewihr is a vital stop on any wine tour. It has an unrivalled collection of 16th-, 17th- and 18th-century half-timbered and stone buildings. The surrounding vineyards are some of the region's finest, and one of the reasons for the early settlement and importance of the town. Its old ramparts and defences remain in evidence and many old-established wine firms still do business here.

A good example is **DOPFF & IRION**, and you can visit the estate in two ways. If you turn up on spec you are invited into a long, decorative tasting-cellar. Here you can stand at the bar and sample the range. If you make an appointment, however, you can make a half-hour tour of the cellars. This takes you through the fermentation and maturation areas, avoiding the more 'industrial' sights of wine production such as storage pallets, and includes a room with old winepresses apparently supporting the ceiling. The room also contains large wooden barrels, the oldest dating back to 1783, which were last put into service in 1982. In that year the harvest was one and a half times the usual size and every available container was commandeered, including railway tankers and even swimming-pools.

The wines at Dopff & Irion are firm and dry, and very well made. Generics start at FF22 for an Edelzwicker and prices rise steeply thereafter. The Crémant, at FF42–49, is impressively rich. They'll also sell you *eaux-de-vie* and plenty of gifts packs.

From Riquewihr or Zellenberg you can follow the Grand Cru vineyard footpath. It's about 15km long, and leads you through the main vineyards with some stunning views. The path is waymarked and you can pick up a map at one of the local tourist information offices or at properties nearby. The map also shows ways of shortening the route.

From Riquewihr the wine route itself passes through Bennwihr and Mittelwihr. These villages were heavily bombed in the closing stages of the Second World War and have little charm, so I suggest taking the narrow vineyard road from Riquewihr direct to **Kientzheim**, which is very picturesque. (It's easier to find when coming from the other direction, so you may prefer to incorporate it in your return journey. To do this, drive past the fountain in Kientzheim and take the road straight ahead of you heading out into the vines.)

Kientzheim has a wine museum in the château which houses the Confrérie de St-Etienne, the local brotherhood (sisters occasionally allowed) devoted to the promotion of Alsace wine. A good place to stay is at the Abbaye d'Alspach, attractively converted in rustic Alsace style, with a tower and open wooden walkways. There's no restaurant but plenty of advice is given on where to eat locally. I think it's a better bet to stay here than in boisterously touristy Kaysersberg up the road.

The estate to visit in Kientzheim is **PAUL BLANCK & FILS**. Its tasting-cellars are full of curiosities, including a collection of caged puppets whirring around on the tops of barrels. There's a relaxed atmosphere for the tasting and explanation of the wines – which are extremely good. If you're keen to learn, allow one and a half to two hours. Marcel Blanck, the winemaker, is big and generous; so are his wines.

There's another informative wine trail from Kientzheim, taking you through the Grand Cru vineyards. Local properties can provide a map. Look out for a slightly surreal, three-part sculpture in memory of Josef Schwartz, guiding force behind the introduction of the Grands Crus.

Cooperatives are particularly significant in Alsace, where many growers produce on too small a scale to vinify their grapes themselves. Co-ops supply a large percentage of the wines we drink in the UK and there's a tendency to think they produce quantity rather than quality. Sometimes I believe that's true, and whereas co-ops are easy places to buy wine, particularly for the novice, they won't give you the personal contact a small-scale grower can. The **CAVE VINICOLE DE KIENTZHEIM/KAYSERSBERG**, however, has an outstanding reputation for quality. Formed in 1955 with 150 members, it was the first in the region to install electronic quality-selection and -monitoring equipment, in 1976. Now it produces an average of 1.7M bottles a year.

Dealing with huge volumes of grapes arriving at the cellar each day throughout the harvest used to leave farmers queuing up with trailer-loads of grapes until well past midnight, waiting for them to be graded and weighed – bad for the farmer who had to be up and out again at the crack of dawn, bad for the grapes which suffered a deterioration in quality when exposed for hours to the air. Now everything is computerized and the grapes are vinified separately according to their variety, quality and place of origin (and farmers are paid strictly in accordance with the quality of what they produce). The separate wines are tracked by computer right through the cellar.

A free multilingual tour is offered each week during the summer and it's well worth attending just to see the complexity of an operation on this scale. There's excellent Crémant (kept on its lees twice as long as the law demands) and good varietal character in all the wines, which can be tried in two tasting-rooms: a modern one, in the main building at Kientzheim (signposted off the Kientzheim bypass), and another, in rustic style, on the main street in Kaysersberg.

Ammerschwihr was 'compulsorily redeveloped' in the last days of the Second World War and most of its ancient centre destroyed. There's a small hotel, A l'Arbre Vert, with good regional cooking and topiary in the dining-room. The village is also worth stopping at for the small family firm of **Sick-Dreyer** (on the D11i between Ammerschwihr and Kientzheim).

One of the first winegrowers I ever visited, because I'd enjoyed her wines from a UK merchant, Mme Dreyer offered a warm, friendly welcome despite my breaking most of the rules by turning up unannounced in the middle of the harvest (it was probably lunch-time, too). These are wines of great finesse, particularly those from her beloved Kaefferkopf vineyard (plenty of politics here, for those who are interested, on why this isn't a Grand Cru site).

Mme Dreyer takes the opposite view to those producers who like to keep separate the wines made from different sites: she believes that mixing grapes grown on all the various soils within the vineyard produces a richer, more complex, harmonious wine. Faced with the evidence in the glass, how can I disagree? The firm no longer exports to the UK, after an unhappy business experience. Redress the balance by buying direct.

The wines of the **Zind-Humbrecht** estate, on the other hand, are widely available in the UK and regularly walk off with batches of prizes in international wine competitions. Father and son Leonard and Olivier Humbrecht make wine together. Olivier has studied winemaking all over the world and is one of the first non-British Masters of Wine.

They have recently built a new winery among the vines on the D11 just outside **Turckheim** and it's an architect's dream – a brilliant, striking, modern design. Indeed, while I was there about a hundred architects were being shown round, a little the worse for wear after lunch and looking enviously at us while we were tasting.

English language tastings are conducted by Olivier's Scottish wife Margaret (they met on a London bus). The domaine isn't prepared for impromptu visits and doesn't encourage tourists. It's vital to make an appointment. You'll be rewarded by a tasting of four or five excellent wines, depending on what is open, and a careful explanation of the range, tailored to your level of interest. Margaret prefers to devote an hour to explaining the wines in detail in this way than to cater for casual visitors.

Here is a graphic example of just how much you can save by buying direct from the vineyard: a '91 Sylvaner is on sale in Wine Rack for perhaps £6.50 but you can buy the '92 from the domaine for just FF30. At the other end of the range, the '90 Clos Windsbühl Gewurztraminer costs about £16 in Wine Rack and the '92 is FF80 at source. If you taste the '90, or the '93, you might be forgiven for thinking that the estate is keen to produce very powerful, intense, overblown Gewurztraminer. The '92 is much more restrained, however, and closer to the domaine's preferred style.

Fans of American wine guru Robert Parker may recall that he awarded the '89 Clos Windsbühl Gewurztraminer his ultimate accolade, 100/100. This threw the estate into confusion. The Humbrechts had only recently acquired the Windsbühl vineyard and 1989 was the first year they made wine from it. By the time Parker's rating was published all the wine had been shipped, and the first they knew of their success was when irate customers began to phone, demanding to know why they hadn't been allocated more of it. Robert Parker considers the Humbrechts to be among the great winemakers of the world, and I couldn't disagree.

From Turckheim to **Wintzenheim** is a short, if dull, hop. Wintzenheim has little of the charm of most Alsace villages but in the main street, well hidden, is the estate of JOS MEYER. A charming, small tasting-room off a cobbled courtyard offers high-quality, elegant wines, on the dear side. There's very good Pinot Blanc, and Riesling Les Pierrets '88 at FF62.

Colmar is next on the agenda. The prospect of driving into Colmar deters all but the brave but it's worth it for the atmosphere and architecture of the pedestrianized old town. The faint-hearted could consider parking on the outskirts and walking in (the town is fairly compact) but if you feel like staying here try the Hôtel St-Martin, which comes complete with a 16th century spiral staircase and Renaissance turret. The hotel is well signposted – you're directed to park in a square outside the police station, a couple of minutes' walk away. Rooms are comfortable and spread over a wide price range.

The St-Martin doesn't have a restaurant, so head for one of Colmar's many *winstubs*. My favourite is S'Parisser Stewwele, five minutes from the hotel. It heaves with local couples and parties who come for terrific food such as *schieffala* (shoulder of pork) and wonderful *crème brûlée*. Alsace wines are available in jug or bottle; the staff are jovial and efficient. Do book. And don't miss Maison des Têtes, a beautiful 17th-century building with about a hundred carved heads decorating the front. The food doesn't quite live up to the surroundings, but at least take a look. Good picnic *charcuterie* can be found at Glasser on Rue des Boulangers and at La Ferme on Rue des Têtes; there's excellent bread at Léonard Helmstetter on Rue des Serruriers.

Walk through the old town and look out for the painted façade of Maison Pfister, the Tanners' Quarter and Little Venice down by the river. Then there is also the famous Isenheim altarpiece in the Unterlinden Museum... best to visit the tourist information office, or ask the hotel to show you where everything is, if you have time to spend half a day here.

The next port of call is **Eguisheim**, one of my favourite villages for the perfectly preserved ramparts which encircle it. (You can walk right round, following the signs marked *circuit de visite*.) It gets very busy in season, so in summer I would go early. As you stroll through the streets, open courtyards reveal modern winemaking equipment squeezed in under half-timbered buildings. This is still a working village. In the central square is a good restaurant, Le Caveau d'Eguisheim, offering traditional dishes in very large helpings.

Husseren-les-Châteaux, above Eguisheim, is the starting-point for the diversion along the signposted Route des 5 Châteaux. It's also the home of **KUENTZ-BAS**, offering a small, rustic tasting-room and a selection of two ranges. Cuvée Tradition is made from bought-in grapes and designed to be drunk young; Réserve Personnelle is from Kuentz-Bas' own vineyards and has more ageing potential.

The wine route now meanders through some rather uninteresting villages and eventually forces you onto the main dual carriageway (the N83). Since you've got to use this road in the end, I suggest you join it sooner rather than later, bypassing Pfaffenheim and Rouffach and heading direct for **Westhalten**.

Just as you turn off the dual carriageway for Westhalten you come to the estate of **RENÉ MURÉ**, which is well worth a visit. It has a series of small, elegantly-furnished tasting-rooms, the main one with a glorious view overlooking the estate's principal vineyard, the Clos St-Landelin, facing up the valley to Westhalten. A tour of the cellars reveals a 13th-century winepress, the oldest in Alsace, and a family tree dating back to 1620. This is a very easy place to visit; you don't need an appointment, there are several English-speaking staff dedicated to visitors and they're as happy giving a beginner's guide to the wines as comparing particular vintages and soils. These are excellent wines, with a recognizable, soft, fruity house style.

From here it's a short drive up to Westhalten to my favourite Alsace hotel, the Auberge Cheval Blanc, which has a dozen rooms in an annexe built five years ago, looking out over the valley. I find a great sense of contentment gazing at this view in the evening. The restaurant is Alsacien in furnishing and food – the FF150 menu is good value and the *foie gras* and *rognons de veau* (calves' kidneys) are excellent. The family makes its own wine – honest generic appellations – which you can try out over dinner and maybe buy a case of. A generous buffet breakfast is provided, if you still have room, and then perhaps you could try the lovely vineyard walk (the hotel has maps). They don't get many British visitors here, and those that do arrive receive a very warm welcome.

And for me, this is where the road ends. The wine route carries on for 30km yet, but the scenery becomes less attractive and the towns not so interesting. The character becomes less Alsacien, more Vosgesien, and by the time you get to Thann you're surrounded by pine forests, logging yards and sawmills – it almost looks as though you've strayed into Twin Peaks. You can either cut through the Vosges mountains and head up to the motorway via Nancy (which is really doing things the hard way) or, better, turn around and visit the places you missed on the way down – perhaps picking up the Route of the Fried Pike-Perch.

Listings

When telephoning France from the UK, first dial 00 33 then the number shown. Producers are listed in the wine route order, and hotels/restaurants by town or village according to the route. Accommodation prices are per room, meal prices are per head.

Producers

Domaine Klipfel
1 rue Rotland, 67140 Barr
Tel 88 08 94 85, Fax 88 08 53 18
Open Mon–Sun 10–12, 14–18
Credit cards accepted
Some English

Domaine André & Rémy Gresser
2 rue de l'Ecole, 67140 Andlau
Tel 88 08 95 88, Fax 88 08 55 99
Open Mon–Sun 10–12, 14–19
Good English

Domaine Ostertag
87 rue Finkwiller, 67680 Epfig
Tel 88 85 51 44
Visits by appointment
(for tutored tasting on Sat, in
French only, phone 2 weeks in
advance)
Good English

Klein aux Vieux Remparts
Route du Haut-Koenigsbourg,
68590 St-Hippolyte
Tel 89 73 00 41, Fax 89 73 04 94
Visits by appointment
Good English

Rolly Gassmann
1 rue de l'Eglise, 68590 Rorschwihr
Tel 89 73 63 28, Fax 89 73 33 06
Open Mon–Sat 8–12, 13–19
No English

Marcel Deiss
15 route du Vin, 68750 Bergheim
Tel 89 73 63 37, Fax 89 73 32 67
Open Mon–Sat 10–12, 14–18
Credit cards accepted
Some English

Jean Becker/Gaston Beck
2–4 route d'Ostheim
68340 Zellenberg
Tel 89 47 90 16, Fax 89 47 99 57
Open Mon–Sun 8–12, 14–18;
possibly also open lunch-time
Good English

Dopff & Irion
Au Château de Riquewihr,
68340 Riquewihr
Tel 89 47 92 51, Fax 89 47 92 51
Tasting-cellar open Mon–Sun 8–18
incl lunch-time; tour of cellars
by appointment
Credit cards accepted
Some English

Paul Blanck & Fils
32 Grand-Rue
68240 Kientzheim
Tel 89 78 23 56, Fax 89 47 16 45
Open Mon–Sat 9–12, 14–17.30
Some English

Cave Vinicole de
Kientzheim/
Kaysersberg
68240 Kientzheim
(& 68240 Kaysersberg)
Tel 89 47 13 19, Fax 89 47 34 38
Open at Kientzheim Mon–Thurs
8–12, 14–18, Fri 8–12, 14–17,
Sat & Sun 10–12, 14–18; cellar tour
July & Aug Wed at 15.00,

lasts approx 1 hour, no booking
necessary, multilingual
Open at Kaysersberg Easter–11 Nov
Mon–Sun

Sick-Dreyer
17 route de Kientzheim,
68770 Ammerschwihr
Tel 89 47 11 31, Fax 89 47 32 60
Visits by appointment
No English

Zind-Humbrecht
4 route du Colmar, 68230
Turckheim
Tel 89 27 02 05, Fax 89 27 22 58
Visits by appointment Mon–Fri pm
English: 'like a native'

Jos Meyer
76 rue Clémenceau,
68920 Wintzenheim
Tel 89 27 01 57, Fax 89 27 03 98
Open Mon–Fri 10–12, 14–17
Good English

An additional visit:
Robert Schoffit
27 rue des Aubépines
68000 Colmar
Tel 89 24 41 14, Fax 89 41 40 52
Open Mon–Sat 8.30–12, 14–17;
visits by appointment Sun
Some English
(A rising star using traditional
methods)

Kuentz-Bas
14 route du Vin,
68420 Husseren-les-Châteaux
Tel 89 49 30 24, Fax 89 49 23 39
Open autumn & winter Mon–Fri
9–12, 13.30–18, Sat 10–12;
spring & summer also open pm
Good English

René Muré
Clos St-Landelin,
Route du Vin, 68250 Rouffach
Tel 89 49 62 19, Fax 89 49 74 85

Open Mon–Fri 8–18, Sat 8–12,
14–18, Sun 10–12, 14–18; closed
Nov–spring on Sun (except last 2
Sun before Christmas)
Good English

Hotels and Restaurants
H Hotel   *R* Restaurant

Hinsingen
R La Grange du Paysan
8 rue Principale
67260 Hinsingen
Tel 88 00 91 83
FF65–245

La Petite-Pierre
HR Auberge d'Imsthal
Route Forestière d'Imsthal,
67290 La Petite-Pierre
Tel 88 70 45 21, Fax 88 70 40 26
Rooms FF220–600, Meals FF80–230

HR Aux Trois Roses
67290 La Petite-Pierre
Tel 88 89 89 00, Fax 88 70 41 28
Rooms FF315–530, Meals FF97–245

Strasbourg
HR Sofitel
Place St-Pierre-le-Jeune,
67000 Strasbourg
Tel 88 32 99 30, Fax 88 32 60 67
Rooms FF650–995, Meals
FF130–210

H Hôtel des Rohan
17 rue Maroquin,
67000 Strasbourg
Tel 88 32 85 11, Fax 88 75 65 37
FF350–595

R Maison Kammerzell
16 place Cathédrale
67000 Strasbourg
Tel 88 32 42 14
FF190–260
(There are also a few rooms
upstairs, in Hôtel Baumann, for
FF420–630.)

R Zum Strissel
5 place Grande Boucherie
67000 Strasbourg
Tel 88 32 14 73
FF56–130

R S'Klosterstuewel
16 bis rue Sanglier
67000 Strasbourg
Tel 88 23 59 84
FF75–95

Andlau
H Zinck-Hôtel
13 rue de la Marne
67140 Andlau
Tel 88 08 27 30
Fax 88 08 42 50
FF250–500

R Au Boeuf Rouge
6 rue Dr-Stoltz
67240 Andlau
Tel 88 08 96 26
FF165–245

R Le Relais de la Poste
1 rue des Forgerons
67140 Andlau
Tel 88 08 95 91
FF65–135

Itterswiller
HR Hôtel Arnold
98 route du Vin
67140 Itterswiller
Tel 88 85 50 58
Fax 88 85 55 54
Rooms FF440–695
Meals FF150–385

St-Hippolyte
HR Aux Ducs de Lorraine
16 route du Vin
68590 St-Hippolyte
Tel 89 73 00 09
Fax 89 73 05 46
Rooms FF450–600
Meals FF100–300
(member of Relais du Silence)

Sélestat
HR Hostellerie de
l'Abbaye La Pommeraie
8 avenue Foch, 67600 Sélestat
Tel 88 92 07 84, Fax 88 92 08 71
Rooms FF690–1,500
Meals FF230–450

Thannenkirch
HR Auberge La Meunière
30 rue Ste-Anne
68590 Thannenkirch
Tel 89 73 10 47
Fax 89 73 12 31
Rooms FF250–310
Meals FF95–180

Bergheim
R Wistub du Sommelier
51 Grand'Rue
68750 Bergheim
Tel 89 73 69 99
Fax 89 73 36 58
FF150–230

Ribeauvillé
R Zum Pfifferhüs
14 Grand'Rue
68150 Ribeauvillé
Tel 89 73 62 28
FF140–190

Zellenberg
HR Le Schlossberg
59A rue de la Fontaine,
68340 Zellenberg
Tel 89 47 93 85, Fax 89 47 82 40
Rooms FF300–550
Meals FF85–230

R Maximilien
19A route d'Ostheim
Tel 89 47 99 69
FF185–360

Kientzheim
H L'Abbaye d'Alspach
2–4 rue Foch
68240 Kientzheim
Tel 89 47 16 00, Fax 89 78 29 73
FF220–400

Ammerschwihr
HR A l'Arbre Vert
4 rue des Cigognes
68770 Ammerschwihr
Tel 89 47 12 23, Fax 89 78 27 21
Rooms FF100–350, Meals FF70–210

Colmar
H Hôtel St-Martin
38 Grand'Rue, 68000 Colmar
Tel 89 24 11 51, Fax 89 23 47 78
FF300–620

R S'Parisser Stewwele
4 place Jeanne-d'Arc
Tel 89 41 42 33, Fax 89 41 37 99
FF120–320
R Maison des Têtes
19 rue Têtes
Tel 89 24 43 43
FF130–300

Eguisheim
R Le Caveau d'Eguisheim
3 place Château
68420 Eguisheim
Tel 89 41 08 89, Fax 89 23 79 99
FF130–335

Westhalten
HR Auberge Cheval Blanc
29 rue Rouffach, 68250 Westhalten
Tel 89 47 01 16, Fax 89 47 64 40
Rooms FF300–450, Meals
FF150–400

Champagne

Champagne is a pretty miserable place. It rains nearly half the
year – for 160 days on average. It's cold, damp and often misty.
The average temperature is a meagre 10°C (50°F). It produces
thin, neutral, acidic, low-alcohol wines. If someone hadn't
worked out how to put bubbles in the bottle the wine
wouldn't have a great deal going for it, but someone did. Now
Champagne makes some of the world's most expensive wines,
and has attached to these an aura of glamour, celebration,
sophistication and extravagance. Pretty clever stuff, eh?

Attila the Hun fought a major battle on the plains of
Champagne in the 5th century AD, and the First World
War's first Battle of the Marne laid waste to the vineyards
just before the 1914 harvest. In between these acts of war
there are two important names to know in the romantic
version of the winemaking history of Champagne: Dom
Pérignon, a 17th-century monk, and Veuve Clicquot, who
lived a century later.

To start with, the wines sparkled by accident and bubbles
were frowned upon as a fault. The wine would stop fermenting
in vat in the cold of winter and start again after it had been
bottled, when the cellars warmed up in spring, trapping the
carbon dioxide given off by the fermenting yeast. The wines
themselves, from red grapes, were probably an insipid pink in
colour, weak and harsh.

Dom Pérignon changed all that. Although he may not
have been the person who sorted out the making-it-sparkling
question, which is a shame for fans of romantic legend, he
was certainly responsible for developing the art of blending
wines from different areas and vintages to make the end
product smoother, and for maturing the wine long enough for

it to acquire a mature richness. He also made white wine from black grapes by using very gentle pressing.

Dom Pérignon showed how to turn a problem – weak, insipid sparkling wines – into an advantage. (Admittedly he was helped by the English invention of stronger, more reliable bottles.) Later champagne-makers learned how to control the production of the bubbles, and how to remove the by-products of the process, which is where Mme Clicquot comes in.

All wine ferments once – that's what creates the alcohol. Champagne ferments a second time while in bottle, but these days it's no longer an accident. Technologists have worked out how to induce a second fermentation by adding a dose of sugar and yeast to a bottle of once-fermented wine. The dose is carefully regulated: too little and you have a very weak sparkle, too much and the bottle explodes under the pressure.

The yeast creates bubbles; it also leaves dead cells, or lees, at the bottom of the bottle. For years champagne was drunk 'off its lees' because no-one could work out how to remove them. You had to be very careful how you poured the wine, or the lees would cloud it (it was worse than pouring White Shield). Then Widow Clicquot and her cellar-master invented the *pupitre*, a hinged board with holes cut into it at a 45° angle. Legend has it that she devised the prototype by cutting holes in her kitchen table.

You put the bottles in the holes horizontally and every day give them a jolting twist, which gradually, over two or three months, raises them until they stand vertically on their corks. The jolt loosens the sticky lees from the side of the bottle, the twist turns the bottle upright, easing the lees onto the cork. The process is known as *remuage*, inadequately translated as 'riddling'. Then you disgorge the lees. The original method simply allowed the cork to shoot out of the bottle and wasted some of the wine as well as removing the dead yeast cells. Today, you freeze the sediment into a pellet by upending the bottle neck into a brine bath. Open the bottle and the pellet flies out, complete with all the unwanted lees. Then you top up the bottle with a *dosage* of wine and sugar and recork it. Simple, really.

While all these refinements to the technical process were taking place, the champagne sales force wasn't idle. Zany stunts and flamboyant salesmen created the image that no party was complete without champagne. At the same time, the great champagne houses were formed. With the wine's increasing success, vineyards were planted beyond the original area, including in the Aube to the southeast. The big houses even began to buy in grapes from outside the region. A series of riots followed as irate growers tried to establish who was allowed to make champagne – at which point the First World War intervened. The Second World War saw the occupation of Reims and the formation of the CIVC, an interprofessional committee created to liaise with the occupying German army. It now represents the interests of champagne at home and abroad.

WHO MAKES THE WINE?

After the war, sales grew rapidly and the advertising efforts of the big champagne houses established their names worldwide. Today many of the most illustrious names are owned by multinational conglomerates and 'traded like playing Monopoly', as one grower put it.

At the other end of the spectrum you find the small-scale champagne maker, who bottles the wine made from his or her own vineyard. In between come the cooperatives and a huge group of nearly 20,000 growers who own on average little more than a hectare each and who sell grapes to the big houses and the cooperatives. Relatively few growers own enough land under vine to make a living from it.

You can tell from the label who has made your wine if you know how to decode the abbreviations used, as listed below. These are handy to remember because over 10,000 champagne brands, or different names, appear on the labels. (The figures in brackets show approximately how many brand names there are in each category.)

RM (Récoltant-Manipulant) A grower producing champagne from his or her own grapes (3,000)

RC (Récoltant-Coopérateur) A grower selling wine made by a cooperative (3,350)

R (Récoltant) A small-scale grower producing up to 500 bottles a year maximum under his or her own name (12)

ND (Négociant-Distributeur) A *récoltant* wishing to become a little more commercial can use these initials (8)

SR (Société de Récoltant) The term used by a company created by growers from the same family. The number of these is expected to increase (17)

NM (Négociant-Manipulant) A champagne house (1,170)

CM (Coopérative de Manipulation) A cooperative (200)

MA (Marque d'Acheteur) The term for shops' or restaurants' own-label brands, ie the buyer's own brand (2,500)

Since there are over 10,000 brands in total, you can't learn all the names, but the abbreviations at least tell you whether the wine was made by a grower, a négociant or a co-op, or, in the UK high street, if it has a name invented by a supermarket. RC, for instance, is a particularly cheeky one: the label will give every appearance of the wine being a grower's champagne, when in fact it was made by a co-op.

Twenty-eight of the champagne houses have formed themselves into a marketing group known as the Grandes Marques, or 'great brands'. This doesn't mean they're the best on offer, it's simply a name. Some great houses are members, but other equally fine houses are not – and a few members could be said to be trading on past glory rather than present quality.

A number of the champagne houses own vineyards, others buy in grapes; some, like Moët & Chandon, do both. Each will tell you its way is best. Vineyard owners say they can control quality from start to finish and are not dependent on the vagaries of the market; buyers-in point to the flexibility of being able to choose only the best grapes on offer and of being able to buy according to the quality of the harvest, of not being landed with loads of underripe or rotten grapes, say, in a bad year. Take your pick.

HOW THE WINES ARE CLASSIFIED

Champagne is made from three grape varieties: Chardonnay, Pinot Noir and Pinot Meunier. The two Pinots are black grapes and together account for roughly three-quarters of planting. If you see *blanc de blancs* (white of whites) on the label, the wine has been made only from the white grape, Chardonnay. *Blanc de noirs*, conversely, is made only from black grapes. You can make white wine from black grapes (with care) but you can't, of course, make red wine from white grapes. Pressing the black grapes gently and quickly ensures that next to no colouring escapes from the skins.

Rosé champagne is made either by allowing more colour to come out of the black grape-skins, or by making a separate still red wine and blending it in before bottling. Some still red wines are sold, called Coteaux Champenois; the village of Bouzy is best known for them. I think they are wildly over-priced in most cases. There's also a still pink wine, Rosé des Riceys, made at Les Riceys in the Aube.

The region's main product, by a huge margin, is white champagne. Most of this is non-vintage, shown on the label by the initials NV. This is a blend of wines from several vintages, hence no date. Vintage champagne on the other hand, does put a year on the label and must be made exclusively of wines from that vintage. The vintage champagnes are more expensive and need to spend much longer in bottle as they don't have the softening influence of older wines to help them along.

Top of the quality ladder is the Cuvée de Prestige, or deluxe champagne. Led by Moët's prestige brand, Dom Pérignon, most houses make an expensive, top-of-the-range wine. Unless you don't need to ask the price, I would suggest steering clear of these as better value is usually to be had elsewhere.

There are three wine districts in what the big houses would like you to think of as the 'classic' area of champagne, the Marne, and of these only two are held in really high esteem. The Montagne de Reims is between Reims and Epernay, the Côte des Blancs lies to the south of Epernay, and the Vallée de la Marne is to the west of Epernay.

The last of these is looked down on because it grows mostly the less-favoured Pinot Meunier grape. When you tour the big champagne houses, you'll be surprised how often you hear that the house uses no Pinot Meunier, or that it has no holdings in the Vallée de la Marne and other unfashionable areas. Meunier accounts for over a third of all planting, however, so somebody must be using it. Why don't they admit it?

The other two regions, Sézannais and the Aube, are so unfashionable as to be beyond the pale. The Aube is sufficiently unregarded that it doesn't even merit inclusion on the wine route. I think differently; there are some very good wines being made down there, and because the area is unfashionable the

CHAMPAGNE

wines are often much better value. The Aube lies closer to
Chablis than to Epernay, so I've included it as part of the
Golden Triangle wine route.

Back at the fashionable end, the growers and houses have
established a pecking-order for which villages produce the best
grapes. This is called the Echelle des Crus, the 'ladder of villages', and is divided up on a percentile basis. Top of the heap,
the best villages are said to be Grands Crus and rank at 100%.
Each year, up to 1990, the CIVC fixed a price per kilogram for
the grapes, and this was the price the 100% villages got.
Moving down the scale, villages rated between 99 and 90%, the
Premiers Crus, received the equivalent percentage of the price,
and so on down the ladder. The price was fixed according to
the expected size and quality of the harvest but also took into
account the level of unsold stock lying in Reims cellars and the
current world economic situation – 'charging what the market
will bear', again.

This system was abolished with the intention of letting
market forces rule. Now a 'reference price' is announced, but
people follow it almost as closely as the old regulated price and
continue to use the percentage scale. Grapes can account for
up to £6 of the bottle's price. That's just one reason why
champagne is so expensive.

The Champagne way of making wines sparkle – with that
second fermentation in bottle – has been adopted as the top
method all over the world and until recently has been acknowl-
edged as such on labels with the term *méthode champenoise*,
champagne method.

Is imitation the sincerest form of flattery? Not a bit of it. So
jealous of their own region's product are the Champenois that
they have succeeded in forbidding the rest of the world from
using the name of champagne to describe the production
process. Now others making sparkling wine by this method
must describe their wine in a different way. The term currently
adopted by most is 'traditional method'.

WHAT YOU'LL SEE IN THE CELLAR

The champagne method of making sparkling wine – or the
traditional method for that matter – offers the most to see
in the cellar. It's a closely controlled process.

Regulations determine the yield, in other words the weight of grapes you can grow per hectare, and the amount of juice you can press from a given weight. These rules have recently been tightened up so that 160kg of fruit, rather than 150kg, may produce a maximum of 1hl of juice. That means the grapes are pressed less hard to release the juice. Previously there was also a difference between the first-pressed juice, which is the best quality, known as the *cuvée*, and the second and third pressings, known as the *premier* and *deuxième tailles*. Now there is only one *taille*. (The second *taille*, in particular, used to produce pretty inferior wine.) Grand champagne houses will tell you during a tour that they, of course, only use the *cuvée* for their wines; but somebody somewhere must be using the *taille*.

The law also states that grapes must be picked by hand in Champagne so that the grape-skins are unbroken when they arrive at the press house. Some press houses, such as Ayala's (qv) in Ay, are exactly designed to deal with the old pressing equation. The traditional vertical champagne press holds 4,000kg of grapes, and if you go down beneath one you'll see concrete containers for collecting the precise amount of juice that was permissible at each stage. Ayala positively welcomes harvest visitors, and I watched teams of workers moving between the old wooden presses, dismantling and cleaning them between operations. Modern presses can be set automatically to produce the correct quantities of juice for each stage.

The juice, or must, rests in a holding tank for a day or so to let any particles settle, then it's fermented. Almost everybody uses stainless steel these days, with more, or less, sophisticated temperature-regulation equipment. The finest wines, however, are generally believed to be those fermented in oak barrels. (The Champagne *pièce* holds 205 litres, which equates to the 2,050 litres of *cuvée* juice which used to form the first pressing – ten barrels' worth. All very handy.) Top champagne house Krug ferments in barrel, and so do two of the producers recommended below, Vilmart and Alfred Gratien. Fashions change, and producers are gradually returning to the idea of barrel fermentation, at least for their top wines. It's worth looking out in the cellar to see what your host's philosophy is.

Frequently the wine is chaptalized. That means extra sugar is added to boost the grape's often poor natural sugar content. Chaptalization is rather like reading the *News of the World*:

I won't admit to it, but of course there are a lot of other people who do it all the time. It's not the kind of thing that's brought up easily in the course of polite cellar conversation.

Once first fermentation is over the wine might 'do the malo'. (Not every producer believes in softening the wine by malolactic fermentation, allowing sharp malic acid to soften into smoother lactic acid.) Malo or no, at this point you have a fermented wine. It's low in alcohol because Champagne is so far north that the grapes don't get the chance to ripen as fully as elsewhere. It's also thin and neutral, which paradoxically is just what you need for champagne. Too alcoholic a base wine and you'd have too boozy a brew once you'd fermented it again – the bottle fermentation sends the alcohol content up as well as making bubbles; it also reduces acidity, so you need a bitingly acidic wine to start with.

One of champagne's most distinctive characteristics is the biscuity, yeasty taste and smell that come from the second fermentation. Too strong a base wine and these delicate aromas and flavours would be overwhelmed. So champagne makes a virtue out of necessity twice over, and turns highly unpromising raw materials that no-one would want into something that on a good day is quite splendid.

The wine is then blended and bottled. To induce second fermentation, you add a dose of sugar and yeast dissolved in wine to the bottle and close it with a crown cap. Some houses, as a mark of respect for their top wines, use wired cork closures for this process – worth looking out for during a visit. The bottles are stacked horizontally in the cellars on *lattes* (thin, wooden laths) and left, disturbed only by parties of tourists, to ferment once again.

The process takes longer than first fermentation because the temperature is cooler in the cellar. These days hardly any bottles burst, but most cellars will lose a couple; look out for jagged-edged gaps in the banks of bottles as you go by. Once second fermentation is over the wine sits on the dead lees and acquires more depth of flavour from the decomposing yeast cells. This is called autolysis. The longer you leave the bottle – it can be as long as five years – the richer and more complex the wine will be. Also, the longer you leave it the more you tie up your capital, so the more the bottle costs.

Next you remove the lees by *remuage* (riddling). These days the romantic sight of the troglodytic *remueur*, turning thousands of bottles a day as he (usually) progresses through the *pupitre*-filled cellars, is becoming rarer (although some big firms do still employ one to keep the tourists happy). Even in the smaller, artisans' cellars you're likely to see pallets of 500 bottles on Star Wars-like pods, called *gyropalettes* or *pupimatiques*, being shaken and turned en masse. Some of these are computer-controlled and run 24 hours a day, reducing a two- or three-month process to a week. Your host will debate the pros and cons of each method with you; those who still do it by hand will tell you the mechanical method is harmful in some way, the mechanists will tell you it's beneficial.

There's a good chance you'll see a disgorging line in action, as they run according to demand for most of the year. In most cases the process is mechanical, although in some small houses and for deluxe brands it may still be done by hand. The necks of the inverted bottles pass through a freezing brine solution, the crown cap is flipped off and the lees, frozen into a pellet of ice, shoot out with the force of a bullet. There's an inspection to make sure no debris is left in the bottle, then the wine is dosed with more sugar dissolved in wine (unless it's to be a totally dry champagne) and finally corked.

Get a good look at the cork; in its manufactured state it's completely cylindrical, so you can imagine the force exerted to get it into the bottle. A champagne cork is a composite of bits of cork, with two discs of better quality cork at the business end, nearest the wine. It will have the word 'champagne' stamped on it somewhere where it can't be tampered with once the cork is in the bottle. You may be given one as a souvenir.

A metal cap is fitted on top of the cork to prevent the wire cutting into it. The wine is then left to rest and to assimilate the sugar *dosage* evenly throughout itself; this can take up to another 18 months. Finally it's labelled. Non-vintage champagne must be at least three years old, vintage a minimum of five years old.

Much is made within the great champagne houses of the art and skill of the blender in mixing a set of harsh, raw, acidic young wines from three different grape varieties, and perhaps from all over the region, into the house style, something that people will recognize as being uniquely yours, year in year out.

Everyone is making wine from the same grapes and the same vineyards. In order to make your brand stand out you have to emphasize the special character of your blend.

Unfortunately, this argument trips over something called the '*sur-lattes* scandal'. When champagne sales were booming, say in the late 1980s, some houses ran out of wine to sell. They thought nothing of buying in bottles from other suppliers' '*sur-lattes*', from the maturing laths in someone else's cellars. The purchaser then simply slapped on his or her label and pushed them out. Now you're not going to have much influence over creating the unique house blend if you've bought in the wine as a finished product, are you?

The big champagne houses' attitude to blending is unique in French winemaking; their intention is to iron out any sense of where the wine has come from. The small-scale grower, on the other hand, can reflect local characteristics more directly. As you follow the wine route there are certainly opportunities to spot these different attributes. Discovering the growers is also one of the best reasons for visiting Champagne. Although they account for perhaps a third of all champagne produced, only about 7% of their wine is exported. The big houses dominate the export market, so getting out there yourself is the best way of discovering individual growers' wines.

HAS THE BUBBLE BURST?

A few words on visiting Champagne

Champagne is expensive. Huge price hikes at the beginning of the 1990s put off a third of us buying it at home. Prices are beginning to come down, but not enough for me. Although the formula of buying at source for half the high street price just about applies, you can still buy New World sparklers in the UK for less than you'll pay per bottle in Reims or Epernay for the Grandes Marques. With the small-scale producers I recommend, however, you'll find champagnes that offer quality for your money way above that of the New World sparkling wines.

These producers are in most cases not the well-known names, but small- or medium-scale growers who have something special to offer. If you want to visit the glossy Grandes Marques by all means do so, remembering all the time that

their multi-million pound investment in tourist facilities is paid
for by you every time you buy their brand. Here you'll be
treated like a tourist; there's nothing wrong with that, but you
won't get close to either the process or the people, and you
<u>will</u> be treated to a large dose of the glamour-and-magic-of-
champagne message, which I for one would rather avoid.

The Champenois are said to be worried about the decline in
sales, and the fact that nearly a million bottles lie stockpiled in
their cellars. (It's good news for us, though; the longer they
languish, the better the wines will taste when sold.) They're
also said to be worried about the decline in tourism, as fewer
people leave the motorway to visit their region now the link to
Burgundy is open. But if they are concerned, they're not
showing it; hotel and restaurant prices are still steep. Money
just doesn't seem to go as far in Champagne.

Nevertheless the region heaves with tourists from every part
of Europe. It's particularly popular with the British as it's the
first wine region we come across in France. Unlike the other
regions I cover, most of the hotels and restaurants I recommend
in Champagne are thoroughly 'discovered' by British tourists,
although there are one or two that are new.

PLANNING THE ROUTE

Reims is the obvious starting-point as the motorway carves
right through it. You can be there from Calais in two to three
hours, depending on whether you observe the speed limit.
(Please do. Brits are terribly conspicuous on this piece of road,
and I know several people who have been caught speeding.)
From Zeebrugge the journey is equally easy – you simply drop
down via Lille.

Reims is a very useful stopover point for longer journeys to
Alsace or Burgundy. There are a couple of hotels just five
minutes from the motorway which are relatively easy to find.
Ambonnay is close to the Epernay motorway exit, and Epernay
itself is feasible for an overnight stop. (For hotels, see Listings
pages 82–3.) It's even possible to add a 'mini-tour' of
Champagne to your exploration of another region. As little
as one day can allow you to visit some of the recommended
producers and explore a stretch of the wine route – before
heading on to better weather perhaps.

If you wouldd like to explore Champagne in more depth, however, you could consider up to a day in Reims, a day touring the route to Epernay, and another in Epernay and covering points south or west. Then I'd suggest driving down to the Aube, where the scenery is very attractive, the tourists are scarcer and the prices on the whole more affordable (see The Golden Triangle).

EXPLORING CHAMPAGNE

The starting point is **Reims**. Pronunciation first: the English way is 'Reams' whereas the French say 'Rams', preferably swallowing the 'm' in a nice, guttural, mid-throat snarl.

You can base yourself just outside if you're passing through. Near the motorway, on the outskirts of the city, is the Assiette Champenoise (take the Tinqueux exit from the A26 and then the N31 in the direction of Reims; it's on the left before a Mobil garage). This has large, comfortable rooms with brilliant beds, an indoor swimming-pool (in deference, no doubt, to the weather) and a Michelin-starred restaurant. The dining-room is very welcoming and attractive, with flocks of attentive staff. There's delicious lobster, but I must warn you about the chicken, which managed to be both tough and tasteless. These days many top chefs are absent from the stove half the year, so it was good to see the main man firmly in control (and at the bar once the meal was over). There's a vast buffet breakfast with exotic fruit salad and the like, and a very warm welcome from Madame, although the receptionist is fierce. The restaurant is very popular with the local business community, and the hotel with international tourists.

I don't usually recommend hotel chains, as I find them rather soulless and regimented, but the Campanile Sud, just outside Reims on the N51 Epernay road, is easy to find and has quiet rooms and a reasonably-priced, basic restaurant. (It's a British tour-operator's base hotel.) Devotees of the shoe warehouse La Halle des Chaussures, purveyors of absurdly cheap footwear to the fascinated, like myself, will find a branch just around the corner.

Overlooking the motorway and the parallel Marne Canal is the Quality Hotel, once the Hôtel Liberté. Alas the landmark plastic Miss Liberty statue has gone. Rooms are well-insulated

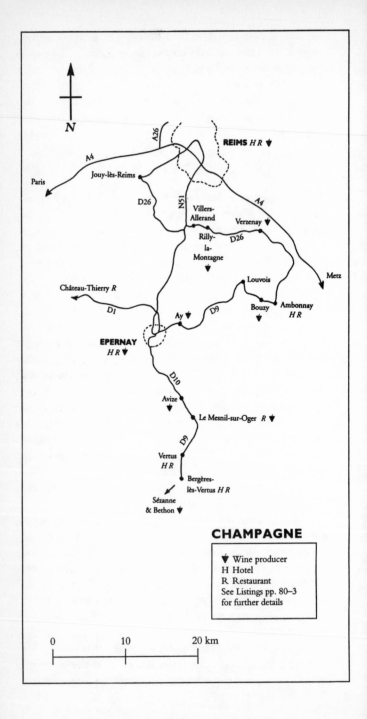

N

REIMS *H R* ♥

Paris

Jouy-lès-Reims

A4

A26

D26

N51

Villers-
Allerand

Verzenay

D26

A4

Rilly-
la-
Montagne
♥

Louvois

Metz

Château-Thierry *R*

D1

Ay ♥

D9

Bouzy

Ambonnay
H R

EPERNAY
H R ♥

D10

Avize
♥

Le Mesnil-sur-Oger *R* ♥

D9

Vertus
H R

Bergères-
lès-Vertus *H R*

Sézanne
& Bethon ♥

CHAMPAGNE

♥ Wine producer
H Hotel
R Restaurant
See Listings pp. 80–3
for further details

0   10   20 km

from noise outside, and it's close to both the motorway and the city centre. It has a restaurant full of modern flavours; for more traditional dishes, head into town.

At Au Petit Comptoir, for instance, there's stylish bistro food under the auspices of the local Michelin three-star chef. Or try Le Vigneron, full of wine curiosities, with an interesting champagne-only wine list and hearty food. Au Petit Bacchus, in an atmospheric old wine building, offers good bistro food at prices much lower than the other two. For a quick *steak-frites*, look no further than the trio of restaurants all under the same management opposite the cathedral, Le Colibri, La Notre-Dame and Le Flamm'Steak.

The cathedral is well worth a visit, and meandering round adjacent streets will reveal plenty that is of architectural merit. Many champagne houses are based here and you can turn up at most of them on spec for a tour. The tourist information centre by the cathedral will give you a map which locates them.

The first visit in Reims I'd recommend, however, is quite unlike these grand tourist operations. In fact there are no wine-making processes to see and the company is so self-effacing that it hasn't even got an address plate outside. I suggest it for those who'd like to experience things done the old-fashioned way, and perhaps imagine they're a wine merchant for half an hour.

To visit **DELBECK** you first need to make an appointment through the firm's UK agent, Sam Gordon Clark of Onslow Pelham. He's happy to arrange everything for you. When you're admitted, you'll be taken into the boardroom and offered a glass of champagne to taste, and you'll have the opportunity to discuss business prospects with a senior member of staff (in immaculate English if required).

Delbeck was originally an old family firm, describing itself as 'Supplier to the former Court of France' and well known half a century ago. The name threatened to disappear, swallowed up in a series of take-overs, but a family company bought it and is re-establishing the firm. Eventually Delbeck will have cellars and a wine museum to show you, but for now just sit back in the elegant boardroom while you work out how many cases you can fit in the boot. The 1985 vintage (an excellent year, not much of which is left) costs FF115–150.

The Montagne de Reims wine route begins at Gueux, but at this point it's pretty dull. If you're staying at the Assiette

Champenoise, I'd pick it up at **Jouy-lès-Reims**. Otherwise leave Reims on the N51 to Epernay (passing the Campanile) and turn left onto the wine route, signposted Villers-Allerand and Rilly-la-Montagne, the D26. Luckily this route isn't shy of announcing itself: enormous signs proclaiming: 'Route touristique de la Champagne' adorn every crossroads.

The road skirts the edge of the Montagne de Reims. Stop in quiet **Rilly-la-Montagne** and above the village square you'll find the house of **VILMART**. Founded in 1890, this family firm is now run by young Laurent Champs, who's taking over from his father. It's open for sales on spec, but make an appointment and Laurent will show you the cellars, with their use of wood. The Champs family is a great proponent of barrel fermentation, even forming a *confrérie* to celebrate it; Laurent's father was a cooper who married into wine. No fertilizer or weed-killer is used in the vineyard but, contrasting with traditional methods, they do use *gyropalettes* for riddling.

These are wines of exceptional quality and at remarkable prices: the NV is under FF80, but it's worth paying the extra for the prestige wines – up to FF112. This is amazingly good value for such high quality. Laurent Champs is extremely committed and passionate about his wines and will take the trouble to explain his philosophy in more depth if you're interested. If you only visit one grower in Champagne, make it Vilmart.

Continue along the wine road, which offers attractive views across the plain towards Reims if it's not foggy. Look out for the windmill, an odd sight amid a sea of vines. The Montagne de Reims is a black grape area and the pretty village of **Verzenay** is renowned for its Pinot Noir, classed as Grand Cru. **MICHEL ARNOULD** owns 12ha of it. This is very much a family business – you're received in the living-room by Michel Arnould himself or, for a little English, his son Patrice. It's a friendly, homely reception and the wines are very good.

The strength of growers' champagne is its ability to reflect its origins more specifically. At this estate, for instance, you can taste the powerful effect of a predominantly Pinot Noir wine, full and rich. They use some Chardonnay, which they don't grow – apparently you can swap up to 5% of your production with another grower; above 5% and you must call yourself a négociant. Prices range from FF67 to FF100.

The wine route now descends into **Ambonnay**, where I'd recommend the friendly Auberge St-Vincent. Bedrooms have been recently renovated, and the rustic dining-room offers good food with more or less authentic regional roots. Don't miss the unique Ceremony of the Car Parking. About 7.15pm all the hotel guests are summoned to their cars by a knock on their doors. (One group of four adults, in separate rooms but travelling in one car, were all summoned to perform the Ceremony jointly and severally.) During the day you park on the pavement near the hotel but in the evening the proprietors have access to an enclosed parking area. Once guests are installed in their cars, a procession forms and proceeds sedately up the high street into this compound. Make sure one of you stays sober long enough to complete the formalities.

A couple of kilometres from Ambonnay, at **Bouzy**, is **ANDRÉ CLOUET**. Bouzy is another village producing Pinot Noir Grand Cru, which also makes the aptly-named Bouzy Rouge. Clouet has very good wines, and the estate is also worth a visit for the little wine museum created in an old attic built centuries ago to house visiting grape-pickers.

Now if you speak French, no doubt you'll be received by the master of the house, Pierre Clouet. No problems there. If you ask for a visit in English, you'll meet his son Jean-François; and if you do, anything could happen. He may tell you he owns the estate; he may open a bottle for you to taste, or maybe not: 'I am not a café' (although he did go on to indicate that if you crossed his palm with silver, corks would fly); he may show you right round the estate. Alternatively he may be on another planet. The visit with Jean-François was, in truth, vastly entertaining; just take along a pinch of salt. His ambition, he says, is to have his photo in *The Times* and he keeps threatening to send his portfolio. I can't wait.

From Bouzy follow the D19 and join the D34 into Louvois. If you want to head back to Reims, follow the narrow D34 as it climbs the Montagne de Reims – a very pretty road. On the right, there's a signpost for the Faux de Verzy, a collection of strange, deformed beech trees, twisted like corkscrews. For the valiant, there's a path the other side of the road leading after an hour's walk to the Mont Sinai viewpoint, a First World War observation post. It's worthwhile only in good weather. You can then rejoin the wine road back to Reims (the D26).

Otherwise, take the D9 from Louvois to **Ay**, and visit **AYALA**. This house is a member of the Grandes Marques but doesn't proclaim itself as loudly as most. By appointment you can have an English-language tour and tasting of its light-bodied, delicate wines. Curious artefacts include an old, ornately-carved vat still used for allowing the wines to 'marry' between *assemblage* (blending) and bottling.

In the cellars, at the end of the rows, I noticed bright circles of lightbulbs. As I grew close I saw that there was only one light bulb, surrounded by a ring of reflectors like flower petals. I thought this was just an economy measure, but no. They're there for safety reasons. Cellar workers driving fork-lift trucks down endless cellar passageways can become mesmerized; when these 'sun' lights change pattern, they know they're getting near to the wall and must slow down.

From Ay head into **Epernay** and brace yourself for traffic jams (I'd advise parking as soon as you see a space, or following signposts for the vast Arcades underground car park – it's one of those where you have to pay a machine before joining the queue to get out). Epernay is home to some of the major names in champagne, such as Moët & Chandon, but I'd like to suggest you visit somewhere on a rather smaller scale: **ALFRED GRATIEN**.

This is a very traditional house and sister company of Gratien & Meyer (qv) in Saumur. It makes very serious champagne by time-honoured methods, including barrel fermentation. You can tour the cellars by appointment and see various old implements which were in use until surprisingly recently. These wines are highly respected within the wine trade but don't receive much publicity. I think they're worth discovering.

In Epernay you can stay at the Champagne and eat at another Petit Comptoir (the same set-up as in Reims) or in the Wine-Bar attached to the Hôtel Berceaux. The latter offers a wide selection of wines by the glass, and good-value dishes and set-price menus. Excellent regional cheeses for picnics are at Les Délices de la Ferme on Place des Arcades, while J M Corda on Rue Mercier has speciality breads and fine *pâtisserie*; also try Charcuterie de la Poste on Place Hugues Plomb.

If this marks the end of your tour, you can head home via Château-Thierry through the Vallée de la Marne. I recommend you keep to the north bank, on the D1, which is quieter than the N road on the south bank. Take the wine-route detours, clearly signposted, if you wish. After lunch in **Château-Thierry** (see Listings page 83) you can be in Calais for a late-afternoon ferry.

Alternatively, follow the wine route south of Epernay into the Côte des Blancs. Here Chardonnay predominates and the wines are lighter and more delicate. Visit the estate of **PIERRE PETERS** in **Le Mesnil-sur-Oger**. This is the first champagne grower I ever visited. It's a small operation producing very good wines, and you can tour the cellars with an English-speaking guide by appointment. Prices are very fair, too, with non-vintage from FF76 and vintage from FF96. There's also a good restaurant in the village, Le Mesnil.

For wines of a very different style, visit **ALAIN ROBERT**, who is also in Le Mesnil. Here you'll find very attractive, rich champagne of the kind sometimes known in France as 'English-style'. M Robert is dapper and extremely charming; a visit here, particularly for advanced students, is a truly delightful experience.

The route now leads you through **Vertus**, where you can stay at the Hostellerie La Reine Blanche, which has an indoor swimming-pool and basic food; or the really brave can try the Mont-Aimé, in **Bergères-lès-Vertus**. I've stayed here twice, my visits separated by some seven years, and in that time the welcome has gone from frosty to downright hostile. The food's deteriorated, too. Why am I suggesting you stay here? Well, the rooms are comfortable and good value, and there's a pool. Perhaps this is the venue for a sneaky picnic to compensate for earlier overeating. That's what I did, anyway.

After Vertus you could follow the wine route on to Sézanne, but I wouldn't recommend it. The scenery is dull and so is Sézanne itself, although the local cooperative, **LE BRUN DE NEUVILLE**, does offer very good quality wines at reasonable prices as well as the chance to see a major operation in action. (To reach the co-op, follow the signs in **Bethon** for Chantemerle.)

Instead, I'd suggest heading on down the motorway to the Champagne section of The Golden Triangle, the Aube, to see if you think the bigwigs in Reims are right to look down their noses at it.

Listings

When telephoning France from the UK, first dial 00 33 then the number shown. Producers are listed in wine route order, and hotels/restaurants by town or village according to the route. Accommodation prices are per room, meal prices are per head.

Producers
Delbeck
51067 Reims
Credit cards accepted
Good English

To make an appointment
at Delbeck, contact UK agent
Sam Gordon Clark
Onslow Pelham & Co
23 South Terrace
London SW7 2JB
Tel 0171 584 5420
Fax 0171 225 1006

Vilmart & Cie
5 rue des Gravières
(Place de la Mairie)
51500 Rilly-la-Montagne
Tel 26 03 40 01, Fax 26 03 46 57
Open Mon–Fri 8.30–12, 14–18;
Nov and Dec also open Sat;
visits by appointment to cellar
Credit cards accepted
Good English

Michel Arnould
28 rue de Mailly
51360 Verzenay
Tel 26 49 40 06, Fax 26 49 44 61
Open Mon–Fri 9–12, 14–18;
visits by appointment Sat and Sun
Some English

André Clouet
8 rue Gambetta, 51150 Bouzy
Tel 26 57 00 82
Visits by appointment
Good English

Ayala
2 boulevard du Nord, 51160 Ay
Tel 26 55 15 44, Fax 26 51 09 04
Visits by appointment Mon–Fri;
also Sat and Sun during harvest
Credit cards accepted
Some English (by appointment)

Alfred Gratien
30 rue Maurice-Cerveaux, BP 3,
51201 Epernay
Tel 26 54 38 20, Fax 41 51 03 55
Visits by appointment
Some English

Pierre Peters
26 rue des Lombards,
51190 Le Mesnil-sur-Oger
Tel 26 57 50 32, Fax 26 57 97 71
Open Mon–Sat 9–12, 14–18
Credit cards accepted
Some English (by appointment)

Alain Robert
25 avenue de la République
51190 Le Mesnil-sur-Oger
Tel 26 57 52 94, Fax 26 57 59 22
Visits by appointment
Mon–Fri 9–12, 14–17
No English

Le Brun de Neuville
Route de Chantemerle,
51260 Bethon
Tel 26 80 48 43, Fax 26 80 43 28
Visits by appointment Mon–Sat 8–12,
14–18 (arrange with M di Florio)
Credit cards accepted
Some English

Grandes Marques

The following is a selection of big champagne houses which I believe are worth visiting, either because they offer an interesting tour or because the wines are good – although the two may coincide. There may be an entrance fee (typically FF20–40), for which you usually get a glass of champagne and perhaps something special like a miniature train to save you the effort of walking round the cellars. Treat the visit as you would any tourist attraction – you'll get something for your money, the champagne will be cheaper here than in a bar, and the entrance fee absolves you from any obligation to buy. Always make a quick phone call in advance, to confirm arrangements, even if an appointment isn't mandatory. I'd be very surprised if any of these houses could not answer you in English.

Reims
Piper-Heidsieck
51 boulevard Henri-Vasnier,
51100 Reims
Tel 26 84 41 94
Ride the *circuit de visite*, a hugely expensive installation – not a train, more a series of individual cars passing through various exhibits including outsize bunches of grapes.

Pommery
5 place du Général Gouraud,
51100 Reims
Tel 26 61 62 63
Mock Scottish baronial exterior, very elegant surroundings, enormous wall-carvings, rather like Cheddar caves turned into a stately home; plenty of glamorous hostesses, and vast, recently-refurbished visitors' areas. Watch out for the descent into the cellars or, more to the point, the ascent out of them: you're climbing a staircase from a depth of 30m.

Louis Roederer
21 boulevard Lundy, 51053 Reims
Tel 26 40 42 11
You must make an appointment to visit. Brilliant champagne; Cristal retails in the UK for £60-odd.

Epernay
De Castellane
57 rue de Verdun, 51204 Epernay
Tel 26 55 15 33
Plenty to see here: various museums (including one showing ancient means of champagne production), posters, a vast collection of labels and, for an extra charge, a heated butterfly garden (closed in winter). There's also a tower with a panoramic view.

Mercier
75 avenue de Champagne,
51333 Epernay
Tel 26 54 75 26
An all-singing, all-dancing tour, with audio-visual show, glass lifts, laser light show, train ride through the cellars, wall sculptures and the largest champagne cask ever made. The wine? Hmm…

Moët & Chandon
20 avenue de Champagne,
51333 Epernay
Tel 26 54 71 11
The largest champagne house and the one receiving the most visitors. Very well organized tours.

Perrier-Jouët
28 avenue de Champagne,
51200 Epernay
Tel 26 55 20 53
You must make an appointment to visit. See the Maison Belle Epoque with its splendid collection of art nouveau furniture. Lovely wines, and the most beautiful champagne bottle, the Belle Epoque.

Ay
Bollinger
16 rue Jules Lobet, 51160 Ay
Tel 26 55 21 31
Bollinger recently produced a
Charter of Ethics and Quality, the
first Grande Marque to do so, with
the implication that the great houses
should take a lead in improving
standards in the champagne trade.
These are some of the best champagnes, with prices to match.

Avize
Bricout
Ancien Château d'Avize,
29 Rempart du Midi, 51160 Ay
Tel 26 57 53 93
Brought to fame by our dear
departed Chancellor, Bricout is a better wine than the 'cheap champagne'
the tabloids claim he bought. The
château is very attractive.

Hotels and Restaurants
H Hotel *R* Restaurant

Reims
HR L'Assiette Champenoise
40 avenue P-Vaillant-Couturier,
51430 Tinqueux
Tel 26 04 15 56, Fax 26 04 15 69
Rooms FF500–785, Meals
FF250–460
(member of Relais du Silence)

HR Campanile Sud
Avenue Georges Pompidou,
Val-de-Murigny
51100 Reims
Tel 26 36 66 94, Fax 26 49 95 40
Rooms FF268, Meals FF80–102

HR Quality Hotel
(*R* Orphée)
55 rue Boulard, 51100 Reims
Tel 26 40 52 61, Fax 26 47 27 38
Rooms FF390–420, Meals
FF155–370

R Au Petit Bacchus
11 rue Université
Tel 26 47 10 05
FF60–150

R Au Petit Comptoir
17 rue Mars
Tel 26 40 58 58
FF150–220

R Le Vigneron
Place P Jarnot
Tel 26 47 00 71
FF155

Ambonnay
HR Auberge St-Vincent
Rue St-Vincent,
51150 Ambonnay
Tel 26 57 01 98, Fax 47 57 32 50
Rooms FF290–360
Meals FF120–350

Epernay
H Champagne
30 rue E Mercier, 51200 Epernay
Tel 26 55 30 22, Fax 26 51 94 63
FF255–390

R Au Petit Comptoir
3 rue Dr Rousseau
Tel 26 51 53 53
FF160–225

R Wine-Bar
13 rue de Berceaux
Tel 26 55 28 84
FF60–120
(The Hôtel Berceaux, to which this
restaurant is attached, is under new
management and standards may
change.)

Le Mesnil-sur-Oger
R Le Mesnil
2 rue Pasteur
Tel 26 57 95 57
FF100–350

Vertus
HR Hostellerie La Reine Blanche
18 avenue L Lenoir, 51130 Vertus
Tel 26 52 20 76, Fax 26 52 16 59
Rooms FF395–495, Meals
FF135–290

Bergères-lès-Vertus
HR Le Mont-Aimé
4–6 rue Vertus,
51130 Bergères-lès-Vertus
Tel 26 52 21 31, Fax 26 52 21 39
Rooms FF230–410, Meals
FF100–350

Château-Thierry and Domptin
R Auberge Jean de la Fontaine
10 rue Filoirs, Château-Thierry
Tel 23 83 63 89
FF120–350

HR Le Cygne d'Argent
Domptin (8km southeast of
Château-Thierry)
Tel 23 70 43 11
Rooms FF 250, Meals FF66–325

Burgundy

Burgundy wines are some of the most expensive in the world. And some of them are worth the money, while others trade emptily on their name. Yet there are bargains, or at least better value wines, to be had if you know where to look. This chapter will do three things: explain why these wines are so expensive, describe a route that takes you through some of the world's most evocative wine names, and tell you who to call on to buy well-made wines at fair prices.

Winemaking in Burgundy goes back to the Greeks, the Romans or the early years AD, depending on who you believe. It was built up by the Church, with several monastic orders establishing major vineyard holdings, and by the State in the form of the Dukes of Burgundy. These dukes controlled most of northern France and the Low Countries, and were great patrons of the arts, which is one of the reasons Burgundy is so rich in art treasures today.

The French Revolution wiped out the land ownership of both church and aristocracy, splitting up the huge vineyard holdings. Then the Napoleonic Code decreed that on death, a man's landholdings be split equally among all his sons. Small vineyards became progressively smaller with each succeeding generation, creating today's crazy patchwork of tiny holdings. The often quoted example is that of the Clos de Vougeot vineyard, which covers 50ha and is owned by about 80 people. No wonder you can't rely on the name of the vineyard to guarantee good wine.

Burgundy wines come from five regions: Chablis, the Côte d'Or, the Côte Chalonnaise, the Mâconnais and Beaujolais. The Chablis wine route is described in The Golden Triangle chapter; the Mâconnais and Beaujolais have their own.

The Côte d'Or, or Golden Slope, is the heart of great Burgundy winemaking. It is also tiny. From just south of Dijon it runs a mere 50km down to its southern border at Santenay. The region pivots around Beaune, roughly its centre. From just north of Beaune up to the suburbs of Dijon is the Côte de Nuits, while Beaune itself and south to Santenay is known as the Côte de Beaune. Stretching above these two regions, higher up the slopes, are the Hautes Côtes de Nuits and the Hautes Côtes de Beaune. The Côte d'Or is a narrow outcrop of rock, and grapes are grown all along its side and on the valley floor beneath, but the best wines come from a slim strip that runs along the slope roughly halfway down.

Wine production on the Côte d'Or and neighbouring Côte Chalonnaise totals about a fifth of the amount produced in rival region Bordeaux. So one of the main reasons burgundy is so expensive is simple supply and demand. We want more of it than they've got. And they know it, which is the second reason it's so expensive – a case of 'charging what the market will bear' again. Luckily the market is currently proving that it won't bear so much, and prices are slipping back from their late 1980s heights.

The third reason is that the red grape of burgundy, Pinot Noir, is extremely difficult to grow. It's sensitive to frost, to rot, to over-production… you name it, it's offended by it. The cost of preventative measures is high and this in turn adds to the price you pay.

When everything goes well, however, Pinots from Burgundy outclass those from the rest of the world. So there's really no competition: burgundy is the best and you have to pay accordingly. Not surprisingly, about three-quarters of the Côte d'Or is planted with Pinot Noir, leaving less and less room for the great white burgundy grape, Chardonnay. Now this one is easy to grow, so there are no cost problems here – but the problem lies in scarcity value. Supply and demand come into play again. Everybody wants the rich, unctuous white wines of Burgundy and of course there are not enough to go round.

However, where Santenay ends, the Côte Chalonnaise begins, running for perhaps 25km as far south as Buxy. Worldwide demand for these wines is less intense, and if anywhere can be said to represent good value in Burgundy winemaking, it is here.

WHO MAKES THE WINE?

Because of the way land has been divided and subdivided there are thousands of winemakers in Burgundy and, ooh, dozens of them are making really good wine. Most of the producers I suggest you visit grow their own grapes and make and bottle their own wine, but not all. The négociant, or merchant, has had a huge role to play in shaping Burgundy's recent fortunes and influencing what the wines taste like.

The négociants were powerful at the end of the last century, when a louse called *Phylloxera vastatrix* (because its destruction was so vast) laid waste to nearly all Europe's vineyards. This plague destroyed many livelihoods. By the time they discovered how to graft the old vines onto phylloxera-resistant American rootstocks many producers had gone out of business. Gradually the vineyards were replanted, but young vines don't produce grapes with much oomph, and the resulting wines were pale and watery. The merchants began to import wines from the south, from the Midi, and especially from French Algeria, to blend with the feeble burgundy and add colour and body.

This practice spread, and continued long after the newly-planted vines had reached maturity. It became the dominant winemaking style for Burgundy reds, so much so that today, long after this adulteration has been banned and (for the most part) stopped, there's a generation of wine-lovers, not least in the UK, who sigh softly in remembrance of the deep red, thick, alcoholic, robust burgundy of yesteryear. Never mind that it was an impostor, that's the way it was when they grew to love it, and they want it back. All the growers described below, however, will show you light, elegant wines of great finesse, and I hope you'll like them. I have included in my suggestions a couple of négociants of very differing styles, as examples of what they have to offer and of the benefits and problems you might encounter when buying wines from the négoce – the collective body of merchants.

Négociants operate in several ways: they can buy grapes from the grower, or buy the fermented young wine in cask and keep it while it matures (known as *élevage* – literally 'upbringing'). Selling to a négociant has many advantages for the grower, not the least of which is cash upfront. No tedious waiting around while the wine matures in cask and then in bottle; the money is in within months of the harvest (it's almost as good as making Beaujolais Nouveau). If you grow grapes on many different parcels of land, all needing to be vinified separately, the négociant's economies of scale make a great deal of sense. Unfortunately négociants' wines can taste more like all the other wines they produce than like other wines made from that village or vineyard.

On the other hand, retailers and restaurants want to buy wines in sufficiently large quantities to ensure continuity of supply. They want their customers to build up 'relationships' with the wines sold. A few hundred cases per year is no use to them, thank you very much. And if you know the names of good, reliable négociants, such as Latour, Jadot or Drouhin, it does help when you're desperately scanning the wine list in a restaurant or searching along a wine merchant's shelf for a name you can trust.

In Burgundy, perhaps more than anywhere else in France, you need to be able to trust the producer's name. The source of the wine – the vineyard – is not enough. Take the Clos de Vougeot again: it may be a Grand Cru, but, alas, this fact is not nearly enough to guarantee that what's in your glass will be worth the inordinate price you paid for it. The equation has to be 'site' plus 'producer' equals 'worth buying'.

Vintage plays a part, too. It's certainly true to say that a good producer will make good wines in a bad year, but the effect of the vintage will have some bearing on the keeping qualities of the wine, and on how long you have to wait before it's ready to drink. Luckily there's been a succession of good vintages since 1987 (which was written off as a bad year only because it was bad in Bordeaux).

HOW THE WINES ARE LABELLED

The ladder of classification in Burgundy moves from the general, covering the whole region, to the specific, covering only one named vineyard. Nearly all the wines in Burgundy are *appellation contrôlée*, or AC, meaning they are made to specific regulations.

The broadest classes, the regional, reveal little about the wine. The most basic reds are Bourgogne Grand Ordinaire (probably made from Gamay, more ordinary than grand, ho ho) and Bourgogne Passetoutgrains, which is at least one-third Pinot Noir. The safest place to start is with Bourgogne Rouge, which is usually 100% Pinot Noir. Even the greatest estates often produce a little generic burgundy, and you'll frequently find that a plain Bourgogne Rouge from someone good is better than a fancier label from someone you've never heard of.

For the basic whites, Bourgogne Blanc must be 100% Chardonnay or Pinot Blanc. Although no-one shouts about it, a fair amount of Pinot Blanc is grown in these parts. A lively alternative is Bourgogne Aligoté. The Aligoté grape at its best makes crisp, fresh, fruity wines and is the classic base wine for making Kir (although whatever you do, don't tell the top Aligoté producers that you intend to adulterate their lovely wine in this way).

Kir is the Burgundy aperitif, made with *crème de cassis* from locally-produced blackcurrants. A sparkling version, known as Kir Royal, is made with Crémant de Bourgogne. Crémant is another generic appellation, for sparkling wine made in the same way as champagne, in other words by second fermentation in bottle. I find these very good value indeed, at half the price of a bottle of champagne.

The above classes of wine apply to the whole of Burgundy. Some regional appellations, however, are more specific, applying just to one part. The Hautes Côtes de Beaune and Hautes Côtes de Nuits appellations offer red and white wines made from grapes grown above the main Golden Slope. Then there is the little Côte de Beaune area, just outside Beaune, and the village of Bouzeron in the Côte Chalonnaise which is allowed to attach its name to the production of Aligoté. The appellations Côte de Beaune-Villages and Côte de Nuits-Villages cover wines from the less important villages on one or other half of the Côte d'Or. (The name of the village may be added as a suffix.)

Now things become much more specific. The next level up is called *village* or AC *communale*. Here you put only the name of your village or commune on the label. If you wish, you can also show the name of the specific vineyard the wine came from but, if you do, the name must be in smaller letters. This may seem pedantic, but it's supposed to prevent the consumer from confusing these wines with the two top-quality levels, Premier Cru and Grand Cru.

Premier Cru wines have the name of the village and the name of the vineyard on the label, usually in letters the same height. Sometimes the grower streamlines the issue by putting only these two pieces of information on as a title, but if so you'll always find the words 'Premier Cru' somewhere on the label to reassure you that this isn't simply a village wine masquerading as something better.

Top of the pecking order, the Grand Cru wines disdain to tell you what village they're from; here all you get on the label is the name of the vineyard. The words 'Grand Cru' will also appear somewhere, if in smaller print. Incidentally 'Grand Cru' is not to be confused with 'Grand Vin de Bourgogne', which many growers put on their labels. 'Grand Cru' is a legally-controlled designation; 'Grand Vin', or 'great wine', is simply the grower's opinion.

Certain villages have annexed the name of their most famous Grand Cru vineyard onto the village name, for promotional purposes. Aloxe hyphenated Corton, its best vineyard, onto its name; Puligny and Chassagne both claimed Montrachet; Gevrey added Chambertin. This causes confusion because you also have Grand Cru vineyards with hyphenated names. Chambertin is a Grand Cru vineyard, for instance. So, too, is Charmes-Chambertin. But the words 'Gevrey-Chambertin' on a label simply indicate a village wine. Hyphenation alone is no guide to what is a village wine and what is a Grand Cru. If you intend to move in these rarefied circles you need to know which is which.

WHAT YOU'LL SEE IN THE CELLAR

Burgundy has much to offer the cellar visitor because of the different techniques growers practise. As the domaines are often very small, you're unlikely to be confronted with rows of gleaming stainless steel towers. Things are done on a small scale, often by hand, often in wood.

In particular, there are many variants on the Burgundian technique of *pigeage*. The aim of this process is to draw more red colour out of the thin-skinned Pinot Noir grape. The grapes are crushed, and perhaps destemmed, and put into open vats skins and all. When fermentation starts, the vigorous bubbling sends the skins floating to the top of the vat where they form a cap, which is not much use since you need the skins to circulate in the vat to give off more colour. Twice a day, therefore, the cap of skins and stalks is pushed back down into the wine.

There are many ways of doing this: the traditional method was to use the feet while standing in the vat and clinging onto the sides for dear life. This is still the method on many estates, but it's dangerous because of the carbon dioxide given off during fermentation. Three men were reported to have died this way during the 1993 harvest on the Côte d'Or.

Alternatively, you can use a plunger that looks like the thing you unblock drains with on a long pole, or even a tree branch with a cluster of little stumpy branch fingers left on the end. I used one of these to push the cap down in Irancy, near Chablis, and found it surprisingly hard work; the cap offers a good deal of resistance. Then there are mechanical aids: pneumatically- or mechanically-operated cap-busters suspended on ceiling tracks that you can move by motor. These require a large investment of money and a strong ceiling, and are worth looking out for – particularly when in action.

Once fermentation is over, the wines, whether red or white, are put into vats or barrels to mature. The creamy-vanilla taste given by new oak is highly prized in burgundy, in both whites and reds, and the general principle is, the finer the wine the more new oak barrels are used. Some growers use new barrels, old barrels and even stainless steel vats, in different proportions depending on the quality of the vintage and the wine, and assemble a blend of the wines before bottling.

Listen out while you're in Burgundy for strains of a huge winemaking controversy fomented by a Lebanese oenologist, or wine scientist, Guy Accad. He's encouraging makers of red wine to turn their usual methods upside down. It's generally thought necessary to heat the grape juice, or must, in order to get it to fermentation temperature as quickly as possible. A high temperature encourages the colour in the grape-skins out into the wine. Accad's theory demands the reverse of this. He says that the grapes should be left at a cool temperature to macerate before fermentation begins – a method which results in really deeply-coloured grape juice. Opponents of this approach say the resulting wine doesn't taste like proper burgundy, and they liken it more to the darker, spicier reds of the Rhône.

Proponents say that when the wine is mature it will be classic burgundy. It's still a little early to know for certain which is true, but it's worth being aware of this violent diversity of technique and opinion before you visit a Burgundian cellar.

PLANNING THE ROUTE

Getting to Burgundy is easiest via Calais or Zeebrugge. From Calais the journey along the recently-opened motorway from Reims to Dijon via Troyes takes about 5-6 hours (it's 605km). This is a splendid road. It's much quieter than the route via Paris, and a birdwatcher's delight: birds of prey dot the route, sitting on fence posts. I counted over twenty on a recent quiet Sunday.

From Zeebrugge, the route is via Brussels and Luxembourg, dropping down to Burgundy via Metz, and allows you to take advantage of a great deal of free motorway. The toll from Calais to Reims is FF88, and from Reims to Beaune FF115, but there are no tolls in Belgium or Luxembourg, and Metz to Nancy is, unusually, also a toll-free stretch.

One of the joys of travelling in Burgundy is its compactness. This gives you several options. You can move on every night, often with only short distances to travel between hotels; you can base yourself in Beaune, following a different wine route each day; or you can pick three centres as you move south. If taking the last option, I'd suggest Gevrey-Chambertin for the Côte de Nuits, Beaune for the Côte de Beaune, and one of a selection of villages for the Côte Chalonnaise (see pages 109–13). The principal hotel recommendations for the first two stopping places have no restaurant, which I think is better for a multi-night stay as you can try a different place each night, all helpfully within walking distance. The Côte Chalonnaise hotels have restaurants, all offering genuine Burgundian cooking at different levels of price and finesse.

Burgundian food is usually described as 'hearty'; take this to mean large pieces of meat in rich, unctuous sauces, strange combinations (such as eggs in red wine – I've tried it three times and still can't abide it) and huge quantities. A Burgundian starter is a normal person's main course. Watch out especially for their salads. A 'peasant's salad' may sound innocuous, but it's a trap: a little bit of lettuce arrives crushed beneath the weight of a heap of croûtons and bacon lardons, perhaps even with a poached egg on top. Don't get me wrong; it's really tasty. It's also all I wanted for lunch, but several other equally gargantuan courses followed it. I know this sounds like a complaint, but it's not meant to be, it's just that since I got back my clothes don't fit like they used to.

Naturally a region so well regarded for its cuisine will produce plenty of good picnic food. If eating outdoors is your thing, head for the hills. There are plenty of pretty spots for vineyard picnics, but the views from the wine routes high up in the Hautes Côtes are stunning. In particular look out for the one high above St-Romain.

I don't offer a producer recommendation for every village. There wouldn't be room to discuss them all, for one thing, and producers often own parcels in several communes. Some, indeed, have property from one end of the Côte d'Or to the other. But between them, the producers listed below will be able to sell you wines from nearly every appellation.

They'll also sell you a bottle of wine for about FF40, and some for FF30 or less. No-one recommended will lure you in and then show you nothing but wine at FF200 a bottle. Even if some offer the finest wines from the Côte, with prices pitched accordingly, you should always be able to find others at lower prices – no unpleasant surprises.

There are several *routes du vin* signposted (I use the term loosely) on the Côte d'Or. You'll see signs for the Route des Grands Crus and various sets of markers in the Hautes Côtes; in the Côte Chalonnaise you'll occasionally see old, blue enamel *route du vin* signs. Don't worry if these signs disappear at vital crossroads; the region is so compact that you have to work quite hard to get lost.

The routes I describe don't always follow the official ones. I chose them because I like them and because they link together well. It's easy to use them as a base and then to strike out on your own and just follow your nose. The vineyard roads are very pretty but not always passable by car. Sometimes they peter out into dirt tracks (I was caught out in this way in the hills above Mercurey) and become better walking or cycling territory. I keep promising myself that one day I'll go to Burgundy without dashing from producer to producer and just cycle sedately among the vines. One day...

EXPLORING THE CÔTE D'OR

I suggest leaving the motorway at Nuits-St-Georges, itself an important wine town, and heading north up the main N74 to the first base village, **Gevrey-Chambertin**. If you've taken an early ferry (say at about 8am) from Dover, or an overnight crossing into Zeebrugge, it'll be early evening and all you'll probably want to do is get to the hotel and collapse. If you've had a fair distance to travel before hitting the Channel ports, I advise you to break your journey in Champagne, at one of the hotels I've recommended in that section. (Several of them are near the motorway: see pages 82–3.)

A good base in Gevrey is Les Grands Crus, a modern hotel in the heart of the vineyards, within sight of the cellars belonging to the first producer to visit. All the restaurants I'd recommend are within walking distance. At Le Petit Caveau you'll find cheap Burgundian cooking, while the Bonbistrot has attractive, rustic décor and a short menu of regional dishes. Then there's La Sommellerie, mid-range in price, modern in style and with a warm welcome; and top of the range is Les Millésimes, a very fine table.

As an alternative, a five-minute car journey brings you north to **Fixin**, where the Relais de l'Empereur hides really hearty, peasant dishes and pleasant service behind an unpromising exterior (don't be put off, go to the side entrance).

Gevrey-Chambertin is, for me, where the Côte de Nuits starts to get interesting. This is where the great red wine Grands and Premiers Crus vineyards begin to appear. The most famous Grand Cru here is the Chambertin, and all the others have tacked its name onto theirs to confer additional prestige. Only one, however, Chambertin Clos de Bèze, was deemed sufficiently good to use Chambertin as a prefix; all the others have to add the glamour name as a suffix, such as Charmes-Chambertin. Incidentally, you can drive past the Chambertin vineyard on the D122; there are large signs at either end proclaiming: 'Ici commence Le Chambertin'. They make a splendid photo-opportunity against a backdrop of vines and, I hope, blue sky.

DOMAINE DENIS MORTET is in the heart of the village. M Mortet has invested heavily in building a new bottle cellar and tasting-area, where he receives his visitors. He doesn't speak

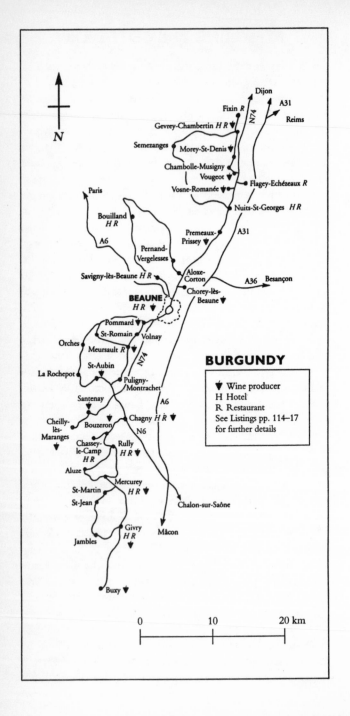

N

Dijon
A31
Reims
Fixin *R*
Gevrey-Chambertin *H R*
Semezanges
Morey-St-Denis
Chambolle-Musigny
Vougeot
Flagey-Echézeaux *R*
Vosne-Romanée
Nuits-St-Georges *H R*
Paris
Bouilland *H R*
A6
Premeaux-Prissey
A31
Pernand-Vergelesses
Aloxe-Corton
Savigny-lès-Beaune *H R*
A36 Besançon
Chorey-lès-Beaune
BEAUNE *H R*
Pommard
St-Romain Volnay
Orches
Meursault *R*
St-Aubin
N74
La Rochepot
Puligny-Montrachet

BURGUNDY

Wine producer
H Hotel
R Restaurant
See Listings pp. 114–17
for further details

Santenay
A6
Cheilly-lès-Maranges
Bouzeron
Chagny *H R*
N6
Chassey-le-Camp *H R*
Rully *H R*
Aluze
Mercurey *H R*
St-Martin
St-Jean
Chalon-sur-Saône
Givry *H R*
Jambles
Mâcon
Buxy

0   10   20 km

English but his wife does; between them they explained a philosophy very much bound up with the soil and simplicity. 'We've got exceptional *terroir* here in Gevrey-Chambertin and it behoves us to do the best we possibly can with its products.' This entails rigorously selecting the grapes you make wine with, throwing out any underripe or rotten ones (known as the *tri*) and keeping yields low for better concentration. He doesn't filter, which he believes removes too much matter from the wine and reduces its concentration. All he does is use egg white to fine the wine, which he says doesn't fatigue it and gives it brilliance. Simple, eh? What I want to know is what happens to all the egg yolks. Perhaps that explains the local popularity of *crème brûlée*.

Truly, the proof of the pudding is in the glass, and you can buy some exceedingly well-made wines here. M Mortet will sell you generic burgundy such as an Aligoté for FF28 and a basic Bourgogne Rouge, which has very good colour and concentration, for FF42.

His '92 Premiers and Grands Crus weren't yet bottled when I tasted them but he made an assembly of each from different casks, just as he would on a larger scale in a few weeks' time when he came to bottle. I was really impressed by the intensity of these wines and the sheer pleasure of tasting them. They'll certainly keep but they were surprisingly enjoyable for ones so young. His top prices range from FF128 for the Premiers Crus to a whopping FF259 for the Chambertin Grand Cru. This is indeed the price league you're in when buying the best that Burgundy has to offer, but bear in mind that you'll probably pay double these prices in the UK. I think Domaine Mortet is a splendid place to begin burgundy investigations.

Leaving Gevrey-Chambertin on the D122, signposted the Route des Grands Crus, you're soon out in the vineyards and the scenery is lovely: you're passing through some of the world's most valuable agricultural land. (The photo-opportunity is coming up on your right.)

Morey-St-Denis, a little-known and somewhat underrated village in the shadow of more famous neighbours, is close by. Here you may like to visit **DOMAINE DUJAC**. Run by Jacques Seysses and his Californian wife Ros, this is one of the finest and most influential estates in Burgundy. It was set up by M Seysses in the late 1960s (Dujac = du Jacques) and makes wines that are elegant and complex, and yet they're similar in price to very inferior burgundy sold elsewhere.

Here's the 'oak equation' in action: he uses 100% new oak barrels for the Grand Cru wines, 50% for the Premiers Crus. It's not as expensive as it sounds, Ros explained, because you can sell the barrels on after you've used them, for half what you paid. So if she paid FF2,000 for a new barrel and can get FF1,000 for it a few years later, she's happy.

Visiting Dujac is strictly by appointment: 'Otherwise the welcome is less than welcoming', as Ros put it. Dujac is also interesting for the connoisseur of red tape. Wine is sold in France with a green *capsule congé* stuck on the top of the bottle, which indicates that tax has been paid and it's authorized for sale. Ros doesn't use these capsules. Her view is that since most of their wine is exported it's too much like hard work putting them on and then having to take them off again if the wine is to be sent abroad.

Instead, she goes down to the local tax official in the village and has the documentation completed for each wine sale to private customers. You might think it was fiddly and time-consuming but Ros doesn't seem to mind. What she usually asks you to do is come back and collect your order the next day. Meanwhile she'll prepare the paperwork and also label and pack your bottles. (Most properties only label enough bottles for their immediate needs. Wine needs to be stored in nice damp cellars, damp enough to peel the labels off in days. It's better to do it on demand.) You'll get a fancy document showing details such as your licence plate and how many hours you'll be travelling with the wine, in an attempt to stop fraudulent double journeys with the same paperwork.

You are likely here to be invited into the cellar to taste the new vintage from cask. Then you can ask to taste one or two wines from the current list. Many Dujac customers return year after year, buying in bottle what they tasted in cask a couple of years before, but the Dujacs only have about five British private customers: 'whom we welcome with open arms'. This estate deserves to be much better known among wine explorers. The village wines cost FF112–118 for the Morey-St-Denis, depending on the vintage, and FF100–106 for the Chambolle-Musigny. The Premiers Crus approach FF200 a bottle, Grands Crus up to FF250. These are really delicious wines, well worth your attention. There are no generic reds, but there are whites: Aligoté for FF42 and Bourgogne Chardonnay for FF60.

The road now leads to Chambolle-Musigny, passing the Grands Crus vineyards Bonnes Mares and Clos de Tart on your right. From Chambolle, head for the Clos de Vougeot, just above **Vougeot** itself and visible from quite a distance.

The Clos de Vougeot is an essential visit, both for its historical interest and for the role it plays today in promoting Burgundy wine. The vineyard was originally planted by Cistercian monks in the 13th and 14th centuries. Then they built the wall around it and finally the buildings known as the **CHÂTEAU DU CLOS DE VOUGEOT**. Both vineyards and château were sold off after the French Revolution and the château was eventually bought in 1944 by the Confrérie des Chevaliers du Tastevin (roughly: The Brotherhood of the Knights of the Wine-Tasting-Cup). This brotherhood was formed a decade earlier to promote the wines of Burgundy, and was and is extremely successful. The members hold massive dinners for 500 guests at the château several times a year and initiate new Knights, who have to dress up in medieval red robes and get through the ceremony without giggling. A visit to the château involves a guided tour (in English by request) including several amazing old wine presses and a slide show full of pictures of other people enjoying themselves at the Brotherhood banquets. The cost is FF15, duration about 45 minutes.

The Knights have no connection with the vineyard, they own only the château. After the vineyards were sold off in 1789, ownership gradually became more and more fragmented, until today when there are about 80 owners (I'm vague because the figure keeps changing as parcels are bought and sold). Eighty people divided into 50ha results in an average annual production of less than 2,500 bottles each, although obviously some own more land than others. A number of these 80 make their own wine, others sell their grapes to négociants and yet others farm their land out under sharecropping arrangements. This chequer-board of ownership is a microcosm of the problems you have in trying to buy a decent bottle of burgundy anywhere in the region, or indeed in any UK high street. How can you rely on knowing the names of the good vineyards? It's not enough. You also need to know the names of good producers.

One of the best in Clos de Vougeot is **CHÂTEAU DE LA TOUR**, and happily it's very well geared up to receiving visitors. It's the only estate situated within the walls of the Clos making and maturing its wines actually on site. Turn right on leaving Château du Clos, and it's about 100m down the road. During the season – Easter to November – English-speaking staff are on hand, but out of season you can be seen by appointment (which also gives you a chance to ring their splendid bell, with an old hunk of vine as a bell-pull). You taste in a first-floor room with a splendid view of the vineyard. Ask to see the cellars, too.

The family-owned property has 5ha in the Clos de Vougeot and also other vineyards, but the other sites' wines, although on sale here, are marketed under different names. In the last century, family ancestors were négociants in Beaune. They owned part of the Clos vineyards and stored the wines at the Château du Clos. In 1891, however, the château was sold and the family had to remove its stocks. Rather than transport 150,000 bottles by horse to Beaune they decided to build a storage cellar within the Clos (the roots of the present property) and then built a little railway to transport the bottles there.

Château de la Tour's Clos-Vougeot wine ranges from FF180 to FF260, depending on the vintage, and it's delicious. (I know, at that price wine should be, but so often in Burgundy it isn't.) The château also offers generics from FF30 and a Crémant for FF40, so you don't have to break the bank in order to visit.

Vougeot itself need not detain you. If you're in need of a sustaining lunch, drop down onto the N74 and cross over to **Flagey-Echézeaux**. There's a bistro here called Robert Losset, rustic in appearance and heavy on the cream. It's hearty, popular and cheap.

Alternatively, loop back up Vougeot's one-way system (by turning left in the village and left again) and continue past the Château du Clos, and the Echézeaux and Grands Echézeaux vineyards, into **Vosne-Romanée**. If you want to pay homage, head high out of the village to the Romanée-Conti and other Romanée vineyards – the dearest in all Burgundy. And I do mean dear. How does £700 a bottle (from a UK wine merchant) strike you?

To set foot more firmly in reality, join the main N74 in the direction of Beaune, and you'll soon see **DOMAINE ARMELLE & BERNARD RION** on your left. This young couple has established a formidable reputation but the wines are as yet relatively unknown and thus better value. Armelle speaks enough English to talk about the estate and its wines, and will guide you through the cellars to a small, cosy tasting-area.

Their generic wines are all of very good quality and at fair prices – FF20 for Grand Ordinaire, FF25 for Aligoté, FF40 for Bourgogne Rouge. They have a range of Grands and Premiers Crus, all very well made and keenly priced, and they also have that rarity, a selection of bottles from older vintages. I know of no better treat than the present of a bottle of wine from a significant vintage (although I did take the precaution of getting married in the bumper year of 1985).

Now you're practically on the outskirts of **Nuits-St-Georges**. Although this is the home of many important figures in the wine world, and its architecture betrays that there has been a lot of money here for many centuries, I don't find it as interesting as what lies just down the road. So if you're staying another night in Gevrey-Chambertin, head back via the D25 (turn right on the northern outskirts of Nuits; the road is signposted – just once – Route des Hautes Côtes). This is a pretty road, through some of the Hautes Côtes vineyards. After about 3km bear right on the D35, and then right again onto the D31 after Semezanges, and descend via the steep, pretty Combe de Lavaux into Gevrey. Incidentally, this road takes you past La Gentilhommière, a very quiet hotel with motel-style rooms, heated swimming-pool and popular restaurant. Alternatively, stop in Nuits if you will, and then head out again on the N74 towards Beaune (I do hope they've finished their interminable roadworks by the time you read this).

The next producer on the route is just south of Nuits, at **Premeaux-Prissey**. Turn off left at the church, and 100m down the road you'll see **DOMAINE BERTRAND AMBROISE** on the left. I really enjoyed my visit here. M Ambroise speaks good English and is a genial host, happy to explain his wines and his philosophy. His tasting-cellar is long on atmosphere, with a wood-fired stove blazing in winter. Generations of grape-pickers have covered the beams with chalked graffiti.

The wines are full and round and have lots to offer. His generic red is a snip at FF32 and he offers a range of smashing wines from various Premiers Crus, including Nuits-St-Georges, Gevrey-Chambertin and Monthélie. M Ambroise also has the white Grand Cru Corton-Charlemagne, and it is gorgeous. He doesn't get many visitors, only about a hundred a year, because: 'Everybody just speeds through on the main road'. Do stop. It's worth it.

Now the N74 heads through some fairly dull scenery, past the industrial areas surrounding Comblanchien and Corgoloin, mainly devoted to quarrying. Here we pass the border between the Côte de Nuits and the Côte de Beaune, and the main road has nothing whatsoever to commend it. You can turn off left onto the D20F at Corgoloin, through Ladoix-Serrigny towards the next stop, Chorey-lès-Beaune.

The small village of **Chorey-lès-Beaune** is often ignored; there are no top vineyards here, not even any slopes. Yet the two growers I'd recommend both make wines at village level which are very good value and will be ready to drink much sooner than the wines at sky-high prices. The first, TOLLOT-BEAUT (I can't resist sounding all the 't's in a robust northern English accent), is a small family firm run by three brothers and their three children, who plan by taking collective decisions at daily meetings. Nathalie Tollot is in charge of sales. Her English is excellent and she'll take you – by appointment – into the cellars to taste a well-made range of wines. Their main production is of village wine from Chorey itself and surrounding villages, although they have very fairly priced generics, some Premier Cru reds, and red and white Grand Cru from Corton.

Tollot-Beaut was one of the first properties to bottle its wines on the estate for shipment to the American market, back in the 1920s when most producers were still shipping in cask. Consequently, it's well geared up to exporting and the wines are widely available in the UK, but not all that widely known, probably because production is concentrated in the mid-priced range. I've been buying wine here for several years and have always been impressed. It's good stuff.

The second domaine to visit, that of **JACQUES GERMAIN**, is located in the Château de Chorey (to find it, just look up; it's the tallest building in town). Here you can taste some very well made, elegant wines in the old cellars (there's another splendid bell to ring if nobody's around) and take the opportunity to walk through the formal park and grounds.

The domaine also offers elegant, expensive bed and breakfast. The setting is very attractive but there are no restaurants in the village and you either have to drive into Beaune or take pot luck with the restaurants on the N74. To me, that's a disadvantage, as I don't like to drive after dinner, although it's no problem for those with a teetotaller in the party (but if you are one, why are you reading this book?).

Now head out of Chorey and cross the N74 to the pretty village of **Savigny-lès-Beaune**. You can taste Savigny reds at Tollot-Beaut (qv), or the splendid, rare white Savigny at Château de la Tour (qv). Leave via the D2, heading north; you'll pass a simple Logis, L'Ouvrée, which has its own cellars (and hence a very fairly priced wine list). The road winds along the side of a lovely wooded valley to **Bouilland**, where there's a temple of gastronomy, Le Vieux Moulin, with well-situated rooms in the annexe opposite.

After Bouilland turn right onto the D18 and the road descends back into Hautes Côtes territory and to **Pernand-Vergelesses**. This is another unappreciated Burgundy village, possibly because of the dangers of pronouncing the name wrongly in restaurants. (Just think of a church without a caretaker, stress the 'less'.)

Turn off the D18 into **Aloxe-Corton** – the road first takes you past the white Grand Cru vineyard Corton-Charlemagne, followed by the beginning of the various parts of the Grand Cru Corton vineyard. The architecture is attractive, with several châteaux and those ornate, mosaic-tiled Burgundy roofs. The area also offers ideal walking territory, up into the hills around the Grand Cru vineyards. Finally, rejoin the N74 and head into Beaune.

Beaune is a very special place for me. Never mind that it's full of tourists during the season. I love stopping here and always manage to find an excuse to travel via the town no matter where in France I'm headed for.

It's a medieval city, built by the Dukes of Burgundy before they moved north to Dijon, and is still surrounded by ramparts; the one-way ring-road circles them, traffic moving anticlockwise. Entering from Dijon, you are confronted as you join the ring-road by the impressive, arched Porte St-Nicolas. Halfway round the ring-road you'll find both the hotels I'd recommend. The Hôtel de la Poste is just before the turning off to Chagny on the N74, the Hostellerie de la Bretonnière is 100m down that turning, on the left.

The Poste is a grand, old-fashioned establishment; I can imagine it as a coaching-inn. It's recently been refurbished and has an elegant piano-bar with something of the air of a 1930s liner (although the pianist is electronic, courtesy of Yamaha). The restaurant serves traditional, expensive food. You might prefer to treat the Poste as a base for exploring some of the excellent restaurants within the ramparts.

The Bretonnière, on the other hand, is modern and without a restaurant; it's an easy walk from here to the town centre. Rooms vary in price; the simplest is FF175 but the ones I prefer are the newest, costing about FF350, set motel-style in a second courtyard at the back. Both hotels offer off-street parking. Beaune is compact, and by far the best way to explore it is on foot.

Top of my current restaurant list is Le Jardin des Remparts for modern, innovative cooking, full of flavour, marred only by rather arrogant young staff. La Ciboulette offers good-value, simple cooking in charming surroundings, and well-chosen, fairly-priced wines. There's also a relatively hip wine bar, Le Bistrot Bourguignon, which has a good selection of wines by the glass and simple *plats*, perfect for a light lunch. The Central hotel – also a decent place to stay – has a restaurant that's well spoken of. Good picnic shops are at hand on the pedestrianized streets off Place Carnot. All these are within the ramparts.

The key wine-tourist visit is the Hôtel-Dieu. This was founded in 1443 by Nicolas Rolin, chancellor to one of the Dukes of Burgundy, who bequeathed all his possessions to endow a hospital for the needy citizens of Beaune. Many people gave vineyards to the hospital and the money raised by the sale of their wines supports the poor of the town to this day. The Hôtel-Dieu functioned as a hospital until very recently but the patients are now rehoused and the building is a museum. Allow an hour to see the beautiful, mosaic-tiled, gabled roof, rooms illustrating hospital life, and the extraordinary polyptych by Rogier van der Weyden depicting *The Last Judgment*. This is a glorious painting and I found myself irritated by the hurried way the guided tour presents it.

All the wines made from the Hôtel-Dieu estates, which are known as the Hospices de Beaune, are auctioned during the third weekend of November. This is a major media event, widely covered on French television and seen as a key price indicator for the rest of the vintage. The marathon auction is the excuse for, and centrepiece of, three flamboyant days of banqueting. The 'Trois Glorieuses', glorious days, commence with a dinner at the Château du Clos de Vougeot and end with a lunch party in Meursault on the following Monday. This last binge is known as the Paulée, and growers vie with each other to provide the best bottles to accompany the massive multi-course meal.

Avoid this weekend unless you're sure of a bed space. The town swiftly reverts to normal, however, and business and tourism continue quietly as usual. Don't miss the informative Musée du Vin de Bourgogne and the Collégiale Notre-Dame. The church houses a series of beautiful tapestries depicting the life of the Virgin Mary.

I also like to take a walk around the ramparts, which run for about 2km, more or less continuously except for a stretch in the northwest corner. Then it's just a question of wandering the streets, following your nose; it's difficult to get lost and there's plenty of beautiful architecture to attract the eye.

To the north of the town centre are two négociants to visit who between them illustrate very neatly the role of the merchant in Burgundy winemaking and wine marketing. If you've been walking or driving around Beaune you can't possibly have missed the signs to the cellars of **PATRIARCHE PÈRE & FILS**: they offer you a visit to 'The biggest cellars in Burgundy'. I do believe these cellars are well worth a tour, although I must be honest and say it's worth it more for the experience of tramping along a kilometre or so of dimly-lit cellars, past stacks of bottles and into a candlelit tasting-room, rather than necessarily for the wines themselves.

Admission costs FF50 and, although they say this fee is donated to charity and the tasting is free, I'm inclined to treat this strictly as a commercial transaction; taste the wines they're showing but don't be seduced by the atmosphere into buying what by daylight may not seem such good value. They give you a *tastevin* to taste in. This is a shallow dish made of silver (or plated) to reflect as much light as possible into the wine when it's being tasted in a dark cellar.

For a very different view of the négociant's role, call at **CHAMPY PÈRE & CIE**. This house was established in 1720, making it the oldest négociant in Burgundy, buying in wines for maturation alongside the production of its own vineyards. It was sold in 1989 to the American-owned négociants Louis Jadot, but they were only interested in the vineyards; the house and name of Champy were bought by father and son Henri and Pierre Meurgey. They've set about revitalizing the firm and have a very worthwhile selection of wines on sale.

You can taste and buy in an attractive mini-museum here, surrounded by collections of winemaking implements. But ask, preferably in advance, to see Vat 17 and the railway, and you'll be taken on a tour of some of the most interesting cellar items in all Burgundy.

Vat 17 is a tasting-room built into an old barrel. There's room for about six inside, complete with table and stools, and walls lined with photographs of celebrities enjoying the facilities. (I gather these days it's used not so much for tasting as for serious drinking.) You can shut the barrel door and no-one would know you were there.

The 'railway', on the other hand, is in the attic, a floor above the vats, and was an integral part of the vinification process a hundred years ago. A decade after phylloxera had devastated Burgundy's vineyards in the 1880s, replanting had produced new vines giving light-coloured juice, which the winemakers didn't know how to handle. The company's head at that time was a friend of Pasteur and he devised the idea of heating the must to 60°C/140°F (that's the same as for colour-fast cottons) to draw out the maximum colour and start the fermentation. Once the cauldron of must was heated, it was rolled along tracks in the roof and poured down into one of the waiting vats in the floor below. There was a lift and other machinery, all powered by steam – you can still see the boiler. The area was last used in 1989 and the last vintage to be boiled up was the '87.

The rest of the buildings and cellars are well worth a visit. The honeycomb of cellars contains bottles dating back to the mid-19th century. With the end of the last century proving to be a strong period for the négociants, they had plenty of money to invest in building work. Eiffel (of the Tower) was born in Dijon and his ironwork can be seen here and in the next property to visit, DOMAINE ALBERT MOROT.

This is on the outskirts of Beaune, on the D970 in the direction of Saulieu, past the Lycée Viticole (itself open for visitors and to sell the wines made by pupils and teachers). Run by the indomitable Mme Choppin, great-granddaughter of the founder, with just three vineyard workers, you can taste a selection of well-structured Beaune Premiers Crus. Her generic red Bourgogne is declassified Premier Cru and also good value.

She's helpful with guiding you towards the wines you want to buy, asking whether you are looking for fine wine or a stronger style, wines for drinking now or to keep, and knowledgeable burgundy fans will be able to learn a great deal from her. Her barrel cellars, supported by Eiffel ironwork, are above vaulted bottle storage cellars. Wine, from the ground-level open fermentation vats (*pigeage* done by feet), is fed down to the barrels by gravity – there's no pumping to upset the wine, and no filtration either.

Mme Choppin will sell you wine practically any time: 'If my door is closed people open it, so it's easier to leave it open.' Saves having to beat it down.

For a panoramic view of Beaune and its vineyards continue along the D970 and turn right up to the Montagne de Beaune. Then retrace your steps to the ring-road and turn south onto the N74. The road divides as you clear the suburbs and you should turn right onto the D973 to Pommard, but before doing this fans of cooperatives may like to turn left into the CAVES DES HAUTES-CÔTES.

The modern sales area has plenty of wines available to taste, although when I visited some were a little faded after being open too long. This is the major outlet for wines from the Hautes Côtes and a source of good-quality, basic-level generics. You can also buy wine *en vrac*, with corks and labels thrown in.

Now follow the D973 to **Pommard**. My heart never fails to lift as I follow this road out into the vines, with its trail of famous names. On the outskirts is the CHÂTEAU DE POMMARD, an imposing 18th-century building and one of the few châteaux in Burgundy, in an enclosed vineyard. A tasting and tour costs FF20. The wine is a good village wine, but not cheap at FF157 the bottle upwards. Luckily, as this is a paid tasting, you need feel under no obligation to buy.

Head next into the village, park in the central square and look for the signposts to DOMAINE ANDRÉ MUSSY. M Mussy is 79, and I confidently expect him to be around to welcome you for the lifetime of this book; he's a walking advertisement for the life-enhancing properties of working with vines and wine. He speaks no English but if your French is up to it you can learn much about his philosophy and discuss it with him. Descend into his cellars on an industrial platform-lift. Space is limited, filled to the brim with barrels and bottles. He keeps yields low, and practises minimum intervention in the cellar – fining with egg-whites, filtering only if necessary, without pumping to tire the wine. He is very conscious of the weight of history; he's the 11th generation of a family going back to 1746, and 1993 was his 67th vinification. His son-in-law is gradually taking over from him. These wines are very attractive and fairly priced, and this is an excellent visit for advanced students. Pommard's wines are fuller and heavier than either of its neighbours' and Mussy makes excellent examples.

On the square you'll also find a shop, Les Domaines de Pommard, which sells the wines of 16 producers at cellar prices. Some of these are very good indeed, such as those from Jean Garaudet and Virely Arcelain. No English is spoken here.

The next stop is **Volnay**, home of lighter, silky reds. It's worth parking in the square for a stroll around this ancient village, which is the only one on the Côte to be sited above its vineyards.

From Volnay drop down into **Meursault** and be prepared to get lost in its meandering maze of roads. CHÂTEAU DE MEURSAULT is owned by the same group as Patriarche (qv), and the two visits have several things in common: a paid tour, a route through atmospheric cellars, a souvenir *tastevin* and a selection of wines to taste. There is also a small modern art gallery. Again, take advantage of the fact that this is a paid tasting; you may find a wine here that's very much to your taste but, if you don't, you are under no obligation to buy. It's dear, too; Aligoté for FF59 is the cheapest white and prices rise to a stratospheric FF450 for Meursault.

Tasting on a more human scale is available every afternoon from grower and négociant JEAN GERMAIN. His capable English-speaking staff offer very good wines and advice from a small tasting-room.

The large négociant house of Antonin Rodet (qv), based in Mercurey on the Côte Chalonnaise, has a 50% interest in the Meursault domaine of JACQUES PRIEUR. Quality has greatly improved since this négociant became involved. You can arrange a visit via Rodet's offices (see Listings page 116). There's plenty to see, not least the pneumatic *pigeage* equipment.

From Meursault head for **Puligny-Montrachet**. Meursault and Puligny, together with Chassagne-Montrachet two minutes away, are responsible for the great white wines of Burgundy. I don't find the village itself of great interest and think it's much more fun to get out among the vines, on foot or by bike, and see the Grand Cru Montrachet vineyards. These are situated above the village and offer another photo-opportunity with a walled gate.

This is the home of the most expensive dry white wine in the world, retailing in the UK for perhaps £700 a bottle. Who pays this kind of money? American wine-writer Robert Parker points to persistent rumours that there's a big market for it among the drug barons of Miami, although he notes that given their short life expectancy they're unlikely to wait for it to age properly. (In south London, the equivalent tipple seems to be Moët & Chandon. A poor second, if you ask me.)

Parker also relates a story about a Second World War French general fighting the Germans as they retreated through the Burgundy vineyards. Apparently he wouldn't attack them while they were in the Grand Cru vineyards for fear of damaging the precious vines. Only when he heard the Germans had moved down to the inferior lower slopes would he give the order to open fire. A similar attitude was demonstrated more recently when the French government amended the route of the A6 motorway to avoid the Montrachet vineyards.

From Puligny, turn right onto the N6 and turn off again almost immediately into Gamay, the village that named the grape. Next along is **St-Aubin**, an underestimated appellation full of dynamic young growers making very fine wine. Typical of these is **HENRI PRUDHON**, who offers remarkably good wines at very fair prices indeed, such as a St-Aubin Premier Cru for FF54. No English is spoken, although the son is learning. St-Aubin's steep, narrow, winding streets are worth exploring on foot.

Climb out of St-Aubin on the D33 (it's signposted Route des Hautes Côtes) and you can look back on some lovely, wide valley views. You also pass the château of La Rochepot, with its Burgundy-tiled roof. Turn right in La Rochepot, and left shortly after onto the D17i. The route is signposted Cluny à

Beaune par la Vignoble. There are waymarked walks in Baubigny and the road passes through Orches, clinging to the side of the mountain. Look out for the parking area above **St-Romain**, where the views are quite stunning.

Now you can either drop down into St-Romain, where attractions include a marked trail up to the 13th century castle, or continue along the extremely pretty D17 into Pommard. Head back into Beaune, if that's where you're staying.

Otherwise head for Meursault, via Monthelie and Auxey-Duresses, and down to the N74. I'm not usually keen on taking the main roads but this one is exceptional; as you drive towards Chagny you'll see a quite beautiful panorama of the Côte unfolding. It's lovely even in winter, as curls of smoke rise from the little portable braziers, looking like punctured wheelbarrows, used to burn vine prunings. Incidentally there's a bustling restaurant on the other side of the N74 in Meursault. Follow the signs to the railway station and you'll find the Relais de la Diligence à la Gare, where the food is good, plentiful (of course) and remarkably cheap.

Follow the N74 under the N6 and turn off to **Santenay**. This sprawling, attractive village is the last major stop on the Côte d'Or (strictly speaking, the last port of call is Cheilly-lès-Maranges). The village is in two parts, lower and upper. Nestled in among the upper village houses is **DOMAINE PRIEUR-BRUNET**, with its distinctive, tiled roof. I can't recommend this visit highly enough. For a start, the wines are splendid and remarkably well priced: generic red for FF31, Santenay Maladière Premier Cru for FF63–82, depending on the vintage. The whites, too, are excellent, including Santenay Clos Rousseau Premier Cru for FF74–94 and Meursault-Charmes Premier Cru for FF102–121.

Parts of the cellars are 15th century but much of the building is new. They are adherents of the cool maceration school and even chill the whites to -3°C (27°F) for a week to precipitate the tartrates – which is somewhat interventionist but the wines don't seem to have suffered. Visits include a cellar tour as a matter of course and there's a comfortable, well-lit tasting-room. These wines are concentrated, rich and well balanced, at prices very favourable for the quality. Dominique Prieur speaks excellent English and pitches the visit at your level of knowledge. Sassy, attractive wines.

From Santenay cross the canal and turn right onto the D974. This quiet road follows the Canal du Centre, popular for narrow-boat holidays. Cruisers like the next stop, the CAVES DE CHEILLY, on the D974 just outside **Cheilly-lès-Maranges**, because they can fill up with wine from the top burgundy appellations to *vin* very *ordinaire* at FF8 the litre.

Although it sounds like a cooperative, the Caves de Cheilly mainly sells the produce of one man, René Martin. It does offer higher appellations from other producers, but more to fill out the range for the holiday-makers than as a serious sales drive. M Martin's admirable assistant, Nathalie de Grange, speaks good English and will show you the cellars (selling, not working, space with large vats of *en vrac* wines) and explain as much as you'd like to know about the area, its wines and its tourist attractions. Maranges is a new appellation, seldom seen; there are good examples at the Caves plus honestly-made generics. It's a friendly, easy place to visit – right on the main road, with easy parking and help if you need it.

Cheilly is officially still part of the Côte d'Or but it doesn't feel like it. The scenery has changed, we're moving into the more mixed agricultural setting of the Côte Chalonnaise.

EXPLORING THE CÔTE CHALONNAISE

The nearest place to stay is the Auberge du Camp Romain in **Chassey-le-Camp**; this is a rapidly developing tourist hotel offering modern, quiet, very good value rooms with a view right out across the valley. There's an outdoor pool (barbecues in summer) and there'll soon be an indoor one, too. I wish they'd get a new chef, though; the food lets them down and the wine list is a disgrace. (It's a perfect illustration of the pitfalls of choosing Burgundy wine.) But stick to basic dishes and house wine, and you'll have a peaceful, reasonably-priced stay.

At the other end of the scale is the imposing Hostellerie du Château de Bellecroix, off the N6 south of **Chagny**. Elegant, expensive bedrooms and the prettiest dining-room I encountered in Burgundy, set in the great hall. I ate a very enjoyable meal, aided by a splendid waiter with a real sense of theatre.

In **Rully** there's the Hôtel Commerce, with Restaurant Le Vendangerot (the grape-picker's basket) attached. This is a small establishment, with rooms traditionally furnished, slightly

faded but great on atmosphere and value. The food is of a high
standard and the wines (including by the carafe – rare in
Burgundy) are very reasonable.

Mercurey has the Hôtellerie du Val d'Or. There's a very
friendly welcome here. The food gets a Michelin star and has a
strong regional accent, with the emphasis on game in season
and offal. Their desserts are brilliant; I must mention the *soufflé
glacé*, which had a creaminess the likes of which I haven't tasted
since I was about six. Caveat: sound insulation in the rooms is
poor and the hall floors are very creaky.

Finally, in **Givry**, there's Hôtel de la Halle, long popular
with the British for its honest regional cooking and over-
decorated bedrooms at tiny prices.

I mention all these places at the start of the section to give
you an overview. There's a good variation of price and you can
pick one as your base for visiting all the properties or move
around as you wish. (You could even, if you've become
addicted to Beaune, an understandable affliction, travel out to
the Côte Chalonnaise from there; the drive from Beaune to
Chagny takes about 15 minutes.)

The first wine village to visit is **Bouzeron**. This village is
best known for producing the most successful wine from
Burgundy's lesser white grape, the Aligoté. This success is
recognized: the village, alone of Aligoté winemakers, may put
its name on the label as AC Bourgogne Aligoté de Bouzeron.
It's also a good source of well-priced generic red and white.

The finest maker of Aligoté de Bouzeron is **A & P DE
VILLAINE**, part owner of the Domaine de la Romanée Conti
which makes the most expensive wines of Burgundy. The
Aligoté is priced at the other end of the scale, but is still excellent. The generic reds and whites are also well worth having.
This is not a visit I've yet been able to make, but the wines are
widely available in the UK and I've often enjoyed them.

The **DOMAINE DE LA FOLIE**, just off the D981 on the outskirts of Bouzeron (officially it's in Chagny) will sell you a
lively, fresh Aligoté and also some well-made Rully whites.
They also make an extraordinary cassis liqueur. The domaine
charges a small sum if you only want to taste, but if you buy a
dozen bottles you get one free, and other quantity discounts
can be negotiated.

From Bouzeron head for the village of **Rully**, dominated by an impressive château. Antonin Rodet (qv) makes **CHÂTEAU DE RULLY** wine and you can arrange a visit through his firm (see Listings page 116).

In the village itself **MICHEL BRIDAY** is establishing himself as a winemaker with a growing reputation. His vineyards are all rented – he can't afford to buy and anyway no-one's selling. He invests every spare penny in improving his equipment and cellars, which he's built up from scratch over the last 15 years. His difficulties illustrate the problems of the would-be winemaker without a family holding to inherit. It's generally accepted that Rully's whites are better than its reds and that the reverse is the case for Mercurey, but here I found the Rully reds more successful than the whites.

From Rully there are two pretty routes to **Mercurey** but neither is well-signposted, so it may end up being pot luck which you take. One runs down behind the Château de Rully to Aluze, from where you turn left onto the D978. The other meanders southeast, bringing you out on a hill east of the village (keep turning right).

Mercurey at first sight seems to be little other than a long, dull main drag; but get off the main road and climb up into the village and you'll find a charming spot. There are also some very attractive walks in the vineyards either side of the village; nothing is waymarked, just follow your instinct.

The two properties to visit in Mercurey are next door to each other but they couldn't be more different. **DOMAINE JEAN MARÉCHAL** makes only red wines: a generic Bourgogne Rouge, Mercurey and a Cuvée Prestige, with prices ranging from FF36 to FF60. M Maréchal works with extreme care and pride in his job, and gives freely of his time to visitors who come to taste: 'If you love your work you have pleasure in sharing it with others.'

I watched him packing wine into boxes with great precision, not reaching for the sealing tape until the edges of the box were perfectly aligned. Such care over a small detail reflects his meticulous winemaking. He prefers a long, slow fermentation, believing that quick fermentation gives short-term aromas in bottle but nothing for the long term. If you speak good French, have plenty of time and want to know the fine detail of a winemaker's philosophy, don't hesitate to visit here.

Just next door is the house of négociant and grower

ANTONIN RODET. Rodet can take a large part of the credit for gaining greater recognition for Côte Chalonnaise wines. Call here for a tasting and you might feel you've entered some-one's elegant home (it was indeed the first house built by the founder). You'll be escorted downstairs to a small, attractive tasting-cellar, where you can try wines from the Rodet properties, Château de Chamirey in Mercurey, Château de Rully (qv) and Domaine Jacques Prieur in Meursault (qv). You can make appointments to visit all these properties by phoning Rodet (see Listings page 116), and they are all well worth the visit. At Château de Chamirey, for instance, you can see yet another *pigeage* system: internal paddles agitate the grape-skin cap several times a day.

This is winemaking of excellent quality, a fact that hasn't gone unnoticed among major restaurants and airlines, where Rodet has found an important market. You won't meet the winemaker at Rodet's tasting-cellars (although you may well if you visit the domaines – there's an oenologist at each), but you'll get an insight into an organization which is becoming a significant player in the region and is still selling very good value wines.

One word of warning: beware of going to Michel Juillot's estate, on the other side of the road. They were so worried about upsetting their importers by selling direct to us Brits that it was all I could do to extract a price list.

Leaving Mercurey towards Chalon-sur-Saône, turn off right past the Château de Chamirey and head towards Givry via **St-Martin**, **St-Jean** and **Jambles**. This partly follows the official wine route and you may see some signposts. It's a very attractive road, through rolling countryside with mixed agriculture and vines only on certain favoured slopes.

From Jambles you can cut across to Givry, or head down to **Buxy** and its **CAVES DES VIGNERONS**. This is a large, modern cooperative that will sell you wines from the pump, or well-made Montagny by the bottle – elegant, reasonably-priced white wines. Montagny is the southernmost appellation on the Côte Chalonnaise and, alone of all French wines, can call itself Grand Cru solely on the merits of its alcohol content; if it reaches 11.5% it's a Grand Cru. Rodet (qv) also offers excellent examples of Montagny.

If you'd like to step back in time, go to St-Gengoux-le-

National, south of Buxy, off the D981. There's a branch of the Buxy co-op there, as dank and old-fashioned as the head office is bright and modern. I loved it.

Head north now, or across, to **Givry** for the wines of **DOMAINE THÉNARD**. Here you can buy red or white Givry, both extremely well made and excellent value. You can also visit the estate's 14th century cellars by arrangement (it's easier off-season, when the workforce isn't out in the vineyards). I've bought very reliable wine here for several years.

Givry is plagued by a one-way system; if you've passed the Hôtel de la Halle, then you've missed the turning for Thénard, so keep turning left until it comes up again. After Givry the Chalonnaise tour is complete. The D981 will take you straight up to all points north; but the Mâconnais and Beaujolais are only half-an-hour's drive south, so why not keep on going?

Listings

When telephoning France from the UK, first dial 00 33 then the number shown. Producers are listed in wine route order, and hotels/restaurants by town or village according to the route. Accommodation prices are per room, meal prices are per head.

Producers

Domaine Denis Mortet
22 rue de l'Eglise,
21220 Gevrey-Chambertin
Tel 80 34 10 05, Fax 80 58 51 32
Visits by appointment Mon–Sat
9–12, 14–18; closed Sun
Credit cards accepted
Some English

Domaine Dujac
7 rue de la Bussière,
21220 Morey-St-Denis
Tel 80 34 32 58, Fax 80 51 89 76
Visits by appointment
Good English

Château du Clos de Vougeot
21640 Vougeot
Tel 80 62 86 09, Fax 80 62 82 75
Open April–Sept Mon–Sun 9–18.30
incl lunch-time; Oct–March
9–11.30, 14–17.30; closes Sat at
17.00
(admission FF15)
Tours available in English (can book)

Château de la Tour
21640 Vougeot
Tel 80 62 86 13, Fax 80 62 82 72
Open Easter–Nov Mon–Sun 9–12,
14–18; visits by appointment in
winter
Credit cards accepted
Good English

Domaine Armelle & Bernard Rion
8 Route Nationale,
21700 Vosne-Romanée
Tel 80 61 05 31, Fax 80 61 34 60
Open Mon–Sat 9–12, 14–18;
occasionally open Sun
Credit cards accepted
Some English

Domaine Bertrand Ambroise
Rue de l'Eglise,
21700 Premeaux-Prissey
Tel 80 62 30 19, Fax 80 62 38 69
Open Mon–Sat pm;
appointment preferred
Credit cards accepted
Good English

Domaine Tollot-Beaut & Fils
Rue Alexandre Tollot,
21200 Chorey-lès-Beaune
Tel 80 22 16 54, Fax 80 22 12 61
Visits by appointment Mon–Sat;
closed Sun
Good English

Domaine Jacques Germain
Le Château
21200 Chorey-lès-Beaune
Tel 80 22 06 05, Fax 80 24 03 93
Open Mon–Sun 9–12, 14–19;
appointment preferred for
extended visit
Credit cards accepted
Good English

Patriarche Père & Fils
7 rue du College, 21200 Beaune
Open Mon–Sun 9.30–11.30,
14–17.30; closed 15 Dec–1 March
(admission Mon–Sat FF50, Sun
FF80)
Some English

Champy Père & Cie
5 rue du Grenier à Sel
21200 Beaune
Tel 80 24 97 30, Fax 80 24 97 40
Open Mon–Fri 9–12, 14–18
Credit cards accepted
Good English

Domaine Albert Morot
Château de la Creusotte
21200 Beaune
Tel 80 22 35 39, Fax 80 22 47 50
Open Mon–Sun 10–12, 14–18;
appointment preferred
Credit cards accepted
Good English

Les Caves des Hautes-Côtes
Route de Pommard, 21200 Beaune
Tel 80 24 63 12, Fax 80 22 87 06
Open Mon–Sat 9–12, 14–18;
5 April–21 Nov; also open Sun 9–12
No English

Château de Pommard
21630 Pommard
Tel 80 22 07 99
Open 1 April–22 Nov Mon–Sun
9–18
incl lunch-time; closed winter
(admission FF20)
Some English

Domaine André Mussy
Rue Dauphin, 21630 Pommard
Tel 80 22 05 56, Fax 80 24 07 47
Open Mon–Sat 9.30–12, 14.30–19;
visits by appointment Sun
No English

Château de Meursault
21190 Meursault
Tel 80 21 22 98, Fax 80 21 66 77

Open Mon–Sun 9.30–12, 14.30–18
(admission FF50)
Some English

Maison Jean Germain
11 rue de Lattre-de-Tassigny,
21190 Meursault
Tel 80 21 63 67, Fax 80 21 64 66
Open Mon–Fri pm;
visits by appointment in winter
Credit cards accepted
Some English

Domaine Henri Prudhon & Fils
Place de l'Eglise, 21190 St-Aubin
Tel 80 21 31 33/80 21 36 70
Visits by appointment Mon–Sun
No English

Domaine Prieur-Brunet
Rue de Narosse, 21590 Santenay
Tel 80 20 60 56, Fax 80 20 64 31
Open Easter–Nov Mon–Sun;
appointment preferred, essential in
winter
Credit cards accepted
Good English

Caves de Cheilly
Cheilly-lès-Maranges, 71150 Chagny
Tel 85 91 14 51, Fax 85 91 17 57
Open Mon–Sat 9.30–12,
14.30–18.30, Sun 10–12, 15–19
Credit cards accepted
Some English

A & P de Villaine
71150 Bouzeron
Tel 85 91 20 50, Fax 85 87 04 10
Visits (strictly) by appointment
Mon–Fri 8–12, 14–17
Good English (from Mme de
Villaine)

Domaine de la Folie
Route de Rully, 71150 Chagny
Tel 85 87 18 59, Fax 85 87 03 53
Open Mon–Sat 9–12, 14–17, Sun
11–13 (tasting FF30, refundable with
purchase)
Some English

Domaine Michel Briday
Grande Rue, 71150, Rully
Tel 85 87 07 90, Fax 85 91 25 68
Open Mon–Sun 9–12, 14–18
Credit cards accepted
Some English

Domaine Jean Maréchal
Route Nationale, 71640 Mercurey
Tel 85 45 11 29, Fax 85 45 18 52
Open Mon–Sat 8–12.30,
13.30–19.30; visits by
appointment Sun
No English

Antonin Rodet
Route Nationale, 71640 Mercury
Tel 85 45 22 22, Fax 85 45 25 49
Open May–Oct Mon–Fri 9–12,
14–18; visits by appointment in
winter
Credit cards accepted
Good English

Visits by appointment with Rodet:
Domaine Jacques Prieur, Château de
Rully, Château de Chamirey

Caves des Vignerons de Buxy
Les Vignes de la Croix, 71390 Buxy
(and 71460 St-Gengoux-le-National)
Tel 85 92 03 03
Open Mon–Sat 8.15–12, 14–18;
closed Tues at St-Gengoux
No English

Domaine Thénard
7 rue de l'Hôtel de Ville
71640 Givry
Tel 85 44 31 36
Open Mon–Sat 8–19 incl lunch;
visits by appointment in winter to
the *cave*
No English

Hotels and Restaurants
H Hotel   *R* Restaurant

Gevrey-Chambertin
H Les Grands Crus
Route des Grands Crus,
21220 Gevrey-Chambertin
Tel 80 34 34 15, Fax 80 51 89 07
FF350–430

R Bonbistrot
Rue Chambertin
Tel 80 34 33 20
FF150–200

R Les Millésimes
25 rue Eglise
Tel 80 51 84 24
FF295–560

R Le Petit Caveau
4 rue Richebourg
Tel 80 34 32 83
FF80–140

R La Sommellerie
7 rue Souvert
Tel 80 34 31 48
FF130–360

Fixin
R Au Relais de l'Empereur
35 route des Grands Crus
Tel 80 52 45 46
FF68–140

Flagey-Echézeaux
R Robert Losset
Place Eglise
Tel 80 62 88 10
FF95–250 incl wine

Nuits-St-Georges
HR Hôtel La Gentilhommière
13 Vallée Serrée, Route Meuilley,
21700 Nuits-St-Georges
Tel 80 61 12 06, Fax 80 61 30 33
Rooms FF400, Meals FF180–240

Savigny-lès-Beaune
HR L'Ouvrée
Route de Bouilland,
21420 Savigny-lès-Beaune
Tel 80 21 51 52, Fax 80 26 10 04
Rooms FF240–270, Meals FF92–220

Bouilland
HR Le Vieux Moulin
21420 Bouilland
Tel 80 21 51 16, Fax 80 21 59 90
Rooms FF380–800, Meals
FF190–500

Beaune
HR Central
2 rue V-Millot, 21200 Beaune
Tel 80 24 77 24, Fax 80 22 30 40
Rooms FF330–450, Meals FF99–185

HR Hôtel de la Poste
1 boulevard Clémenceau, 21200
Beaune
Tel 80 22 08 11, Fax 80 24 19 71
Rooms FF500–850, Meals
FF160–320

H Hostellerie de la Bretonnière
43 rue de la Bretonnière
21200 Beaune
Tel 80 22 15 77, Fax 80 22 72 54
FF175–350

R Le Bistrot Bourguignon
Rue Monge
Dishes up to FF40, Meals FF60

R La Ciboulette
69 rue Lorraine
Tel 80 24 70 72
FF87–119

R Le Jardin des Remparts
10 rue Hôtel-Dieu
Tel 80 24 79 41
FF125–290

Meursault
R Relais de la Diligence à la Gare
(opposite the station)
Tel 80 21 21 32
FF63–148

Chassey-le-Camp
HR Auberge du Camp Romain
71150 Chassey-le-Camp
Tel 85 87 09 91, Fax 85 87 11 51
Rooms FF145–342, Meals
FF113–164

Chagny
HR Hostellerie du Château
   de Bellecroix
71150 Chagny
Tel 85 87 13 86, Fax 85 91 28 62
Rooms FF550–920, Meals
FF220–330
(member of Relais du Silence)

Rully
HR Hôtel Commerce &
   Restaurant Le Vendangerot
Place Ste-Marie,
71150 Rully
Tel 85 87 20 09
Rooms FF140–250, Meals FF70–160

Mercurey
HR Hôtellerie du Val d'Or
Grande Rue, 71640 Mercurey
Tel 85 45 13 70, Fax 85 45 18 45
Rooms FF310–390, Meals
FF160–370

Givry
HR Hôtel de la Halle
Place de la Halle, 71640 Givry
Tel 85 44 32 45
Rooms FF200–230, Meals FF55–205

The Mâconnais

Religion brought wine to Mâcon; the first vines were planted by the monks at Cluny Abbey, which once rivalled Rome in power and grandeur. The monks have gone, and so have most of their buildings, ransacked in the Revolution, but the vines live on and the winemakers prosper.

Mâcon wines were put on the map by a man called Claude Brosse. This local hero was, according to legend, so fed up with lack of sales that he loaded up his ox-drawn wagon with barrels of Mâcon wine and, braving brigands and bad roads, travelled to Versailles to present his wines at court. At six foot six tall he stood head and shoulders above the courtiers; the king, Louis XIV, noticed him and asked him to present his wines. They found favour, and from that day on the success of Mâcon wines was assured. Claude Brosse is, as a result, often depicted on cellar-wall paintings: there's a large mural devoted to him at the Hameau du Vin in Romanèche-Thorins.

Today, Mâcon is Burgundy's bargain basement. It makes three times as much white wine as its more illustrious northern neighbour, and often you might think it's about a third as good. At its worst it's dilute, insipid stuff, trading on the Burgundy name without offering much in return. Happily, at its best it can be lively, fresh and fruity, offering reasonably good to excellent value.

The Mâconnais region also offers attractive touring countryside; the gentle rolling hills of the north gradually giving way to more dramatic, steep crags as you move south. The architecture takes on a more Mediterranean feel, and the climate becomes milder, and, as a side issue, there's plenty for the lover of prehistory or Romanesque churches to discover.

HOW THE WINES ARE CLASSIFIED

Mâcon makes two reds, and the labelling is sufficiently confusing to make me wonder whether they're doing it on purpose. There are two different grape varieties grown, just like the rest of Burgundy: posh, temperamental, can-be-wonderful Pinot Noir and easy-to-grow, uncomplicated Gamay. Wine made from either grape can be labelled Mâcon Rouge (or Mâcon Supérieur which indicates slightly higher alcohol levels). It gets complicated because wines made in Mâcon from Pinot Noir can also be labelled Bourgogne Rouge. And with the magic word Bourgogne on the bottle the wine can command a significantly higher price. So, not unsurprisingly, the bottles labelled Mâcon will in practice contain Gamay. These can be fresh and fruity, but in most cases they're not as attractive as those made in nearby Beaujolais. Watch out for stunning exceptions, though, and some very creative work.

Whites at their most basic are also labelled Mâcon – Blanc and Blanc Supérieur. These will be made from the Chardonnay grape, and come from the least-favoured vineyard sites. Mâcon (Blanc)-Villages is better quality and can be good value. Some villages tack their names on the end: frequently-seen examples are Viré, Lugny, Prissé, Clessé. At their best these are lively, fresh, mostly unoaked wines for everyday drinking, at maybe FF30 a bottle.

Now we're firmly in hyphenate territory. Pouilly-something is a name most people have probably noticed, -Fuissé being the most common add-on. Pouilly and Fuissé are two villages whose combined names are found on wine lists all over the world, especially in America, and there's a high price to be paid (by us) for this popularity. Some estates make really excellent wines in this appellation, but many producers, I suspect, simply thank their lucky stars they own a vineyard with such a prestigious name and milk the vines for all they're worth. None of whom is listed here.

You'll find other Pouilly-hyphenates: Loché and Vinzelles. These nearby villages are only too pleased to tag themselves onto their illustrious neighbour, but the wines are made in small quantities. One difference with Pouilly-something wines is that many producers do use oak, maturing their wines for longer than is standard practice elsewhere.

Best Buy, in many cases, is a wine whose reputation lies somewhere in between the Mâcon-somethings and the Pouilly-somethings: St-Véran. It's apparently named after the village of St-Vérand, though who knows what they did with the d. This is a newish appellation, relatively unknown. It seems to me that producers of this AC often offer better-priced and better-made wines than many of their neighbours.

Finally, producers of all shapes and sizes make the tradi-tional-method Crémant de Bourgogne, and a sizeable number also produce rosé. The sparklers are generally well made but most of the examples I tasted were pretty neutral – fine for party fizz or for mixing with *crème de cassis* for a Kir Royal. The rosés are lower in acidity than the average Loire pinks, worth laying in if summer turns out hot again.

The co-operatives are major players in Mâcon, particularly in the north of the region where received wisdom states that good producers are few and far between because soil and site aren't as good as further south. Visits to a couple of the north-ern producers mentioned below will demonstrate yet again how dangerous generalisations can be.

One final point: watch out for a tendency in these parts to promote the wines on the glass itself. You'll often find in tast-ing cellars the name of the appellation inscribed on the tasting glasses, in green ink. I fell over this several times, peering intently at the wine in poor light and thinking, sagely, that the wine was rather green, only to realize that I'd been deceived by the ink.

EXPLORING THE MÂCONNAIS

Arriving either fresh/jaded from the Côte Chalonnaise, or direct from the motorway, Tournus makes a good jumping-off point for exploring this region. If you're coming from Givry, stay on the D981 as far as **Cormatin**, where you'll pick up the first of the wine route signs, which will become very familiar: a woman's head, with a vineleaf hat and golden grapes for hair, enjoining you to 'Suivez la Grappe!' So do so: turn left onto the D14 and head into **Tournus**. The 10th-century former abbey is a two-star attraction here, and a gentle meander through the old town is architecturally very rewarding.

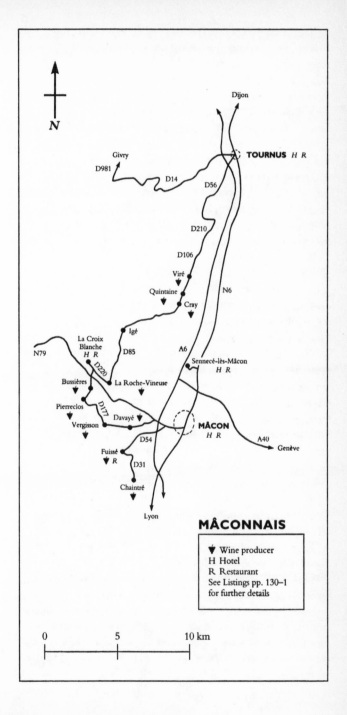

N

Dijon

Givry

TOURNUS *H R*

D981

D14

D56

D210

D106

Viré

Quintaine

N6

Cray

Igé

La Croix
Blanche
H R

D85

N79

A6

D220

Sennecé-lès-Mâcon
H R

Bussières

La Roche-Vineuse

D177

Pierreclos

Davayé

Vergisson

MÂCON
H R

A40

Genève

D54

Fuissé
R

D31

Chaintré

Lyon

MÂCONNAIS

♥ Wine producer
H Hotel
R Restaurant
See Listings pp. 130–1
for further details

0   5   10 km

Stay at the Hôtel Les Terrasses, on the N6 on the south side of the town. Unprepossessing on the outside, the newly-refurbished rooms for under FF270 will restore your faith in value for money. And the dining-room offers excellent bourgeois cooking, a fact which hasn't gone unnoticed locally. After a fortnight in winter getting used to being the only guest in the hotel, it was extraordinary to be in a heaving restaurant – not a spare table in sight. If the local townsfolk are packing a place out you know you're onto a good thing.

Leave Tournus on the D56, through Chardonnay. (This is the village which probably gave the grape its name, and leads to the confusion of seeing Mâcon-Chardonnay on a label. Not an enlightened move towards varietal labelling, but good old geography. They simply expect you to know what the grape varieties are.)

Next, pass through Uchizy and take the D210 and D106 to **Viré**. **DOMAINE ANDRÉ BONHOMME** is on your left. M Bonhomme makes mostly Mâcon-Viré on his 9-ha estate, and it is really fine stuff. He differentiates between his old and new vines, producing cuvées from each. No prizes for guessing that the *vieilles vignes* produce a much richer, more concentrated wine. He has invested in his own bottling line, despite the relatively small production, so that he can have complete control over when and how the wine is bottled, rather than having to rely on trying to get hold of the mobile bottler when you need him. (Rather like trying to find a plumber, I suppose.)

André Bonhomme's wines are in demand at top French restaurants. He reckoned the big boys told him to put up his prices – 'then we could sell more'. So he makes a very special cuvée for these restaurateurs, with more oak, which then presumably sells for a fabulous price (he became curiously reticent when I asked just how much).

Visitors taste in a very atmospheric ground-level cellar, with glasses cunningly concealed in a barrel. Ask to see the wine-making cellars, and you'll be led into a mould-encrusted vaulted barrel cellar. Not, as I thought, ancient: he enjoyed pointing to the date of 1985 above the door. He'll also sell you honey, and Marc and Fine de Bourgogne, two spirits well worth getting to know. The wines are priced at FF34–47, the spirits around FF140. 'We want our clients to depart happy', M Bonhomme says. You will, you will.

Head south: you'll come to **Quintaine**, where you'll find **DOMAINE JEAN THÉVENET** in the centre of the village (parking space opposite the domaine). But I'd advise you to ignore him for the moment and keep going to the next visit in Cray, doubling back afterwards. It's only a mile or so to **DOMAINE MICHEL,** and believe me, Thévenet's wines will swamp Michel's delicate flavours.

René Michel farms his 12ha with his three sons – the sixth generation. The average age of their vines is 60 years, which means they're offering good concentration, although one vineyard dates back to around 1885, replanted with resistant rootstock after phylloxera had devastated the vineyards. The Michels make two styles of wine, oaked and unoaked, a useful choice. Their aim is to release wine for sale only when mature enough to be drunk, so, unusually, they have several vintages on sale, which is good for us consumers and bad for their accountants. With whites from around FF31–36, a Gamay red at FF29 and a Crémant at FF38, these wines are extremely good value. The floor of their neat barrel cellar is strewn with immaculately-raked pea gravel. Not a single stone was out of place in the elaborate pattern. We all stood respectfully at the door gazing in; I for one couldn't bear to walk in and disturb it.

So now head back to Quintaine and prepare to taste the most extraordinary Mâcon wines you're ever likely to encounter. Jean Thévenet sells his wines under two names: Domaine Emilian Gillet and Domaine de la Bon Gran. And they're a snip at between FF65 and FF85, because they are gorgeous. How does he do it? No chemical treatments; manual harvesting; very little chaptalizing; no commercial yeasts, only what is on the grape naturally; and, crucially, yields of almost half the permitted maximum. Thévenet also prefers to harvest when the grapes are slightly overripe, which means the wines appear to have lower acidity than most (I say 'appear'; he puts this down to getting the balance between alkaline and acidity right; all to do with the wine's pH.) He leaves the wine in vat to mature for two years after the harvest, which is a good year longer than most.

Jean Thévenet's family has worked these vines for generations, and, with this inherited tradition, he's clearly a perfectionist. And also, reflecting on the as-the-winemaker-so-the-wine question, I remember that he's a gentle, courteous, softly-spoken man with an obvious depth and passion about the wines. Just so: the wines are gentle on you in their low acidity, but have great depth and richness. Difficult to explain, but once you meet him I think you'll see what I mean.

You're received in the front of his new bottling cellar: ask to go inside. The architect won a prize for it and M Thévenet, as the client, shared in the prize money; nice to be rewarded for sponsoring creativity. It's full of unobtrusive creative touches, an excellent example of how a functional building can be transformed by that extra thought. (The Zind-Humbrecht cellars in Alsace are a more dramatic example, and the quality of the winemaking comparable.) At the back of the cellars, the architect has designed a cowl surround for a spring rising there, illuminated from below. Very striking – like the stage in the Hollywood Bowl.

Even if you only buy a bottle or two, don't pass up the chance to visit. I looked on it as an unmissable part of my education – what Mâcon wines can be with a genius at the helm. If you're lucky, you may find a special cuvée available, or even a botrytized wine, but the wines are in such demand that stock levels are low. Thévenet's wines are completely unlike any other Mâconnais wine, and advanced students will enjoy questioning him about the truly typical wines of the region, a subject on which he has strong opinions. They're not cheap compared to the norm, but frankly they're a snip.

For a complete contrast, visit the **CAVE DES VIGNERONS D'IGÉ** (signposted from Clessé). There's a cheery atmosphere here, honest winemaking and – what I liked best – a tasting area right inside the cellars. Instead of being in one of those sterile little shops, you're surrounded by vats and pipes and can see cellar workers actually making the stuff. Much more fun. Note that on Saturday afternoons and Sundays tastings and sales switch to a converted chapel in the village, where you have to pay after the first glass. I'd stick to weekdays, with the bonus of cellar tours by appointment. Prices start at FF24.

From Igé the D85 takes you straight into **La Roche-Vineuse**: **DOMAINE DU VIEUX ST-SORLIN** is signposted in the village, perched high up on a steeply-climbing road past the church. Here Olivier Merlin brings his respect for traditional methods and expertise acquired in the Napa Valley to bear on an excellent selection of reds – from both Gamay and Pinot –

and whites. This is a great visit to make if you want to learn about hand-made wines; M Merlin ploughs between the vines to force the roots down, away from the surface, to seek better nourishment. He uses no chemicals in the vineyards, and has an experimental patch under organic cultivation. He picks by hand, in common with only 20% of Mâcon growers, and ferments 80% of production in barrel – most unusual hereabouts as it costs a fortune. He also employs the old burgundian technique of *battonage*, stirring up the lees inside the barrel to extract more flavour. As a result he reckons to devote an entire day each week to working with the barrels, an expensive way of spending his time.

Normally the reds aren't filtered, and the best of the whites aren't either. Most producers profess themselves scared to leave their wines unfiltered, fearing bacterial problems will emerge later. M Merlin has no such qualms. 'There's no sugar left in the wine, the malo is complete. There's nothing else that can happen to the wine, so why filter?' I agree. This is a fascinating visit.

M Merlin is charming and speaks good English after his years in California. So what's the catch? It seems that he isn't too keen to sell you the finished product. His idea is that you visit his domaine and taste the wine in situ, then go back and buy it in the UK to stop him getting into trouble with his importers. Fair enough. We wouldn't want to upset anybody. But on the other hand these wines are too good to miss. Don't say I said so, but I don't think it would take too much arm-twisting to get hold of a few bottles. And well worth the effort.

Time for a rest. **La Croix Blanche** is a couple of miles away, on the old route nationale, and the Relais du Mâconnais is a charming place to stay. It has comfortable rooms with views over rolling hills, and offers some of the best food in the neighbourhood; the stunning dessert trolley made a particular impact on me (don't think you'll get away with just one selection). There are other restaurants in the village, but the hotel discourages experimentation with a notice on the bedroom door informing you that a table has been 'obligatoirement' reserved for you for dinner. I'm not at all sure this is legal but would hesitate to argue the toss. Anyway, the food's really good; I just don't care for the element of compulsion.

The next visit is in **Bussières**: retrace your steps towards La Roche-Vineuse and it's signposted to your right, crossing under the N79. **DOMAINE DE LA SARAZINÈRE** is in the village, a tiny property where young owner Philippe Trébignaud is doing some endearingly eccentric things with his old Gamay vines. He vinifies his wine like Pinot Noir and ages it in oak. This gives it an extraordinarily powerful gamey animal nose, and it tastes nothing like a Gamay. Great fun, and a perfect bottle to take home to confuse your wine-buff friends with. They'll never guess. He also makes a more normal style Gamay, and two Mâcon-Villages, one oaked the other unoaked, both full of fruit and flavour. These wines are very tasty, and very good value at FF25–36. I really warmed to M Trébignaud's enthusiasm for what he's doing. Half an hour tasting and talking in his barrel cellar is time very well spent.

In the next village, **Pierreclos**, you'll find **JEAN-CLAUDE THÉVENET**. His cellars are signposted in the village, just up from the post office. (You pass his house, which confusingly seems to suggest you should call there. Instead, look for a lane further up.)

Confession time: five years ago I bought some Thévenet wine from Adnams in Southwold, and wrote to him – having found the address in a French guide – saying how much I'd enjoyed his wines and could I visit. An appointment was arranged and I duly presented myself, saying how much I'd enjoyed his wine from Adnams, etc, etc – but was met with puzzlement. He didn't export to the UK. Then it occurred to me that he didn't actually look much like his photo in the Adnams catalogue. Realization dawned, but I didn't like to mention that I was confusing two Thévenets and really should have made an appointment up the road. By then we were halfway through the tasting, and I found I'd stumbled on some really good-quality stuff. My Best Buy is his St-Véran from old vines, FF34.

Prices now start to rise as we move south, straying into Pouilly-something territory. You begin to have to pay for the name, and may even sometimes get what you pay for. Touring down here in the southern end of the Mâconnais you'll notice the skyline dominated by sharp crags; at the base of the most prominent of these, Solutré, is a macabre mass grave stretching out over a wide area. It contains a thick layer of animal bones – horse, deer and bison. Maybe prehistoric man killed the animals by driving them over the sheer cliff. Another theory is that gangs of hunters annually waylaid the animals here as they migrated south. For more information there's a museum at Solutré devoted to the subject. It's well-signposted.

From Pierreclos take the D117 to **Vergisson**. **DOMAINE DANIEL BARRAUD** is on the road leading out of the village towards Davayé: look for a big orientation board on your left. Here the St-Véran costs FF37, the top-cuvée Pouilly-Fuissé FF75. These wines are very well made, with good concentration of fruit – worth keeping.

Prices are more restrained at **DOMAINE CORSIN**, on the right of the main road through Davayé. The Pouilly-Fuissé is FF64, St-Véran FF34-37, and a very honestly-made Mâcon-Villages for FF30. I can wholeheartedly recommend the wine-making here, as well as the welcome in the low-ceilinged tasting-room. M Corsin is particularly proud of his Pouilly-Fuissé and will be happy to demonstrate the differences in taste that derive from the different weather in each year. (Watch out for the vipers in the *eau-de-vie*. Yes, literally. Apparently it's a local custom.) The fermentation cellars are in Fuissé, and you can view them by appointment. M Corsin reckons he doesn't speak English, but he's widely-travelled, and I doubt you can get through working the harvest in New Zealand speaking French, so have a go with English if necessary.

Outside Davayé on the road to Charnay you'll find the **DOMAINE DES DEUX ROCHES**, a medium-sized estate of 32ha, well-represented on UK shelves. A tour of the cellars reveals considerable recent investment (or bank loan) and the resulting wines are very good quality. Prices range from FF27 for a ripe Mâcon rouge to FF52 for their top St-Véran, which will need several years' patience before being ready to drink.

From here it's a short hop into **Mâcon**, a town I enjoy visiting, particularly on Saturdays for its busy quayside market. I've stayed at the Hôtel Bellevue, which has comfortable if hideous sixties decor and soundproofed views across the river. Plenty of places to eat: cross the river for the lively bistro-style St Laurent. As you cross the bridge, look back for a splendid view of the quayside. Or stroll in the old town just behind the hotel for the quieter restaurant Pierre or – one of Jean Thévenet's favourites – L'Amandier.

Then there's the **MAISON MÂCONNAISE DES VINS**, on the N6 just north of the town centre. You can eat simple meals here with a glass of Mâcon wine, or taste and buy from a well-chosen selection in the new shop: friendly, English-speaking staff. Plenty of maps and guides on sale, and tasteful postcards. If it's quiet, nip into the children's play area and have a go on the 'smell test' computer game.

Further north, at **Sennecé-lès-Mâcon**, there's the Hotel-Restaurant de la Tour. I haven't stayed there but so many producers recommended it I thought it worth mentioning. (Though of course that may be because the hotel had the perspicacity to sell their wines in the restaurant.)

The other thing to mention about Mâcon is its pride in its native son, the Romantic poet Lamartine. There's a museum devoted to him and any number of streets, restaurants and artefacts named after him. Just so that you know. I'd also like to draw your attention to the Centre Commercial to the south of town on the N6 at Crèches-sur-Saône. There's a revamped Carrefour hypermarket here with cheap petrol and self-service café, a gloriously-tacky Halle des Chaussures and other monuments to consumerism, plus a large Campanile hotel (dinner terrible, breakfast good.) Crèches doesn't appear on the wine route, but when visiting the Mâconnais or Beaujolais the N6 becomes inescapable and you're almost bound to pass it at some point, if only when rejoining the motorway.

Leave Mâcon on the N79 and turn off on the D54 to **Fuissé**. Here you'll find the main man in Pouilly-Fuissé, Jean-Jacques Vincent of **CHÂTEAU FUISSÉ**, on the D209 at the edge of the village. This elegant domaine has trademark double topiary wine bottles in front of the château tower (originally planted to stop people falling off the dangerous tower steps). It's a tranquil spot, surrounded by its own vines. The 19th-century barrel cellars are built at ground level as the water table is too high for the traditional subterranean approach, and there's water everywhere, even a series of trout pools in the courtyard.

If your shopping-list includes Pouilly-Fuissé this is the place to come. M Vincent aspires to place his wines on the same level of depth and richness as the top Côte d'Or whites, Puligny or Meursault, and I reckon they stand comparison. You'll pay FF120 for the top of the range – which is sold under the brand name of Château Fuissé – but for FF44 you can walk away with a bottle of absolutely exemplary St-Véran. It's not really one for casual visitors, but be prepared to give these wines the respect they deserve and you'll enjoy a very informative visit here with a courteous host.

In Fuissé you'll also find one of my favourite local restaurants, Au Pouilly-Fuissé. I first ate here many years ago when it was packed with locals enjoying simple, good food on red checked tablecloths. Then the son-in-law took over and the red tablecloths disappeared as the place moved upmarket. The food may be more refined now, but the value is still good and the place still crowded. Happily they've also retained one traditional touch – *crêpes parmentier*. These little potato pancakes are often served in this part of the world, either with the main course or as a separate dish afterwards (you can sprinkle them with sugar). I think they're brilliant.

The last Mâconnais visit links us seamlessly with Beaujolais, which by now is not even on the doorstep but has begun to overlap into the Mâconnais. (No such thing as a clear dividing-line down here.) **ROGER DUBOEUF** has a surname which might be familiar; he's the elder brother of Georges, and there's a strong family resemblance. Georges, known these days as the king of Beaujolais, left his brother running the family estate in **Chaintré** to make his own career, of which more – much more – in the Beaujolais chapter. But a visit to his big brother is very worthwhile. In common with many small growers, Roger sells part of his production to local négociants – in his case, naturally, to his younger brother. But he bottles part of his production himself, and makes a very ripe, distinctively-flavoured Pouilly-Fuissé for FF50.

His tasting cellars are terrific, full of dusty wine bric-a-brac and a wood fire in winter. Sit on long rickety benches to taste at an ancient oak table. His overriding interest, though, is local history. He's involved with the museum at Solutré and with the design of his brother's magnum opus, the Hameau du Vin. In a large workroom behind the winery he has a huge collection of stone age arrowheads, and fragments of artefacts dating back many thousands of years. If you're interested in the subject, and speak French, M Duboeuf will be delighted to share some of his prodigious knowledge with you.

Listings

When telephoning France from the UK, first dial 00 33 then the number shown. Producers are listed in wine route order, and hotels/restaurants by town or village according to the route. Accommodation prices are per room, meal prices are per head.

Producers
Domaine André Bonhomme
71260 Viré
Tel 85 33 11 86
Fax 85 33 93 51
Open Mon–Sat 8–19, Sun by
appointment
No English

Jean Thévenet
Quintaine, 71260 Clessé
Tel 85 36 94 03, Fax 85 36 99 25
Visits by appointment Mon–Sat
Credit cards accepted
No English

Domaine René Michel
Cray, 71260 Clessé
Tel 85 36 94 27, Fax 85 36 99 63
Visits by appointment
Good English

Cave des Vignerons d'Igé
71960 Igé
Tel 85 33 33 56, Fax 85 33 41 85
Open Mon–Fri 7.30–12, 13.30–18,
Sat 7.30–12

Domaine du Vieux St-Sorlin
La Roche-Vineuse, 71960 Mâcon
Tel 85 36 62 09, Fax 85 36 66 45
Visits strictly by appointment
Good English

Domaine de la Sarazinière
71960 Bussières
Tel 85 37 80 06, Fax 85 3762 71
Open Mon–Sun 8–18, appointment
preferred
No English

Jean-Claude Thévenet
71960 Pierreclos
Tel 85 35 72 21, Fax 85 35 72 03
Open Mon–Sat 7.30–12, Sun
13.30–18.30
By appointment
Credit cards accepted
No English

Domaine Daniel Barraud
71960 Vergisson
Tel 85 35 84 24, Fax 85 35 86 98
Open Mon–Sun 9–11.30, 13.30–18
Appointment preferred
No English

Domaine Corsin
Les Plantés, 71960 Davayé
Tel 85 35 83 68, Fax 85 35 86 64
Open Mon–Sat 7.30–19, Sun a.m.
by appointment
Some English

Domaine des Deux Roches
71960 Davayé
Tel 85 35 86 51, Fax 85 35 86 12
Open Mon–Sat 9–12, 14–18
Appointment preferred
Some English

Château de Fuissé
71960 Fuissé
Tel 85 35 61 44, Fax 85 35 86 98
Mon–Fri 8–12, 13.30–18
By appointment
Credit cards accepted
Minimum purchase 12 bottles
Good English

Roger Duboeuf
71570 Chaintré
Open Mon–Sun 9–18
(9–20 in summer)
No English

Hotels and Restaurants
H Hotel *R* Restaurant

Tournus
HR Aux Terrasses
18, avenue du 23 Janvier
71700 Tournus
Tel 85 51 01 74, Fax 85 51 09 99
Rooms FF245–270, Meals FF90–230

La Croix Blanche
HR Le Relais du Mâconnais
Ancienne N79
71960 La Croix Blanche
Tel 85 36 60 72, Fax 85 36 65 47
Rooms FF270–360, Meals
FF130–270

Mâcon
H Bellevue
416 quai Lamartine, 71000 Mâcon
Tel 85 38 05 07, Fax 85 38 54 60
Rooms FF320–590

R Le St-Laurent
1, quai Bouchacourt
71000 Mâcon
Tel 85 39 29 19, Fax 85 38 29 77
FF98–200

R Pierre
7, rue Dufour
71000 Mâcon
Tel 85 38 14 23, Fax 85 39 84 04
FF98–295

R L'Amandier
74, rue Dufour
71000 Mâcon
Tel 85 39 82 00
FF98–260

R Le Matefin
4, rue de la Liberté
71000 Mâcon
Tel 85 29 02 50
FF49–98

Maison Mâconnaise des Vins
484, ave Mal-de-Lattre-de-Tassigny
71000 Mâcon
Tel 85 38 36 70, Fax 85 38 62 51
Meals from FF50

Sennecé-lès-Mâcon
HR De la Tour
71000 Sennecé-lès-Mâcon
Tel 85 36 02 70, Fax 85 36 03 47
Rooms FF235–300, Meals FF95–210

Fuissé
R Au Pouilly-Fuissé
71960 Fuissé
Tel 85 35 60 68
FF75–205

Beaujolais

Beaujolais is a delight. The spectacular scenery rivals the best Alsace has to offer, and the winemakers give the most genuinely friendly welcome you'll find anywhere. The wines are fresh, fruity, unpretentious and good value, and local cuisine has an exuberance to match it. This is wine tourism at its best, as far removed from the condescension of Bordeaux as you can possibly imagine.

For reasons that have puzzled many, Beaujolais is lumped in with Burgundy by people who like to keep things neat and tidy, such as government departments. This doesn't make a lot of sense, because the Beaujolais grape is the Gamay, which is very much the poor relation in Burgundy, and Beaujolais wine is made by means of a unique fermentation process quite unlike the way in which Burgundy wine is made.

If you go to wine appreciation classes, or open a learned wine book, you'll almost certainly be told that this process is called carbonic maceration. Which is what I learned in my youth. And which is, I subsequently discovered, totally wrong. Ask anyone who actually makes the stuff, and they're likely to throw up their hands in horror at this misapprehension. And when I asked the chap in charge of promoting the wines of Beaujolais, he shook his head ruefully and conceded that they were having problems in getting their message across. Carbonic maceration, he says, was an experiment which failed (it involved very long fermentation with the injection of carbon dioxide, apparently).

It's like this. The grapes are harvested by hand and the whole bunches dumped unceremoniously, uncrushed, in closed vats. The weight of grapes crushes the berries at the bottom of the vat, which begin to ferment. The fermentation warms up the vat, and releases carbon dioxide. This rises and envelops the other berries. As oxygen can no longer reach these berries they can't breathe, so the juice in each individual berry starts to ferment – inside the skin – macerating (that is, extracting colour and flavour from the skin) as it does so. This method of fermentation is called 'semi-maceration' because only about half the berries are affected by this process. The other, lower, half of the vat is fermenting away in the usual fashion.

This goes on for five to ten days, after which the 'free-run' juice (ie the juice that is squeezed out of the berries under the weight of the overlying bunches) is drawn off. Then the grapes are mechanically pressed and the resulting juice added to the free-run. The pressing usually releases a little more sugar from the skins, so fermentation will then continue for a while longer. A second fermentation, known as malolactic fermentation, follows, then the wine is bottled immediately (to be sold as Beaujolais Nouveau) or left to mature for weeks or months, depending on the vintage and the winemaker's philosophy.

This is *la vinification beaujolaise* and it makes use of a number of factors. Firstly, because the Gamay grape has black skin but white juice (its full name is 'Gamay Noir à jus blanc'), you need to find an effective way of keeping the fermenting juice in contact with the skin to extract maximum colour. Fermenting inside the skin is a good way of doing that.

Secondly, you have to harvest by hand, because you need whole bunches. Mechanical harvesters 'vibrate' individual berries off the stalks, which means the berry is punctured and the juice will get out. No good. And just to make sure nobody transgresses, mechanical harvesters are banned throughout the region.

One way of telling which part of the region you're in is by looking at how the grapes are trained. Only grapes for basic Beaujolais can be planted in rows trained along wires known as *guyot*. Higher quality levels (ie Beaujolais-Villages and the crus) have to be kept as individual bushes, known as *gobelet,* because the canes are trained into a goblet shape. This system makes the vine less productive and is supposed to keep yields down. And just to make sure, mechanical harvesters are banned throughout the region making better quality Beaujolais.

I should also mention that a small amount of rosé is produced (from the Gamay), as well as Beaujolais Blanc (from the Chardonnay).

HOW BEAUJOLAIS IS CLASSIFIED

Bottom rung is Beaujolais Nouveau. This is one of those mad exercises where the infant wine is rushed through production in order to be on your table about six weeks after harvesting. I have to admit that I don't actually much like the stuff. No matter what I've been told about the improvements in quality there's still too much sugar-water swilling around, like the bottle I bought at Ouistreham whiling away the wait for the ferry last November. Dreadful stuff, sickly sweet and over-priced.

One of the problems with Nouveau which is often overlooked is that newly-bottled wines suffer from 'bottle sickness'. Wine is a living product – even Beaujolais Nouveau – and it suffers from all the trauma of being pumped about and treated with chemicals and forced into bottles and having a cork shoved down the neck. So newly-bottled wine goes into a bit of a decline, needing weeks or even months to recover. There's such an enormous demand for Beaujolais Nouveau that it never has a chance to recuperate; bottling begins in early November – the bottling lines are working day and night – so the wine arrives on the shelves around the world at precisely the moment when it's not ready to drink. An intractable problem, so I'd suggest waiting a while for the next tranche of wines to appear, Beaujolais or – better – Beaujolais-Villages.

Basic Beaujolais is light, fresh, and should be gulpable and cheap. It has no pretensions and appears around a month after the Nouveau excitement has died down. Supermarket Beaujolais isn't usually terribly interesting, but I've nosed out a couple of producers who'll sell you a 'basic' Beaujolais which is anything but dull. Occasionally you'll see Beaujolais Supérieur, which, as usual, is just a question of an extra degree of alcohol.

Beaujolais-Villages, on the other hand, is a definite leap up the quality ladder. This comes from the granite soils found in the north of the region, and I find it makes a much more interesting wine for not much more money. For everyday drinking, at perhaps FF25 the bottle, it is well worth laying in supplies of -Villages.

Top of the ladder are the ten 'crus', inadequately translated as 'growths'. These are wines from ten named villages (from north to south): St-Amour, Juliénas, Chénas, Moulin à Vent, Fleurie, Chiroubles, Morgon, Régnié, Côte de Brouilly and

Brouilly. These are held to be the best the region can produce, with subtle distinctions of flavour and structure among them. Fun to discover, and at prices in the FF30-something range, an affordable exploration.

One of the debates you might like to follow, and enter into, is how long these wines will keep. Conventional wisdom among wine writers is that even the top crus aren't worth keeping for more than a couple of years, but many producers will disagree. In an inversion of the usual opinion, whereby the French think wines are ready to drink long before the Brits do, there are producers who will tell you to hold on to the Beaujolais crus for five years or more, and claim for them the development of Pinot Noir-style aromas and tastes after that length of time.

You may well think that if you want a wine to smell like Pinot Noir you may as well buy Pinot Noir; or you may be tickled with the idea of getting Pinot tastes for half the Pinot price. It all adds to the fun, especially when you've established such good rapport with a producer that he or she starts opening aged bottles to prove it to you.

Beaujolais is a region of small producers. The wines didn't begin to reach a wider public until after the Second World War, and so the easiest thing was to sell to a négociant or to the local cooperative, and this remains commonly the pattern today. Many of the producers listed here still sell only a portion of their wine direct, in bottle; they're happy to sell maybe half to a négociant, which gives them guaranteed cash up-front, even though it's less profitable than bottling themselves. And it can be a matter of pride for producers to be able to say they sell to some of the top négociants.

EXPLORING BEAUJOLAIS

The first thing to note is that there's no signposted wine route; the Beaujolais interprofessional wine committee, which represents all aspects of the region's wine trade, decided that it was simply too complicated and gave up. For once I don't think that's a cop-out. Beaujolais is a small region, just over 50km long and 10 to 15km wide. It's hard to stay lost for long, and as each bend in the road seems to open up yet another breath-taking view it really doesn't matter if you stray a little. Touring

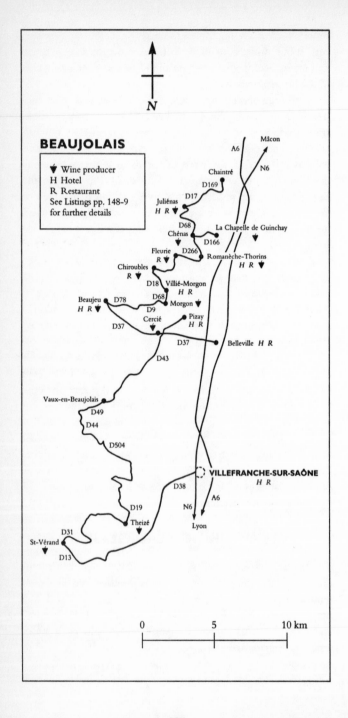

BEAUJOLAIS

▼ Wine producer
H Hotel
R Restaurant
See Listings pp. 148–9
for further details

N

Mâcon
A6
N6
Chaintré
D169
D17
Juliénas
H R ▼
D68
Chénas
La Chapelle de Guinchay ▼
D166
Fleurie
R ▼
D266
Romanèche-Thorins
H R ▼
Chiroubles
R ▼
D18 Villié-Morgon
H R
Beaujeu
H R ▼
D78
D68
Morgon ▼
D9
Cercié
Pizay
H R
D37
D37
Belleville H R
D43
Vaux-en-Beaujolais
D49
D44
D504
VILLEFRANCHE-SUR-SAÔNE
H R
D38
A6
D19
N6
Theizé
Lyon
D31
St-Vérand
D13

0   5   10 km

in Beaujolais gives a whole new meaning to the phrase 'scenic route.' The committee decided instead to develop a series of wine-related sights and exhibitions. Some of these are already open, some still being created. I'll mention what is available en route.

A useful navigational aid is a special IGN touring map. This is large scale and has the different crus helpfully picked out in contrasting colours. True devotees can even search out a plastic relief version of this map and see exactly where the hills are.

Picking up where the Mâcon tour left off, in **Chaintré**, puts you right on track. Newcomers should leave the A6 at Macon-sud: either way, head for **St-Amour**, the most northerly cru village. (Not that we're visiting a producer here, it just means you can cross it off the list.) From St-Amour take the road for **Juliénas**; Michel Tête's **DOMAINE DU CLOS DU FIEF** is signposted from the main road, in the *lieu-dit* of Les Gonnards.

This is a great visit to kick off with. For a start, there's a very attractive tasting room set in a barrel maturation cellar surrounded with stacks of mouldering bottles; and M Tête will pour your tasting samples from behind a genuine *zinc*, the old-fashioned bar counter. He sells Beaujolais-Villages, St-Amour and Juliénas, cru number two, for FF26–36. He makes an additional, prestige cuvée of Juliénas, from 60- to 80-year-old vines and partly matured in wood. Fight for it, it's usually all gone by December, and indeed customer pressure is such that he has very little stock. I'm not surprised; this is everything Beaujolais should be, and provides the perfect benchmark by which to judge the rest of your visits.

There's a lively restaurant in Juliénas, Le Coq au Vin. The owner is Claude Clévenot, who also runs a printers – and she's responsible for the design and production of Georges Duboeuf's much-copied distinctive floral labels. As you might imagine, the décor is dazzling: strong clear blues and yellows, with cockerels a leading design element. This is one of those places where the local business community retires for a good gossip over lunch; try the hearty *pot-au-feu*, but leave room for *pain perdu*, a wonderfully rich concoction of stale bread, soaked in cream and jam, and fried. Just across the road is Chez la Rose, a simple Logis with a popular restaurant. It's recommended and used by one of the stoutest defenders of Beaujolais in the UK, John Thorogood, deputy MD of the redoubtable Colchester wine merchants Lay & Wheeler. He also has a hot tip for a happening restaurant: the Auberge Les Vignerons at Emeringes. 'Well worth a detour. Booking essential.' Emeringes is signposted from Juliénas, just a couple of kilometres up the road.

Leave Juliénas, head towards Chénas, then turn left, signposted **La Chapelle-de-Guinchay**. Denise and **HUBERT LAPIERRE**'s estate is a little over two kilometres along on the left. He left the local co-op in 1989 and now sells a third of his small production to négociant Duboeuf, exporting a third of the remainder.

M Lapierre has parcels of vines in Chénas and Moulin-à-Vent, the next two crus. The name Chénas comes from *chênes*, the French for 'oaks', which were cut down on the local hillsides to make way for vines, and there's a suggestion of an oaky taste to the wine. For confirmation, try Lapierre's oak-aged Chénas; it adds a whole new dimension to what you think Beaujolais can taste like. He reckons his wines are not so agreeable in their first year because he encourages a longer fermentation than average; he believes, though, that the wines will make up for it when they come into their own a year two later, and will last three to five years (ten in certain vintages if you take care of it properly.)

He also produces Moulin à Vent. (It's a cru but not a village: all you can see is the eponymous windmill – it's over 300 years old and has been declared a historic monument.) Chénas and Moulin à Vent are similar in style: deep colour, rich and robust, with the potential to age well. If any Beaujolais wines can be said to resemble a Burgundy Pinot with age, it's Moulin à Vent.

Head back into **Chénas**. **GUY BRAILLON**'s estate is right in the centre of the village. (The wine committee has used Chénas as a guinea-pig for an experiment in comprehensive producer signposting, and as a result of this laudable initiative it's very difficult to get lost. More! More!) M Braillon also produces Chénas and Moulin à Vent (Chénas is the only commune in Beaujolais producing two crus) and welcomes you into a modern cellar with a secret stash of interesting bottles concealed on shelves built into the back of a large old vat. I was given a large silver trophy to use as a spittoon. His wines are rich, ripe and inviting, and if you don't believe they can age he's been known to rise to the challenge of proving you wrong. Go for it.

From Chénas take the **Romanèche-Thorins** road; you'll pass the ancient Moulin. In Romanèche there's only one place to go, and it's well-signposted: **GEORGE DUBOEUF**'s Hameau du Vin ('village of wine') is a simply amazing place, quite the most comprehensive, imaginative wine exhibition I've ever come across. I nearly called it a 'museum'; it is, of course, but it's much more than a collection of implements.

But to begin at the beginning. Georges Duboeuf comes from a family of small winegrowers, but left his elder brother to farm the estate and set himself up as a wine broker, introducing growers to merchants. Then he bought a mobile bottling-line so that growers could put 'estate bottled' on their labels for greater cachet and higher prices. Now he sells wines on behalf of the growers, with both their name and his on the label; he also sells a complete range of own-label Beaujolais. He's now thought to be responsible for almost 10% of all sales in the region, a phenomenal achievement, and to have been largely responsible for putting Beaujolais wines on the map.

You'd think that would be enough for one lifetime, but this man's nothing short of a workaholic. He bought the adjacent railway station and land, and created his wine village. This is an amazing feat of the imagination. You enter through a replica of the Gare du Nord railway station in Paris, complete with buffet serving coffee and light meals from an authentic *zinc*. That bit's free: for the rest it's FF70, not cheap, but there's a lot ahead. The museum exhibition areas are stunningly lit, and contain as comprehensive a collection of implements as you'll ever wish to see. In common with most wine museums, explanations are, sadly, only in French. You move on to one of the highlights, the deeply moving animated tale of Toine the vinegrower and Ampelopsis, a coquettish vine. (One curious thing is that some of the accompanying music is taken from Dvorak's *From the New World* symphony, which, given the threat to French wines from the New World, seems almost like tempting providence.)

Next is a sound and light show, which illuminates the different regions of Beaujolais and Mâconnais. There's a traditional 'bistrot beaujolaise' with wax figures enjoying a glass, and a fascinating film showing exactly what happens inside the vat during traditional Beaujolais vinification. Finally you end up in a room which reminded me of the sort of saloon Mae West might have sung in, dominated by one of those organs which play a paper roll. (Don't let them know you're English or they'll make it play the national anthem.) Here there are bistro tables, and you can sample a glass or two on production of your entrance ticket. Thus fortified, you leave via a large sales area which offers you around sixty different wines, singly or in all manner of pretty presentation packs – design has always been a strong suit here, and you won't find handsomer packaging anywhere. Plus posters, aprons, books... just about any kind of wine ephemera.

Yes, this is a major operation, one of the grandest of its kind (in the mad weeks before the Nouveau is released they bottle 54,000 bottles an hour, 16 hours a day) and no, you won't meet the winemaker here, although you've probably already met several Duboeuf winemakers through the producers listed in this chapter. After all, unlike in Champagne where growers supply grapes to the big houses, here the négociant buys the finished wine, maturing and bottling it himself. And during the harvest M Duboeuf is at the growers' elbows throughout, issuing very precise instructions each year.

I recommend a visit here because the exhibition is about the region as a whole, not Duboeuf in particular and because he produces consistently good wines. These days his empire has burst the bounds of Beaujolais and now encompasses the Rhône and even Languedoc, but his Beaujolais wines win prizes year in, year out. You could actually make this your only visit in Beaujolais, selecting from his range, and be confident that you were buying some of the best available. It wouldn't be as much fun, but for those with a large payload and little time this could be very useful. And for anyone interested in discovering the region as a whole I'd say the Hameau was unmissable.

Once you've walked your feet off (allow an absolute minimum of an hour and a half) sustenance is at hand, just over the road. I've stayed at Les Maritonnes more than once, and always enjoyed its friendly, comfortable welcome and good traditional food. It has a small park and a large pool. It's rather too close to the railway line for complete calm, and I also think the bedrooms are rather highly priced (I really do think that if they want you to pay nearly FF500 for a room they could give you a bed that doesn't sag). It's a very convenient place to stay, though, not only for visiting the crus but also as a stopover for points further south, as it's very close to the N6.

Take a left out of the Maritonnes and drive up to **Fleurie**. This village is so easy to pronounce that the wine has become famous (well, maybe also because it's good to drink). The local co-operative, the CAVE DES PRODUCTEURS DES GRANDS VINS DE FLEURIE, is just on the left on the road to Chiroubles. I once came here during the harvest and got caught up in a massive traffic jam as tractors queued in all directions, jockeying for position to deliver their trailers of grapes.

The co-op was run for many years by Marguerite Chabert, who exerted such influence on the place that after her death in 1988 she was commemorated by a special cuvée, Madame La Présidente. You can also see her wax effigy in the Hameau du Vin – she's one of the figures drinking in the bistrot beaujo-laise. They also produce a *cuvée* called Cardinale; the current director, Marguerite Chabert's nephew, reckons that 80% of Brits will prefer La Présidente whereas 80% of Swiss, his number-one export market, prefer the Cardinale which is supposed to be more 'masculine'. Put it to the test.

One rather curious thing is that the co-op sells 90% of its production in bulk, to négociants such as Duboeuf. M Chabert cheerfully admits that the négociants get first pick, so that the co-op is left to bottle and sell what the merchants don't want. Not the sort of information I'd volunteer to a passing writer, or to a wine-tourist arriving hot-foot from a visit to Duboeuf and his prize-winning Fleuries. Nevertheless, the two wines make an interesting comparison, and the co-op cellars are easy to visit (they charge FF5 a glass, but say that's to discourage casual drinkers and they reckon they won't charge you if you buy).

Just up from the co-op is Auberge Le Cep, a local temple of gastronomy highly rated by the locals (I have yet to try it). Then take a – I don't say 'the', advisedly – scenic route to **Chiroubles** by following the continuation of the road from Romanèche up into the hills. This is the D32, and it takes you past a little hillside chapel which gives its name to Fleurie's most important vineyard, La Madone. Turn left at the inter-section with the D26 and follow signs for Chiroubles. Or not. This is an exceptionally pretty part and you may feel like an aimless potter through the beautiful hills. The more purposeful will make their way to the incredible panorama offered at La Terrasse high up in the hills. Follow the signs – and be bowled over by the view.

Anyway, sooner or later we meet again in Chiroubles, which is itself no mean contender in the good view stakes. If you've followed the route I mentioned you'll pass **ARMAND DESMURES** on the right, sporting a red gate on the edge of the village. M Desmures is president of the local Chiroubles committee, and reflects the local trade structure in that he sells part of his harvest to Duboeuf in bulk and bottles and sells the rest himself. His wines are classic examples, with the characteristic heady aromatic nose and light body. Do ask him some questions, he's an enthusiastic propagandist for the area and 'accepts visitors with pleasure'. He vinifies half a dozen parcels separately, blending before bottling. If you visit while they're still in vat, ask if you can taste them: he'll explain the subtle distinctions, in French, and it can be a very rewarding exploration. He recommends two places to eat in Chiroubles: the traditional Terrasse de Beaujolais, and the simple Chez Marc et Annick.

Make your way by any generally downhill route (the D18, for instance) to **Villié-Morgon**. This is a lively village with plenty of scope for picnic shopping, which is just as well; there's a comfortable modern Logis here, Le Villon, but the food was pretty awful.

From Villié-Morgon take the D68 towards Cercié, and in the small village of **Morgon** stop at the first house on the right. **DOMINIQUE PIRON** vinifies his own grapes and has also expanded into buying in grapes from others. His is a traditional style of working, using oak barrels for a small proportion of the better wines. I think this is an admirable enterprise. M Piron is growing in importance as a force for improvement of the Morgon wines in particular and Beaujolais in general, and is definitely one to watch.

Taste a wide range of wines in his cellars; the glasses are printed with the slogan 'Morgon: the fruit of a Beaujolais, the charm of a Burgundy'. Faced with the evidence, how can you disagree? His Morgons are excellent, characteristically ripe with powerful red fruit tastes. He also offers a Régnié, the newest cru of Beaujolais – promoted from Beaujolais-Villages as recently as 1989. M Piron explained that, in the beginning, 'Régnié was only the best of the -Villages, so we used a short fermentation period to get maximum fruit. Now it's a cru so we want more tannin, so it's fermented for longer. That means we lost the fruit, so we now have a more minerally wine, smelling of the soil.'

You can also buy very good quality Brouilly here, and a fat, fruity Mâcon Chardonnay (Chardonnay the village, that is, though of course it's made from Chardonnay too. How nice they keep it so simple). A wide range, with prices in the low FF30s, makes the wines excellent value. M Piron speaks good English and has a dry sense of humour; this could be a most informative visit.

In the village of Morgon turn right, and pick up the D9 towards Régnié. (No need to stop, the cru has been covered chez Piron.) Take the D78 to **Beaujeu**, and brace yourself for a search; this is the One That Almost Got Away. VINCENT LACONDEMINE's domaine lurks behind the car park for the Shopi supermarket. Go through the college car park until the road runs out. There's a house on the left; its letterbox, showing the name Lacondemine, is the only clue you'll get.

M Lacondemine owns 1ha and rents another five, all in the Beaujolais-Villages appellation. He sells half to the négoce, half direct: 'I don't want to put all my eggs in one basket.' His is a traditional approach, using gentle old wooden presses mechanized by his father. The juice flows underground between vats, avoiding all pumping. He's located right by the river, and uses its water to cool the vats via a heat exchanger. A large part of the Lacondemine production is sold as Beaujolais-Villages Nouveau, and then the traditional Beaujolais goes on sale in the spring. He also makes a charming, fresh rosé. Prices start at FF24 for that and the Nouveau, rising to FF30 for a special *vieilles vignes* cuvée which will keep for several years.

I wondered why there was no signboard. M Lacondemine confessed that he was still not quite sure what to call the domaine, and what logo to use, so he couldn't get a signboard made. He shrugged. 'People seem to find it all the same', he said. With wines of this quality, I'm not the least surprised. He speaks only French but his wife is an English teacher and you can make an appointment for her to show you round at weekends.

Take time to wander in Beaujeu. It's a small town with a straggly main street following the valley floor. M Lacondemine recommends the hotel-restaurant Anne de Beaujeu, set in a charming old building in the high street. Plenty of shops and bistro-style restaurants here, too, and a museum containing wine history exhibits.

Follow the D37 out of Beaujeu towards Belleville. As you enter **Cercié**, look out for **DOMAINE DE LA VOÛTE DES CROZES** on the right. Here Nicole Chanrion will offer you an unmissable visit. She runs the enterprise herself, having taken over from her father, who's still around. In her passionate commitment she reminded me of the women winemakers of Savennières, in the Loire. Like them, she also makes only one main wine, Côte de Brouilly, grown on the hill which rises behind her house. Her eyes light up as she talks about these slopes, and speaks with real enthusiasm about the wines. She related how the growers on the hill slopes decided to secede from the general Brouilly appellation, maintaining that their wines were different in style – and, naturally, superior – to those of the flat Brouilly vineyards which surround Mont Brouilly on three sides. A marketing error, she reckons, as the Brouilly vineyards are now much better known than those in Côte de Brouilly.

Her wines are terrific: lovely, ripe, fragrant fruit, with suppleness and backbone. And what a bargain: just FF34 a bottle, dropping to just FF31 if you buy six or more. Stock up. I did.

And with that we finish the tour of the crus, but not of Beaujolais; there are still some delights in store, which have the additional advantage of being less well-known. Meanwhile, turn right from Nicole Chanrion's estate and take the Pizay turning at the roundabout outside Cercié. This will lead you to **CHÂTEAU DE PIZAY**, about which I have very mixed feelings. The rooms are excellent: large, modern, galleried affairs with lots of space and individual terraces. There are some tiny touches which makes me wonder whether they ran out of money before they finished them: the bed surround in my room was built for a 2-metre bed, but the bed itself was only a large double, leaving a sizeable gap on each side from the built-in bedside tables.

The bedroom block is tacked on to an imposing renovated château with formal gardens and country walks. I suggest you enjoy the rooms and the grounds, and avoid the staff (unsmiling, even hostile) and the food (indifferent, and very expensive).

Plenty of other eating options in nearby **Belleville**. Find the station, and next to it is the Buffet de la Gare, a splendid old-style bistro, open for lunch only, with a no-choice set menu.

This is another haunt of the local business community. Across the street is the well-regarded Beaujolais. Between these two you'll find the Hôtel La Route des Vins, which has simple, very fairly-priced rooms and no restaurant (well, it scarcely needs one.)

If you head north on the N6 from Belleville you'll soon see the **MAISON DES BEAUJOLAIS** on your left. This is one of the 'oenological centres' the local wine committee is developing. Here you can taste and buy local wines, pick up sheaves of leaflets, and eat traditional Beaujolais dishes.

Retrace your steps on the D37 and turn left to St-Lager, eventually joining the D43. From this road you'll see any amount of signs to **Vaux-en-Beaujolais**, immortalized by the author Chevallier as the setting for his comic novel *Clochemerle*. The first time I came to Beaujolais I was reading this, and accidentally left the book behind in the gîte without finishing it. Wonder how it turned out. In the village centre there are photo-opportunities to stand in (or in my case in front of) a small building boldly proclaiming itself the 'Pissotière de Clochemerle', and there's a tasting-room nearby.

Vaux is surrounded on all sides by stunning hill views. It's difficult to go on describing the scenery round here as I fear you'll think I'm getting dull and repetitive, but it really is wondrous. The route now heads south, passing through the remaining -Villages vineyards to the basic Beaujolais appellation which lies beyond. Leave Vaux on the D49, turn left onto the D44 and left again on the D504. (Or take the D489E: the views are just as good.) Turn right for Cogny, and stay on the D19 as far as Theizé.

This route takes you into countryside of different character and quite exceptional beauty, known as the Pierres Dorées, or golden stones. A quick look at the local architecture explains everything; honey-coloured houses nestling among the vines and woodland. This is no longer solely a wine region – mixed agriculture has replaced it. And while this area is popular with tourists in summer, out of season wine-lovers will have it practically to themselves.

Theizé is home to another oenological centre, the **CHÂTEAU DE ROCHEBONNE**. You'll find this at the top of the village – follow the road leading uphill on the right of the village square. The wine committee is organizing the restoration of the château to accommodate exhibitions on winemaking in the region. Meanwhile there's parking and picnicking just opposite, with, oh dear, yet another lovely view. I'm told you can see Mont Blanc from here when it's clear enough.

Leave the car here and walk a short way down to **DOMAINE DE ROCHEBONNE**, on your left. This is very much a family operation: the young grandson has just joined his father, Jean-François Pein, in making the wine, and the grandparents are in charge of sales. The family owned an apartment in the château until being bought out by the heritage department.

They've built a charming new tasting room in the cellars of the family house, and you can also see into the old working cellars, now used for a mixture of storage and show. They haven't got much in the way of signposting yet, apart from the domaine name: the cellars are right round the back – keep going.

Here the appellation is basic Beaujolais, but it's well-made and inexpensive (FF22). They make a special cuvée for three francs more; this is more concentrated and will keep a little longer. Also on sale: a light rosé, an attractive Beaujolais Blanc and a well-balanced sparkling wine. The grandparents don't speak English but the grandson does; all generations offer a warm welcome and take great pride in what they do.

From Theizé take the D96 towards the gloriously-named Oingt, then St-Laurent-d'Oingt and Le-Bois-d'Oingt, a very scenic road. From Le Bois you briefly join the D485, then turn off on the D39 to **St-Verand**. In the village there's a sign for **DOMAINE VISSOUX** just by the church: it's a sharp right turn. Keep going down this narrow road and park opposite the domaine.

A young couple, Pierre-Marie and Martine Chermette, have been working the family property since 1982. Their local vines are in the simple Beaujolais appellation, but they've recently managed to acquire vineyards in Fleurie and Moulin à Vent. It's very hard indeed to buy vineyards here, and the Chermettes were only able to do it because they got wind of the sale before anyone else. The vineyard is tied to a sharecropping agreement, so in buying the land they also buy the sharecropper – who has right of veto over any deal. Careful negotiations were needed. Now the sharecropper tends the vines, and the crop is split 50:50.

Here there's a simple philosophy of non-intervention, using only natural yeasts, and with a very light hand on the sugar, sulphur, and filter machine. Plus the added advantage of old vines, some of which are over 80. A small proportion of wine is aged in oak. All this adds up to fine wine; when you see the prices, FF27 for the old vines or FF23 for younger ones, the value seems amazing. There's also a very fine Beaujolais Blanc, and a *crème de cassis* to die for. Forget the supermarket stuff, this is the real thing (and at FF57 the half litre, so it should be).

This is a great visit to round off Beaujolais explorations, a classic example of what these wines can be if there's a light touch with the sugar bag and no desire to overproduce. Highly recommended.

Drive on past the estate and you eventually come to the D13, which in turn leads you onto the D485. The D38 then takes you into Villefranche, where you can pick up the motorway home. (Or stop overnight, if desired, at the Hôtel Plaisance in the town centre; comfortable if slightly faded rooms, elegant restaurant La Fontaine Bleue across the courtyard. Try the seafood tagliatelle.) If you're interested in linking wine regions, take the D485 in the opposite direction, picking up the D8 to Marcigny. This brings you to the banks of the Loire, which you can follow north to (eventually) Sancerre.

Best advice of all, though, is to continue south through the Coteaux du Lyonnais to the northern Rhône. Which is the next chapter.

Listings

When telephoning France from the UK, first dial 00 33 then the number shown. Producers are listed in wine route order, and hotels/restaurants by town or village according to the route. Accommodation prices are per room, meal prices are per head.

Producers

Michel Tête/Domaine du
Clos du Fief
Les Gonards, 69840 Juliénas
Tel 74 04 41 62, Fax 74 04 47 09
Open Mon–Sat 8–19, Sun 10–20
in August
Some English

Hubert Lapierre
Les Gandelins
71570 La Chapelle-de-Guinchay
Tel 85 36 74 89, Fax 85 36 79 69
Open Mon–Sun 9–12, 13.30–19,
Appointment preferred
Credit cards accepted
No English

Guy Braillon
Le Bourg, 69840 Chénas
Tel 74 04 48 31, Fax 74 04 47 64
Open Mon–Sun 9–20
Appointment preferred
No English

Georges Duboeuf
71570 Romanèche-Thorins
Tel 85 35 51 13, Fax 85 35 56 58
Open Mon–Sat 8–19
Credit cards accepted
Good English

Cave des Producteurs des Grands
Vins de Fleurie, 69820 Fleurie
Tel 74 04 11 70, Fax 74 69 84 73
Open Mon–Sat 9–12, 14–18 and
Sun from 1/4 to 15/10
Credit cards accepted
Good English

Anne-Marie and Armand Desmures
69115 Chiroubles
Tel 74 69 10 61, Fax 74 69 15 12
Open Mon–Sun 9–22 (!)
Appointment preferred
No English

Dominique Piron
Morgon, 69910 Villié-Morgon
Tel 74 69 10 29, Fax 74 69 16 65
Open Mon–Fri 8–12, 14–16 & Sat
by appointment
Credit cards accepted
Good English

Vincent Lacondemine
Le Moulin, 69430 Beaujeu
Tel 74 04 82 77
Open Mon–Sun 9–18
Some English
(Mme Lacondemine can give visits
in English at weekends)

Nicole Chanrion
Domaine de la Voûte des Crozes
69220 Cercié
Tel 74 66 80 37
Open Mon–Sun 8–21
Appointment preferred
Some English

Jean-François Pein
Domaine de Rochebonne
La Roche, 69620 Thiezé
Tel 74 71 21 47
Visits by appointment
Good English (son)

Pierre-Marie Chermette
Domaine Vissoux
Le Vissoux, 69620 St-Vérand
Tel 74 71 79 42, Fax 74 71 84 26
Open Mon–Sat 8–12, 14–18
Appointment preferred
Good English

Hotels and Restaurants
H Hotel *R* Restaurant

Juliénas
R Le Coq au Vin
Place du Marché
Tel 74 04 41 98, Fax 74 04 41 44
FF98–198

HR Chez la Rose
Place du Marche
Tel 74 04 41 20, Fax 74 04 49 29
Rooms FF120–280, Meals FF90–250

Emeringes
R Les Vignerons
Tel 74 04 45 72 Fax 74 04 48 96
FF195–220

Romanèche-Thorins
HR Les Maritonnes
Route de Fleurie, 71570
Romanèche-Thorins
Tel 85 35 51 70, Fax 85 35 58 14
Rooms FF360–500, Meals
FF150–400

Fleurie
R Auberge du Cep
Place de l'Eglise, 69820 Fleurie
FF190–550

Chiroubles
R Chez Marc et Annick
69115 Chiroubles
Tel 74 04 24 87
FF95

R La Terrasse du Beaujolais
69115 Chiroubles
Tel 74 04 20 79
FF85–160

Villié-Morgon
HR Le Villon
69910 Villié-Morgon
Tel 74 69 16 16, Fax 74 69 16 81
Rooms FF260–360, Meals FF80–170

Beaujeu
HR Anne de Beaujeu
69430 Beaujeu
Tel 74 04 87 58, Fax 74 69 22 13
Rooms FF250–350, Meals FF108–350

Pizay
HR Château de Pizay
Pizay, 69220 Belleville
Tel 74 66 51 41, Fax 74 69 65 63
Rooms FF530–1150, Meals FF150–345

Belleville
R Buffet de la Gare
69220 Belleville
Tel 74 66 70 36
Lunch only, FF85

R Beaujolais
40 rue Maréchal Foch, 69220
Belleville
Tel 74 66 05 31
FF75–230

H La Route des Vins
1, place de la Gare, 69220 Belleville
Tel 74 66 34 68, Fax 74 66 19 00
Rooms FF155–250

R Maison des Beaujolais
N6, St Jean d'Ardières
Tel 74 66 16 46
FF58–99

Villefranche-sur-Saône
H Plaisance
96, avenue de la Libération, 69400
Villefranche-sur-Saône
Tel 74 65 33 52, Fax 74 62 02 89
Rooms FF300–400

R La Fontaine Bleu
18, rue Jean-Moulin, 69400
Villefranche-sur-Saône
Tel 74 68 10 37
FF98–220

The Northern Rhône

Why might you want to visit the northern Rhône? It might be to find wine bargains – some of France's finest wines are made here, yet the prices fall well short of those in Burgundy or Bordeaux. It might be for healthy exercise: not even in Alsace are the vines planted on such precipitous slopes. It might also be for the views, which reward anyone fit enough to struggle up to the top of the slope.

But the bargains aren't of the FF20-a-bottle type. This is the place to come to discover wines of first-class quality, made from varieties you'll hardly encounter anywhere else in France and which are less well-known than they deserve to be.

For many years I ignored this region too, zooming down the motorway to hit the sun; and indeed, as far as scenic wine tourism goes it's only fair to say that this is perhaps not right at the top of the list. The main disadvantage is geographical; the vines line the valley sides, the wide river Rhône occupies most of the valley floor, and road, rail and housing squash themselves into the small space remaining. This means the meandering tourist admiring the view has to mingle with the heavy stuff delivering to riverside factories. Here there's no gentle country lanes *à la Beaujolaise*; but occasionally you're rewarded by wonderful views opening up as you round a bend in the river, as at Condrieu.

The French refer to this northern winemaking section as *le Rhône septentrional*, whereas the southern part is called *le Rhône méridional*. We'll stop explorations when we get to the gap which separates Rhônes north and south. While the north is a fairly homogeneous region the south spills over on all sides, forming just part of one enormous wine region, from Gascony and Languedoc-Roussillon in the west to Provence in the east, with all their different grape varieties and wine styles. In order to make sure you can still lift this book with one hand, I've ignored the enormous southern area. There's enough down there for a whole new book. I hope.

Sorry to make this even more complicated, but I've sub-divided it up yet further into the northern northern Rhône and the southern northern Rhône. Which we can call the central Rhône if you prefer. The Rhône septentrional divides itself into two distinct clumps, with a boring bit in between, which it makes sense to drive through as swiftly and painlessly as possible.

Grape-wise, both parts of the northern Rhône are pretty easy to get to grips with. Red wines have only one permitted variety, the Syrah. This is the first time this variety has entered these pages, and with good reason – it needs plenty of sunshine to avoid various nasty grape diseases, and we're only just edging far enough south to hit the right kind of climate.

This variety, widely grown in Australia where they call it Shiraz, is pretty thin on the ground in France. The Rhône, plus some new planting in southern areas emerging from the old wine lake, is just about the only place it stands alone as the sin-gle variety in the bottle. Producers in the (southern) southern Rhône use it to add tannin and structure to their wines. And in Bordeaux until fairly recently they would import Syrah from Hermitage to beef up their weedy wines. You could specify whether or not you desired your claret 'Hermitagé' and those blends with added Hermitage were the more popular. I can well understand why.

For the whites, there are two main groups. In the delicate, fragrant corner we have Viognier, used to make the wines of Condrieu and Château-Grillet; in the richer, rounder corner we have Marsanne and Roussanne, which are used singly or blended to make the whites found elsewhere in the region, such as Crozes-Hermitage and St-Joseph.

So what is made? There's a simple series of appellations, which happily don't overlap. There's also need to mention the generic Côtes du Rhône, which can come from anywhere in the region, meridional as well as septen... – northern. It can be white, or even pink, but in practice is overwhelmingly red. Most of it comes, wine-lake style, from the south, but a small quantity is made in the north and can be very good value from a decent producer. Wine Law rules and regs state that the wine must be a blend of specified varieties except north of the 45th parallel (sounds like something out of the Cold War.) This is the line of latitude which divides the meridional and sept- etc Rhônes. (It is also, of less local significance, the exact half-way point between the Equator and the North Pole.) North of this parallel it's OK to make Côtes-du-Rhône exclusively from Syrah, as the grapes used in the meridional part won't ripen properly north of the line. Phew! That's all right then.

Actually, when you think about it, doesn't it seem daft that a wine with the same appellation can be made from totally different grapes, and therefore taste totally different, if it comes from a different part of the region? All these appellation laws are supposed to standardize things for the benefit of the consumer, but just the opposite seems to be happening here.

No such complication with the other appellations: strictly geographical. The main white is Condrieu, relating to vineyards surrounding that town. The grape here is exclusively Viognier. If you do nothing else in the Rhône get to know this grape. It's gorgeous – overwhelmingly fragrant, reminding some of apricots or pears – and it's expensive. That's largely because it's a bit of a pig to grow, giving small, unreliable yields. And one look at the narrow terraces painfully hacked out of the steep slopes will tell you that it's no picnic to cultivate it either. Many growers with vineyards in Condrieu have simply given up on it. Follow those who've persevered, though, because drinking this wine is a hedonistic experience which'll cost you half what it would cost in England, where £20 a bottle isn't unusual. So it might not be something to acquire a taste for unless your pocket can stand the shock. Alas you may be like me, and get hooked before you know it.

Within Condrieu is Château-Grillet, a tiny single estate with an AC all to itself. It's even more expensive than Condrieu and is somewhat different in style. Whereas Condrieu is bottled the year after harvest Château-Grillet stays an extra year in oak. This should make it last longer, again unlike Condrieu which should be drunk young, within three to five years of the harvest. I didn't include it in my visits because I thought it was too expensive for the quality, but as soon as I got back home I regretted leaving it out, so you'll find the address in the listings. Let me know what you think.

The northernmost red appellation is Côte Rôtie, a name thought to derive from the roasting heat its southeast-facing vineyards receive. The two outstanding slopes are called Côte Brune and Côte Blonde; there are lots of romantic legends surrounding how these names came about, usually centring on two fair damsels, one brunette, one blonde. You know the sort of thing. The more prosaic answer lies in the different coloured soils, brunette clay and blonde limestone. Never mind. It can be very entertaining to ask the producers you visit what they think the true origins are.

Mature Côte Rôtie is just wonderful, my joint favourite Rhône wine. What makes it special is that producers are allowed to add in a small percentage of Viognier. This gives a red wine with an astonishing nose, a heady cocktail of Syrah and all these fragrant fruity aromas all competing to get out of the glass and attack your senses. Terrific.

Of course you can have too much of a good thing, even in Côte Rôtie. In recent years the boundaries of the appellation have been expanded, and now you can legitimately grow Côte Rôtie on the flat land on top of those steep hillside slopes. And flat fertile land does not as a rule produce grapes that are a patch on those that have had to suffer on the slopes. (A little stress is supposed to be good for a vine. Just like managers, we're told.) These attempts to cash in on the AC at the expense of quality are a Bad Thing, and let's hope this reckless expansion is curbed.

Next on the AC list is St-Joseph. This AC is like a halfway house: halfway in both quality and price between the generic Côtes-du-Rhône and the top-notchers like Côte-Rôtie. The second largest AC, it stretches down most of the left bank, covering all the scenically boring bits in theory (but in practice it's sparsely planted there). There's a small amount of white St-Joseph, made from Marsanne.

Cornas follows on from St-Joseph on the left bank, and in good hands can rival the best wines of the Rhône. As in Côte Rôtie, the best wines come from the slopes yet flat land has been planted; in this case the flat land between slopes and river. It's a powerful, intense red, full and rich.

To round off the left bank I have to mention St-Péray, south of Cornas, which makes still and sparkling white wines, the latter using the traditional method, as in champagne.

And on my right... Hermitage. This is the classic wine of the northern Rhône, ranking with the top wines of the world. It grows on the hills surrounding Tain, in the southern end of the region (OK, the southern northern Rhône.) On these incredibly steep slopes they train the vines up individual stakes, to help buttress them against the wind. This training fashion is also followed elsewhere in the region. Hermitage will last and last and last. This is the wine I've laid down for my silver wedding. One needs more optimism for the endurance of marriage than the endurance of the wine.

Surrounding Hermitage is the lesser Crozes-Hermitage, the largest AC in the northern Rhône. The land, in sharp contrast to the precipitous slopes of Hermitage, is flat or gently hilly, and the aspect isn't as good. Both red and white Crozes are produced, and, like so many things, it can be very good in the hands of someone who knows what they're doing.

EXPLORING THE NORTHERN RHÔNE

Actually that heading is a bit of a cheat, because before we get to the banks of the Rhône I intend to route you, if, as I hope, you're coming from Beaujolais, via another appellation. (And indeed intend to take you back via yet another at the end of the tour. But we'll come to that.)

This wine route can be used in sections, obviously, but is also designed to lead you directly here from the golden slopes of Burgundy via Mâcon and Beaujolais. Nice idea, but there's a major obstacle in the way: the urban sprawl of Lyon. And getting through Lyon, via its choked city centre tunnels or round its new eastern bypass, is deeply unpleasant.

But fear not, I've devised a route which winds through some very pretty countryside, completely avoids Lyon, and has the added bonus of nipping though yet another appellation, Coteaux du Lyonnais. This AC is not, in the great scheme of things, terribly important. It only achieved this pinnacle of AC status in 1984, after many years squatting on the next rung down. The wines are like Beaujolais only less so – mostly Gamay with some Chardonnay and Aligoté. Georges Duboeuf will sell you some if you want to find out what they're like without actually having to go there, but I do recommend this route – and I found a smashing young producer too.

For those travelling direct to the Rhône, leave the A7 motorway south of Vienne and head straight to Ampuis, which is on the N86. To pick up where we left off in Beaujolais: head south on the D485 and turn right onto the D596 towards l'Arbresle. Take an almost immediate left onto the D70 and follow this pretty, winding (and indeed pretty winding) road until it intersects with the D489. Cross this, then take the D50 to Brindas, where you turn right onto the D11. In Maltaverne (still with me?) turn left onto the D30, then in St-Laurent-d'Agny take the D105 to **Taluyers**. **DOMAINE DU CLOS ST-MARC** is signposted in the village, located southeast of the village centre.

Here you'll find a newly-opened tasting-room set among the vines. See the world's largest tasting-cup! It holds 1,716 litres, according to my notes, and you can climb into it via a set of steps. It's used in one of those bizarre initiation rituals by the local wine fraternity.

I really don't think you'll find better examples of this appellation than here – and at astounding prices. Try a fresh, light, well-balanced Chardonnay for FF21, or a fine Gamay with good structure (there's some wood-ageing here) for a mere FF19. This isn't just a visit for the sake of completeness, ticking off the appellations – it's good wine in its own right, honestly made and honestly priced.

Turn right out of the domaine and right again onto the main road, the D42. Take a left onto the D34 and follow this through the suburbs of Givors: then take the D59 to **Condrieu**. This leads you through beautiful semi-wooded countryside: vineyards aren't thick on the ground for most of the way, but gradually become more common. The descent into Condrieu is magical as you get your first glimpses of the river and the steep vineyards that slope up from it.

Condrieu is an important stop on the tour, but I make no apology for asking you first to head north; doubling back seems irrelevant when the views are so good. We head straight for the northernmost visits, in Vérenay, north of Ampuis.

As you begin the tour you soon get to know who the major players are – their names stare down at you from huge billboards on the vine-covered hills. You occasionally see large roadside signs announcing that you're in the region of Côtes-du-Rhône. There may also be the name of the relevant AC

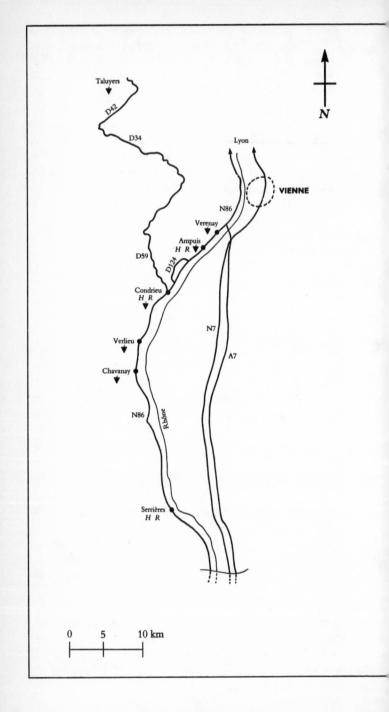

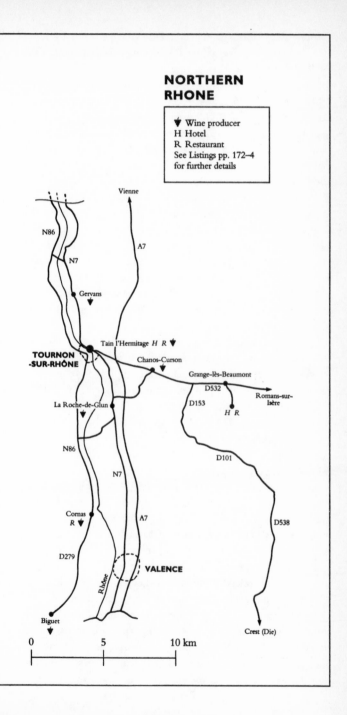

NORTHERN RHONE

♥ Wine producer
H Hotel
R Restaurant
See Listings pp. 172–4
for further details

Vienne

N86

N7

A7

Gervans ♥

Tain l'Hermitage *H R* ♥

Chanos-Curson

TOURNON -SUR-RHÔNE

Grange-lès-Beaumont

D532

Romans-sur-Isère

D153

H R

La Roche-de-Glun ♥

N86

N7

D101

Cornas ♥
R

A7

D538

D279

Rhône

VALENCE

Biguet ♥

Crest (Die)

0   5   10 km

you're passing through beneath. Don't be deceived by these signs: there's far more to the Rhône than the generic Côtes-du-Rhône. I think it's a shame that the whole wine region shares a name with its vinous lowest common denominator.

Take a left in **Vérenay** – it's signposted – and **DOMAINE GERIN** is on your left. Good visit, this. Jean-Marie Gerin has built himself a stylish tasting-room where you sit at the bar to taste his range which, though limited to three wines, is of first-class quality. First of all, there's a Côtes-du-Rhône from vineyards on less-favoured sites lurking between those of Côte-Rôtie; a fine, spicy example. He also owns land in both the other local appellations, Condrieu and Côte-Rôtie. His Condrieu is full and fat, with a gorgeous delicate floral nose. The Côte-Rôties currently on sale will keep a minimum of 20 years (he tasted the family's 1947 recently and reckoned it was still a '*joli bébé*'). A visit to his cellars reveals Bordeaux-style rows of barriques, complete with lees-painted central stripe, and immaculate housekeeping. This is a really good bench-mark-establishing visit, and good value to boot.

M Gerin also offered help of another kind. Driving north to Vérenay I'd passed through Ampuis and spotted a smashing-looking new restaurant in the village. (Spotted? It hits you between the eyes, painted almost fluorescent blue.) Unfortunately Ampuis offers nothing in the way of hotel accommodation, but M Gerin's mother-in-law has just opened several bed-and-breakfast rooms, right by this new restaurant. Naturally the in-laws also make wine. Within five minutes not only was the night's accommodation settled, but also another producer visit had sidled onto the agenda.

But before I could head back to Ampuis M Gerin directed me to the house above his. 'Young producer. Great stuff.' And indeed it was. This is **Domaine Clusel-Roch** (no signposts, just ring the bell), and it's tiny – only three *barriques* of Condrieu and just a few dozen of Côte-Rôtie. But it's delicate and well-made, and well-priced; FF95–145 (believe me, given what they ask round here, that's reasonable; Condrieu ain't cheap).

Now retrace your steps to **Ampuis**, a village dominated by a long, straggly main road shopping area (excellent picnic shops). Turn left at the far end of the village, cross the railway line, and the **JASMIN** estate is on your left. There's no indica-tion on the gate that visitors are permitted – and the welcome committee is likely to consist of loudly yapping dogs. If you've made an appointment, however, persist; ring the bell, and you'll be admitted, to loud cries of the French for 'down, Shep', to a series of low vaulted barrel cellars, and offered a taste of their supple, fragrant Côte Rôtie from cask. Patrick Jasmin now works with his father Robert, and it may be that change is in the offing; I'd recommend tasting carefully before you buy. They're not prepared to sell you more than two cases at a time, preferring larger orders to be routed through the UK importer. Never mind – if you want more bargains there are plenty of good producers on the route.

Such as **DOMAINE GILLES BARGE**, just a few hundred metres away. Retrace your steps to the village square, then take the road leading off the far side up the hill, past a car park. It's signposted. The domaine is along the first road on the left. There's a rustic tasting-room, with some truly dreadful pictures on the walls (note in particular the extraordinary leering trio depicted by the bar). Don't let them put you off – here's wine of deep colour, full of fruit and delicious. Prices, depending on vintage, are around the FF85–90 mark, which is very fair indeed for this quality.

This is the estate offering *chambres d'hôte*, on the top floor of an old town house on the village square. Rooms at the back look out over the high terraced vine slopes. It's reasonably comfortable, very clean and neat, and fairly priced. And the luminous blue restaurant, Le Côte Rôtie, is next door but one, well within tottering distance (no, no, it's the pavements – they're very uneven).

Le Côte Rôtie is new, but already tipped by locals to get its first Michelin star. Food is of high quality, and also very creative – I had a pumpkin soup with little slices of cervelas sausage floating in it, an unusual combination of flavours which worked really well. Excellent value.

Head south from Ampuis to Condrieu, either straight down the N86 or take a little scenic detour. Turn right in **Tupin** on the narrow, twisty D124 for steep climbs but wonderful views of the river. This road rejoins the N86 just before Condrieu.

Look out at the edge of the village for **GEORGES VERNAY**; it's on your left, with a walled garden and an ordinary-looking suburban villa. Drive in through gates on the far corner. (If you miss it, turn round in the Elf petrol station just beyond.) This is a classic visit; no appointment needed, and in the rustic tasting-room you'll encounter just about the finest Condrieu anyone's likely to sell you. Not only that, but there's a range of reds of exceptional quality, including a fine Côtes-du-Rhône with a little Viognier added to the Syrah. It may be FF50, but it knocks spots off most of the rest.

There's something for everyone here; prices start at FF30 and rise to FF160 for the top Condrieu cuvée. M Vernay is theoretically now in retirement – his son Luc is now in charge – but in practice most days will find him in the tasting-room, a genial, welcoming presence, happy to discuss the wines (in French). Direct sales account for 60% of their turnover, so they're well geared up to look after visitors. You can visit the cellars, but they're elsewhere and the owners would like a couple of weeks' notice to arrange things. For quality of both wine and welcome, this is gold star stuff.

In **Condrieu** (signposted on your left) there's the riverside hotel-restaurant Le Beau Rivage, expensive and comfortable, long beloved of Brits. Staying, as ever, on the N86, the next stop south is in the hamlet of **Verlieu**. CAVE YVES CUILLERON is on your right – drive straight in. M Cuilleron offers an unusual range of Condrieu. The first is fruity, for drinking young. The second is barrel-aged, like Château-Grillet, and will keep. And the third is sweet, late-harvested and with some noble rot. This, the old way of making Condrieu, has now nearly died out, so here's a rare opportunity to find out what it tasted like. You may be offered a barrel sample – when I was there he'd sold out of the current vintage. You may have more luck.

M Cuilleron bottles his barrel-aged wine in brown flute bottles, similar to those used by Château-Grillet. This is the old traditional shape for this wine. He complains that when Alsace claimed exclusive use for this shape, banning anyone else in France from using it, only Château-Grillet protested on the grounds that they too traditionally used it. They received special permission to continue to do so but, he claims, Condrieu failed to lodge an objection and missed the boat.

The cellars lead off the modern tasting-room, and M Cuilleron is happy to show you round and explain, in English, his philosophy. This is well worth a visit, to discover what someone with a passion for Viognier – and an unusually large

planting of it – can do with this extraordinary grape. He adds
10% Viognier to his Côte Rôtie, for instance, a much higher
percentage than the norm, giving that characteristic floral nose
and extra complexity. He makes a white and a red St-Joseph for
just FF47; Condrieu ranges from FF110 to over FF200 for the
late harvest, if he has any.

And with that we've come to the dividing line between the
northern and southern northern Rhônes. There's a dull stretch
of road to come now; drive swiftly south, maybe taking lunch
in the restaurant Charles in Chavanay or the Schaeffer in
Serrières (both also have rooms). You can cross the river by any
convenient route: I chose the strange new road via the barrage
at Arras, the D800, which brings you out near **Gervans**.

Here's the first stop, **DOMAINE FAYOLLE**, and I wish I could
tell you which of their two locations to visit. The estate is run
by two ebullient brothers who bear a disconcerting resemblance to Russell Harty. They have a tasting-room on the main
N7 but their cellars are high up in the village (distinguished by
a pub-style swinging sign of a bunch of grapes.). If you want to
make sure you meet them, and see the cellars, then it's best to
make an appointment.

Their parents' way of working was to maintain high stock
levels, which is good for you and me as it means we can buy
wines with a few years' bottle age. (And to keep the brothers in
line, photos of previous generations stare down sternly from
above the bar. Strong family likenesses apparent.) They're
equally attached to their 'old furniture', the ancient large barrels
lining the cellar.

They make Hermitage and Crozes-Hermitage, both white
and red, all four of excellent quality. Had life turned out differently these two could probably have had a career in showbiz –
they love playing to an audience and the audience clearly loves
them back; I was there late on a Friday afternoon and the joint
was jumping with customers wanting something for the weekend. The atmosphere is relaxed and entertaining, with clients
more than happy to enter into the spirit of the place. One
wrote in the visitors' book of the '91 red Crozes that it was as if
'*le bon dieu en culottes de velours*' had descended. I suggest you
walk in there and demand to taste the little baby Jesus in velvet
shorts, which for some reason is how we ended up rendering it.
You should get a warm response, even in that translation.

The Fayolle estate, both arms of it, lies just north of **Tain l'Hermitage**. Tain is an important centre for the big négociants who play an important role in the economics of Rhône wine. It can easily occupy a day of your time, so my advice would be to pitch camp first. In the centre of town there's the Mercure, with comfortable rooms and a reasonable restaurant (and, despite being in the cramped centre of town, a pool.) Although it's part of the Mercure chain the hotel is family-owned, and staff are polite and helpful. Plenty of good picnic fodder on the Rue Jean-Jaurès, and even a decent takeaway pizza place immediately opposite the Mercure.

Just south of town, still on the N7, Reynaud offers the best food in town on a riverside terrace, served by a gliding, pongy waiter, and very spacious, well-appointed rooms, the best of which share the view. Locals complain that the standards here are too variable, while I can only judge on the basis of one night; but I found it good.

In Tain I suggest a selection of visits encompassing the spectrum of local wine commerce: a négociant, a cooperative and a small individual grower. But first, make a pilgrimage to the top of the hill dominating the town, home of the Hermitage vineyards, to get an overview in the most literal sense of the word. Follow signs for the cave cooperative and drive on past it up the hill; signs marked '*circuit touristique*' guide you to the viewpoint. It's steep and twisty, and when the road finally disintegrates into a bumpy dirt track, I'd suggest you park and walk unless you've a four-wheel drive or something very rugged.

As you go over the summit and head down the other side towards the tiny chapel there are magnificent views of the river, north and south; of Tournon on the opposite bank; and of the gently rolling hills of Crozes-Hermitage curving away to your left. All the vines on this prime site surrounding the chapel are owned by Chapoutier, as little signs tell you; but the wine called Hermitage La Chapelle, one of the greatest wines of the region, isn't made by them but by rivals Jaboulet who own the rights to the name. More of them later; for now, retrace your steps and call at the cooperative, **CAVE DE TAIN L'HERMITAGE**.

Until I came here I thought my theory of 'as the winemaker, so the wine' could only apply to an individual. How could wine made by a group of people reflect personality? But somehow, here, I think it works. I've never come across a friendlier group of people, who all seem completely dedicated to their work and their product. All the staff I encountered, without exception, were exceptionally welcoming and helpful. And I do feel it's permeated the wine, even though the grapes come from hundreds of suppliers (480, to be precise), with an average holding of just 3ha apiece, and who are often also growing fruit, such as apricots.

You can tour the cellars by appointment and I think it's well worthwhile. You can see some very sophisticated equipment, such as the computerized selection and grading of the grapes as they arrive, freshly harvested. One man stands guard and judges all the grapes which pass. He decides what grade they are – and, consequently, what the growers will be paid for their crop. His word is law. Not even the director of the co-op is allowed to countermand him. The system appears to work with few complaints, and encourages growers to improve quality as they see the results in the increased size of their cheques.

Connoisseurs of large pieces of stainless steel equipment will enjoy a rare sighting of a '*cuve égoutteuse*', used to drain off the free-run juice before pressing (thus saving the presses to press only what actually needs pressing, if you see what I mean – important when there are huge quantities of grapes coming at you from all directions.)

The co-op is a major player in Crozes-Hermitage, being responsible for two-thirds of all production. They sell around 40% to négociants such as Jaboulet, and bottle and market the rest themselves. There's a comprehensive selection of wine on sale at remarkably fair prices. Excellent Cornas and red Hermitage, good whites; also a selection of non-AC wines for under FF20. I especially liked the fact that they have a good stock of older vintages, going back up to 15 years, and again very fairly priced. If you wanted to trace the evolution of Rhône wines, a selection bought here would be an excellent way to do it.

Head back to the main road to find **MARC SORREL** – his domaine is on the river side of the road. His barrel cellars are on view through glass, right behind the entrance and tasting area, and all the cellar work takes place in full view. Crozes start at FF30, Hermitage is FF85–130. There's no filtration or fining, and the wines are supple, rich and round, and will keep for ages. He's open without appointment, but if you specifically want to meet him to talk about the wines it's better to ring first, in case he's out in the vineyards and someone else is minding the store.

Take the road leading up to the station, past the Mercure, and you'll find the offices of the large producer and négociant **M CHAPOUTIER** on the right. This has been a family business for several generations, each of which has been careful to give the succeeding generation names beginning with M so the labels and signs don't have to be altered with each succession. Current incumbent, young Michel Chapoutier, is an ardent advocate of biodynamics and has (with his brother Marc, in charge of marketing) turned round his family's fortunes in a remarkably short space of time, drastically reducing the yields in some cases to a minuscule four bunches per vine and aiming for a true expression of the *terroir*.

These are wines of stunning concentration and quality, and there was quite a storm in 1993 when, according to wine-writer Robert Parker, Chapoutier was the only grower to pro-duce decent wine – thanks to the use of biodynamics. You can imagine the uproar from other growers. Get the evidence in front of you, though, and I think you'll be impressed by the sheer quality of these wines. There's a wide range, in all price brackets – choose with confidence.

Unfortunately there doesn't seem to be very good visitor provision yet. They've just opened a new wine shop on the premises, replacing the old one on the high street. The range includes wines from bought-in grapes from the meridional Rhône, and a very successful *vin de paille* – 'straw wine' – from Hermitage grapes laid out on straw to dry and shrivel, making a concentrated sweet wine like those of the Jura. You can taste and buy, but sadly opportunities to tour the premises seemed in doubt. Keep the pressure on – theirs is an interesting set-up, and the more visitors ask to visit the greater the chance some-thing will be organized.

Meanwhile take a stroll along the Rue Emile Friol, opposite Chapoutier, and turn right in the square along the Rue d'Hermitage. Pass under the railway bridge and take the path up into the vines. Here you'll see a cleft in the rock: this marks the dividing line between the granite of the Massif Central to the north and the chalk of the alpine massif to the south. Around here there seem to be dividing lines all over the place.

Now we move back to the left bank; cross the river in the centre of Tain to Tournon, and take the N86 south to Cornas. The road hugs the riverbank, making the most of the narrow strip of flat land before the steep slopes begin. Several ruined castles dot the hilltops.

In **Cornas**, park by the (traditional, reasonable) Restaurant Ollier, on the right; **AUGUSTE CLAPE**'s small domaine is just opposite, but he isn't going to betray his presence by even the tiniest signboard. This is a visit strictly by appointment. Ask to see the cellars, and you'll stumble downstairs into a gloomy, dank, mould-encrusted room in which, by common consent, he produces the definitive Cornas. M Clape, about whom the word 'wily' springs irresistibly to mind, professes indifference to it all, indicating that making the wine is simplicity itself; but if it's so easy, why can't everyone else make wine of this quality? And for the absurdly reasonable price of FF85? Drink it before it hits 3 years of age, or wait until it's 8 or 10. In between it goes off in a major teenage huff and isn't worth trying. Meanwhile snap up his rich, thick Côtes-du-Rhône, for FF45.

Upstairs there's a sign sent by an American fan: 'You've got a friend in Cornas'. It may be referring to Pennsylvania, but it clearly holds equally true here. This isn't really a casual visit, but if you want to spend some time hearing how it's done from a master, in French, don't miss this.

Backtracking slightly, you'll see signs at the entrance to the village for the **CENTRE OENOLOGIQUE DES CÔTES DU RHÔNE**. As well as being an oenological laboratory this is home (though I use the term loosely) to Jean-Luc Colombo's own wine-making operation. He also buys in from his lab clients and acts as négociant, forming a marketing group with some of them. He drives thousands of kilometres a year looking after his clients, so you're unlikely to find him at home. Whoever receives you will take you into a charming, small, vaulted tasting-cellar and offer a range of both his and clients' wines.

This man has caused quite a stir in Cornas, partly for using atypical Bordeaux-shaped bottles and arty labels, partly for his winemaking methods which, some say, make all his wines taste the same. He's a firm advocate of new oak *barriques* in an area given to using large old vats, for instance. He's been known to be outspoken about the mistakes and faulty wines his fellow Cornas growers make. In short, he hasn't gone out of his way to endear himself locally – and I have to say his prices didn't endear themselves to me. I think these wines are overpriced. His top Cornas cuvée is FF140. And yes, it's good, but I can buy my favourite Hermitage, La Chapelle, for that price, thank you. Even his Côtes-du-Rhône is FF60. I'm not saying it's not good, just that it's very dear. Nevertheless, he's worth a visit to see what all the fuss is about – he's clearly having quite an impact on the region.

If, for the sake of completeness, you want to go to St-Péray, head back through Cornas and through St-Péray itself, leaving on the D279 towards Toulaud. **Biguet** is on a tiny road, the C4, on your right, signposted Tourtousse. When the road peters out, you've arrived at JEAN-LOUIS THIERS, who makes very respectable still and sparkling St-Péray. The sparkling wine is made by the champ... er, traditional method, and M Thiers does all the *remuage* by hand, increasingly rare in these parts. As indeed it is in Champagne. He also makes a hearty Cornas, for a much more modest FF60.

Back now through Cornas, heading north, and looking for a right turn to **La Roche de Glun**. From here the estate of PAUL JABOULET AÎNÉ is signposted, across on the right bank of the river on the N7. Jaboulet is the other big négociant of Tain. The cellars are still in the town centre, but bottling and admin moved out here in 1983.

They'll show you round by appointment, and with sufficient advance notice you can even see round the Tain cellars. The company owns vineyards in Hermitage, Crozes and Cornas and buys in grapes from many other Rhône appellations. They make the glorious Hermitage La Chapelle, with which you should indulge yourself if you possibly can. (Around FF85–140, depending on vintage.)

There's also a white Hermitage named after the knight who allegedly built the chapel on returning from the crusades, le Chevalier de Sterimberg. Another recommended wine is their Crozes, Domaine Thalabert, and their Côtes du Rhône Parallèle 45, generally reliable in both red and white, costs around FF22. You can see a monument marking this parallel, the exact halfway point between the Equator and the North Pole, a couple of kilometres south of here, on the N7. Some wines are available back to the mid-80s, such as Cornas (from FF52, rising to FF77 for the '85.) Nice to find wines on sale that should be ready to drink. They reckon to open 10,000 bottles a year for tasting purposes, so you shouldn't have too much trouble getting a sample of the wines that interest you.

Cross country now; turn right off the N7 towards Les Sept Chemins, and when you come to this crossroads (actually I think it's only six roads that intersect, not seven) head for **Chanos-Curson**. Here, in the centre of the village, you'll find the One That Got Away on this trip, **DOMAINE DES ENTREFAUX**. The owners have a formidable reputation for their Crozes-Hermitage, and by now you'll have established a sufficiently firm benchmark to know whether that's justified.

From Chanos take the D532 towards Romans-sur-Isère, and turn right on the edge of **Granges-lès-Beaumont**; follow signs for Les Vieilles Granges. I did this at night in thick fog, and it seemed really spooky following these signs, turn after turn, apparently leading nowhere. Suddenly the building appeared, prettily lit and looking very friendly, and it was well worth the strange journey. The restaurant here has been open for several years but the rooms are new. The best ones have a balcony with a wonderful view straight down to the river Isère; the fog lifted the following morning in time for me to enjoy it.

The chic restaurant is a two-person operation; she cooks, he serves. Excellent food, consisting of the best ingredients simply prepared. And, oh wonder of wonders, there's a vegetarian menu. And a very fairly-priced wine list. Monsieur knows the list well, and you might well discover an extra visit to make on the strength of his recommendations. This was one of my favourite stops of the whole trip, with the added bonus of extremely reasonable prices. For some reason it hasn't hit the guidebooks; go now.

Strictly speaking, this is where the tour ends. You can head back to the A7 at Tain if you must. I'd much rather you came with me on this last leg, though, because in the scenic wonderment stakes it outclasses just about anything I've seen in France. We're off to Die. That's pronounced like 'see', as in 'we're off to Die the Wizard'.

Get back on the D532, retrace your steps for a short drive and turn left onto the D153 towards Châteauneuf. Take the D101 to Alixan, and turn right onto the D538. Keep right until you get to Crest, then join the D93 to **Die**. This is a lovely road, with scenery like the Scottish Lowlands, only more so.

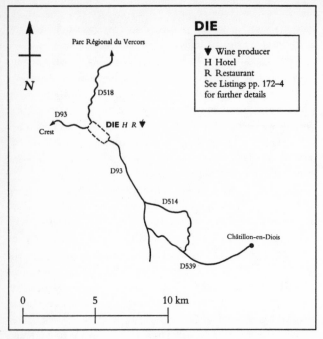

Gradually it comes to resemble the Highlands, and by the time you get to Die the mountains extend up past the snowline. This valley represents the dividing line between the alpine and Mediterranean climates, making it a good place to end the tour.

Clairette de Die is a sparkling wine made of the fairly neutral Clairette grape or the livelier Muscat (known as Tradition). The unique Dioise method stops fermentation at around the 7–8° mark, leaving you with a very fresh, fruity wine you can drink in the heat of the summer sun without getting blotto. Well, not quickly, anyway.

Fermentation is halted by refrigerating the wine. When it's bottled and the wine warms up again, the sugars remaining in the bottle will cause CO_2 to form. I was puzzled by the use of modern refrigeration in a 'traditional' process, but apparently they used to use icy river water instead, plunging the barrels into mid-stream. Pity the freezing, drenched, cellar-workers.

The best place to discover these wines is at the **CAVE COOPERATIVE**, which is on your right as you enter the village. This is a major operation, producing the vast majority of Clairette – and, fortunately, with an eye to quality. There's a comfortable, large tasting-room where you can compare the two styles of Clairette, and also sample the rest of their vast range. They've got deals going with a couple of co-ops in the meridional Rhône, which allow them to sell one another's wine, so there's a vast choice of reds to try from the south. Additionally, and unusually, several growers allow the co-op to vinify their wines and market them under the producer name. Some interesting still wines from Châtillon-en-Diois are made, notably Aligoté, which I found particularly successful.

The co-op also offers a small wine museum, with some splendid old photographs of the region, and an audiovisual film – shown on request. Special equipment freaks will thrill to the band press, specially used to crush the large oily Muscat grapes, and the Italian plaque filter. Wouldn't your dentist just love one? It looks like a giant waffle iron and is used for the first filtration, which is carried out several degrees below zero. As you might gather, this winemaking process demands an enormous investment in equipment, which is why the co-op was founded in the first place – the individual growers simply found it too expensive to go it alone.

The other wine to mention is Crémant de Die, a new appellation first launched in 1993. It's made by the, um, traditional method, from 100% Clairette grapes, and will eventually usurp the Clairette Brut. They'd been hoping they could have used some Chardonnay in the blend, so plantings were made in anticipation. Alas, the national wine law people forbade it. Thus you'll also find vin de pays Chardonnay on their shelves. My advice would be, however, to stick to the Aligoté which is really very successful (and cheap. Under FF20). Clairette de Die comes in at around the same price as most crémants throughout France, ie around the 40FF mark. It's a different taste, and some prefer it for that and for the low alcohol content. I like the Tradition, with Muscat; see which you prefer.

The nice young man from the co-op is keen to encourage visitors to come to Die, which he reckons is more than can be said for the interprofessional committee covering all Rhône wines – including Die. He complained that, although the co-op paid its whack to the committee, they didn't get much promotion – they've been left out of the booklet of wine routes, for instance. Seems a bit unfair to me – don't ignore Die, the scenery is glorious and the wine a novelty.

Where to stay is rather a tricky question. There's nowhere I'd recommend outright. I had a room in the Hôtel des Alpes which was basic, comfortable and reasonably priced, but the welcome left a lot to be desired. It has the advantage of being right in the old town centre. (Charge right in where it appears to indicate pedestrians only. It doesn't really mean it. Park in the central car park – the hotel is reasonably well signposted.) On the outskirts of town – you passed it on the left as you came in – is the Petite Auberge. The welcome here was warm, but the food a good decade out of date – smothering sauces and lots of little piles of messed-about-with veg. Never mind – it's the wine and the scenery I came for, not the food.

You can make a small wine tour down to Châtillon-en-Diois. Leave Die on the D93 and, first of all, turn left on the D514 to Laval d'Aix. This is a delightful drive through mixed agricultural land, vines jostling for space with walnut trees or corn. Take a single-track road on the right signed St-Roman. You'll notice some graveyards amongst the vines. This form of burial was practised by the Protestants who migrated here after the Revocation of the Edict of Nantes. Many of the wine estates you pass, although appearing to be individual domaines, in fact sell to the co-op. It'll generally say so on small letters at the bottom of their signboards.

Pass through the pretty village of St-Romans and turn left onto the main road. This is now the D539 to **Châtillon**. In Châtillon take the right fork up towards the centre, and park near the old communal wash house, the *lavoir*. This exceptionally attractive old village is very popular in the summer – and practically deserted in the winter. Some say it's too cold here then, that life is too harsh. The village isn't thriving. The local café is closed down, for sale. The only place doing good business is the video rental shop. But walk slowly, look closely. You'll see walls painted with false bricks and more creative murals. Tiny alleyways full of interesting little details.

Now for the scenic wonderment. Go back into Die and take the D578. This takes you high up into the mountains, via a series of hairpin bends that make you glad of/long for power steering. You descend again and follow the valley plain, high up in the Vercors. Now the equivalent of a national park, fifty years ago this was the scene of fierce and bloody resistance against Nazi occupation, and a new national memorial to the heroes and victims of this resistance has been opened at Vassieux-en-Vercors (signposted left on the D76). After visiting it, rejoin the route via the D178 to La Chapelle-en-Vercors.

At the village after La Chapelle, Les Barraques, you turn into a most extraordinary series of tunnels and almost-tunnels over-hanging the road, known as the Grands Goulets – great gullies. I found the switchback, twisty road pretty scary and was glad to do it at lunchtime out of season, when it was relatively quiet. (Though now, of course, having done it, I think it was no big deal.) That isn't the end of the excitement, either, as the road snakes down one mountainside and up another and through another, smaller, set of Goulets. Eventually you reach the mountain equivalent of dry land at Pont-en-Roy, and head for the main N532, which brings you out at Romans-sur-Isère.

I thought the Vercors absolutely stunning, and would like to return, even though it's a vine-free zone. From here the motorway beckons, though there's a lot to be said for reversing the route and enjoying the view from the opposite direction. And there are other options, not least the chance to visit Alsace via the A36 to Mulhouse at Dijon. Whatever you do, make sure the car is so full that you're not tempted to stock up on supermarket wines at Calais. That way disappointment lies...

Listings

When telephoning France from the UK, first dial 00 33 then the number shown. Producers are listed in wine route order, and hotels/restaurants by town or village according to the route. Accommodation prices are per room, meal prices are per head.

Producers

Domaine du Clos St-Marc
69440 Taluyers
Tel 78 48 26 78, Fax 78 48 77 91
Open Fri 14–18.30, Sat 10.30–12.30,
14.30–18.30, Sun 15–18.30
Mon–Thu by appointment
Some English

Domaine Gerin
Rue de Montmain, Vérenay
69420 Ampuis
Tel 74 56 16 56, Fax 74 56 11 37
Open Mon–Sat 8–12, 14–19
Credit cards accepted
No English

Domaine Clusel-Roch
Route du Lacat, Vérena
69420 Ampuis
Tel 74 56 15 95, Fax 74 56 19 74
Visits by appointment only
Good English

E.A.R.L. Jasmin
69420 Ampuis
Tel 74 56 16 04
Visits by appointment only
No English

Domaine Gilles Barge
Route de Boucharey, 69420 Ampuis
Tel 74 56 13 90, Fax 74 56 10 98
Open Mon–Sat 8.30–12, 14–18
Credit cards accepted
No English

Georges Vernay
1, route nationale, 69420 Condrieu
Tel 74 59 52 22, Fax 74 56 60 98
Open Mon–Sat 9–12, 14.30–19
Cellar visits by appointment with
two weeks' notice
Credit cards accepted
No English

Yves Cuilleron
Verlieu, 42410 Chavanay
Tel 74 87 02 37, Fax 74 87 05 62
Open Mon–Fri 8–12, 13.30–19,
Sat 10–12, 15–18.30
Credit cards accepted
Good English (by appointment
with Yves)

Domaine Fayolle
Gervans, 26600 Tain-l'Hermitage
Tel 75 03 33 74 or 75 03 34 83
Fax 75 03 32 52
Open Mon–Sat 9–12, 14–19
Sat and Sun by appointment but
caveau on N7 should be open
Credit cards accepted
No English

Cave de Tain l'Hermitage
22, route de Larnage
26600 Tain l'Hermitage
Tel 75 08 20 87, Fax 75 07 15 16
Open Mon–Sat 8–12, 14–18,
Sun 9–12, 14–18. Cellar tours by
appointment
Credit cards accepted
Good English

Marc Sorrel
128, avenue Jean Jaurès
26600 Tain l'Hermitage
Tel 75 07 10 07, Fax 75 08 47 16
Open Mon–Fri 10–12, 14–19,
appointment preferred,
Sat and Sun by appointment only
No English

M Chapoutier
18, avenue du Dr. Paul Durand,
26600 Tain l'Hermitage
Tel 75 08 28 65, Fax 75 08 81 70
Open Mon–Fri 10–12, 14–17, Sat
10–12, 14–16
Credit cards accepted
Good English

Auguste Clape
148, route nationale, 07130 Cornas
Tel 75 40 33 64
Visits strictly by appointment
No English

Jean-Luc Colombo
Centre Oenologique, 07130 Cornas
Tel 75 40 24 47, Fax 75 40 16 49
Visits by appointment
No English

Jean-Louis Thiers
Biguet, 07130 Touland
Tel 75 40 49 44, Fax 75 40 33 03
Open Mon–Sun by appointment
No English

Paul Jaboulet Aîné
Les Jalets, La Roche-de-Glun
26600 Tain l'Hermitage
Tel 75 84 68 93, Fax 75 84 56 14
Open Mon–Fri 8–11.30, 13.30–17,
appointment needed for cellar visit
Credit cards accepted
Good English

Domaine des Entrefaux
26600 Chanos-Curson
Tel 75 07 33 38, Fax 75 07 35 27
Open Mon–Sat 9–12, 14–18

Cave Coopérative Clairette de Die
26150 Die
Tel 75 22 02 22
Open Mon–Sun 8–12.30,
13.30–18.30
Credit cards accepted
English by appointment

Hotels and Restaurants
H Hotel *R* Restaurant

Ampuis
R Le Côte Rôtie
Place de l'Eglise, 69420 Ampuis
Tel 74 56 12 05, Fax 74 56 00 20
FF90–235

Chambres d'Hôte through
Domaine Gilles Barge
(see Producers)
Rooms FF250 for two, including
breakfast

Condrieu
HR Beau Rivage
2, rue Beau Rivage, 69420 Condrieu
Tel 74 59 52 24, Fax 74 59 59 36
Rooms FF500–820, Meals
FF165–600

Chavanay
HR Alain Charles
Route nationale, 42410 Chavanay
Tel 74 87 23 02, Fax 74 87 01 42
Rooms FF200–250, Meals FF
92–290

Serrières
HR Schaeffer
Quai Jean-Roche, 07340 Serrières
Tel 75 34 00 07, Fax 75 34 08 79
Rooms FF165–285, Meals
FF120–320

Tain l'Hermitage
HR Reynaud
82, avenue du President-Roosevelt,
26600 Tain l'Hermitage
Tel 75 07 22 10, Fax 75 08 03 53
Rooms FF350–500, Meals
FF160–350

HR Mercure
69, avenue Jean-Jaurès
Tel 75 08 65 00, Fax 75 08 66 05
Rooms FF380–550, Meals
FF120–280

Cornas
R Ollier
Route nationale, 07130 Cornas
Tel 75 40 32 17 Meals FF85–175

Granges-lès-Beaumont
HR Les Vieilles Granges
26600 Granges-lès-Beaumont
Tel 75 71 50 43 or 75 71 62 83
Fax 75 71 59 79
Rooms FF300–350, Meals FF80–150

Die
HR La Petite Auberge
Avenue Sadi-Carnot, 26150 Die
Tel 75 22 05 91, Fax 75 22 24 60
Rooms FF150–260, Meals FF90–230

H Hôtel des Alpes
Rue C. Buffardel
Tel 75 22 15 83, Fax 75 22 09 39
Rooms FF190–230

The Loire Valley

The vast Loire river runs over 1,000km from trickling beginnings high in the Massif Central to stately, wide Atlantic estuary at Nantes. It's a region well beloved by British tourists, who come for the river views, flat cycling country and splendid châteaux. Many of the châteaux were originally built to keep meddling dowager queens and scheming mistresses at arm's length from the Paris court – far enough away to stop them meddling, not too far to be insulting. Perhaps the Windsors should try it.

The wines of the Loire are, to generalize grossly, more expensive the further inland you go. The region is best known for its white wines, but significant amounts of red and pink are made too. Muscadet, made nearest the coast, in the Pays Nantais, used to be thought of as cheap and cheerful, but bad harvests and a syndrome that could be called 'what the market will bear' have all but put paid to that notion in the UK. In the region itself, however, you can buy a good bottle for about FF20.

Following the river east, the wine region of Anjou, around the town of Angers, concentrates on the Chenin Blanc grape, known in the Loire as Pineau de la Loire, which makes little-known but splendid dry whites and excellent sweet whites – a must for lovers of dessert wines to explore. There are basic rosés and reds, too, some of which are great value.

In Saumur the emphasis is on sparkling wines, stored in caves carved straight into the hillside from the white tufa clay, and in good, chewy reds from Cabernet Franc. Touraine offers more red, particularly in Chinon and Bourgueil, plus sparkling and still whites in Vouvray and Montlouis. The river now heads north, to the city of Orléans, but the wine trail heads across country to Sancerre and Pouilly-sur-Loire, where the white grape changes again, to Sauvignon Blanc. This last wine area nestles in comfortably beside Chablis and the Aube, and is covered in The Golden Triangle chapter.

For this present chapter, I have divided the route into three sections to allow you either to visit one of them for a separate long weekend or to link them together for a proper holiday. After Touraine, it may well seem more convenient to head back to a port rather than to continue overland, but if you do want to link Touraine with Sancerre, a suitable route is described at the end of this chapter. There's more to the Loire Valley, of course, as you'd expect from a river covering such a wide area; but I think these are the areas most worth exploring to start with.

The other fact I should mention at this stage is that this guide will ignore all the blandishments of châteaux etc – well, nearly all. Much has been written elsewhere about these beautiful buildings, and it's easy to nip off the route and follow the signs to Chenonceau if that's what takes your fancy. (And, I admit, it did mine.) But it's not something I'll be concentrating on – there's too much interesting wine about. Pick your own castles and follow me on the wine route.

PLANNING THE ROUTE

This is where the crossings from the UK's south coast ports really come into their own. Whether you take a day or a night crossing depends on where you start from in the UK and whether you prefer to be bored stiff on a six-hour day crossing with the prospect of proper French food and a decent bed at the end of it, or to sleep through the crossing but be woken up at a truly ungodly hour and spend the rest of the day in a daze. I usually take a night crossing but pay for it in drowsiness the following day.

The Brittany Ferries crossing into St-Malo, however, is long enough to let you get a decent night's sleep, and you can be in Nantes by lunch-time via a quiet dual carriageway. As a bonus, the approach to the harbour is very pretty and worth braving the freezing winds on deck for. The longer crossing has not only helped the beauty sleep but brought you closer to your final destination.

For day crossings, on the other hand, the shorter the better. Both Le Havre and Caen have reasonably convenient motorway connections and are better for reaching Saumur and Tours. Cherbourg is further, and the roads aren't so good, but it's a feasible second choice for Nantes or Angers. Dieppe is reasonable too. You can pick up the motorway at Rouen, but driving through Rouen is a horrible experience; it's very badly signposted and not recommended for the first-time visitor – A-level navigation students only.

From Calais or Ostend all roads lead to Paris, I'm afraid, and the western section of the Loire seems dauntingly far. Sancerre is easier to reach from these crossings, as is Touraine, but Anjou-Saumur and the Pays Nantais will need longer than a five-day trip if you're not to see more of the inside of your car than feels comfortable.

The Loire is ideal for 'open-jaw' trips: out on one route, back from another port served by the same company. Consider travelling Portsmouth–St-Malo–Caen–Portsmouth with Brittany Ferries, Southampton–Cherbourg–Dieppe–Newhaven with Stena Sealink, or Portsmouth–Cherbourg–Le Havre–Portsmouth with P&O. All the ferry companies allow you to travel this way on their cheaper tickets as well as standard returns.

The Pays Nantais

WHAT YOU'LL SEE IN THE CELLAR

Muscadet the wine is made from Muscadet the grape, also known as Melon de Bourgogne. There's also a VDQS called Gros Plant du Pays Nantais, made from the Gros Plant, which is related to the grapes used for making cognac. It's like Muscadet only less so, being even more tart and astringent. It doesn't have much going for it, except perhaps its price.

The key factor with Muscadet is the process which leaves the wine *sur lie*, on its lees. Muscadet is by nature neutral-tasting, so you can add more flavour to the wine by allowing it to rest for

a minium of five months over winter on the dead yeast cells –
the lees – once fermentation is over. The wine picks up a
yeasty flavour and more character, and if it's left undisturbed
will retain some of the carbon dioxide produced during fermentation, giving it a lively taste. You don't fine this wine, and you
don't filter it either, preferably. You handle it as little as possible
to preserve the freshness and sparkle, and bottle it straight from
the tank either between 1 March and 30 June or from 15
October to 30 November. Regulations ban the bottling during
the summer as the heat can interfere with the wine.

Wines that aren't *sur lie* can now only be labelled simply
'Muscadet'. These can come from anywhere in the region. *Sur
lie* wines are divided into three areas: the biggest area, southeast of Nantes, is Muscadet de Sèvre et Maine. Then there's
Muscadet des Coteaux de la Loire (northeast of Nantes) and a
new designation, Muscadet Côtes de Grand Lieu, covering
vineyards around the large lake southwest of Nantes.

An interesting quirk in Muscadet winemaking is that the
fermentation/maturation tanks are set into the floor. When you
enter the cellar, which is usually at ground level, very often all
you see is what looks like a series of manhole covers. Beneath
these are tiled or glass fibre tanks, which you may be able to
look inside. This subterranean habit evolved because producers
usually didn't have below-ground cellars but wanted to find
cool conditions for the wine to rest on its lees. A blanket of
earth seemed just the thing. You'd think that underground
tanks would be impervious to disturbance from the elements,
but one producer I met refuses to bottle his wine when the
wind's blowing; he says it unsettles the lees and you have to wait
for absolutely still conditions to make sure that no sediment is
disturbed when you bottle, or you won't get a clear wine.

Like many aspects of wine production, the practice of making Muscadet *sur lie* is open to abuse. Many consumers know
that the term *sur lie* means they are buying a better wine, and
are prepared to pay more for it, but there is no law stating how
great a surface area of wine at the bottom of a tank should be
exposed to the lees. Obviously a wine matured in a tall, thin
tank won't get as much exposure to the lees as wine in a shallow tank with a big bottom, if you see what I mean. The producers I recommend below, however, play fair with their *sur lie*
maturation and you can taste the difference in the glass.

EXPLORING THE PAYS NANTAIS

Working along the Loire from west to east, the Muscadet region is the first to explore. In some ways it's the easiest, too, as it's compact and there's only one main style of wine to investigate. I concentrate on the area southeast of Nantes, because it produces the best wines.

The Nantes and Anjou-Saumur wine committees clubbed together in 1993 and organized a wine route that runs seamlessly through their two regions. This was clearly not an easy task – talk to the women who were instrumental in creating it, and a shadow crosses their faces as they remember all the wrangling over routes that went on. Being on a signposted wine route can make a huge difference to direct sales, and loud were the wails from bypassed producers. The Nantais signs show a bunch of grapes in green and yellow, and are enormous; the Anjou-Saumur signs have the same logo but in orange and purple, and are more modest and therefore harder to spot.

The obvious place to begin the tour is in **Nantes** itself. This city has had a bad press, but I found it reasonably straightforward to drive through and soon found L'Hôtel, a rather faded but welcoming establishment, without a restaurant, well placed for heading out onto the wine route. I also hear good reports of the Amiral.

Staying in the middle of a big city isn't everyone's idea of fun, and I'd offer you suggestions for country stops if I could; but, curiously, although there are plenty of good restaurants on the Muscadet wine route, decent hotels are thin on the ground. You are unlikely to stay in the region more than a night or two unless you develop a passion for the local wines, so perhaps a couple of days in the city will be OK just this once.

Being so close to the coast, Nantes has seafood and fish of unparalleled freshness. I had excellent scallops at L'Océanide, an unpretentious neighbourhood restaurant with the look of a 1930s ocean liner. La Poissonnerie is a new place, close to L'Hôtel, where mountainous *plateaux de fruits de mer*, complete with whole crabs, were the order of the day. Do book; even on a freezing Tuesday night in late autumn there wasn't a spare table in sight. Drink Muscadet, of course; nowhere is wine and food as obviously complementary as here. You can practically taste the salty sea tang in the wine. (Or was I just imagining it?)

Nantes is also a useful place to organize picnic provisions. There's a fine baker, the Boulangerie Chez Marie on Rue de la Fosse, and Pascal Beillevaire's cheese shop on Rue Contrescarpe, where they'll package your cheese for a picnic or to ensure it will survive the rigours of the Channel crossing. There's also a brilliant chocolate shop, G Gautier-Debotte (which is likewise on Rue de la Fosse), where you step back in time into a sales room with a gilded ceiling, mirrors, cut glass, ornate panelling and even an ottoman to sit on while you take it all in. Gifts include chocolates filled with Muscadet and *berlingots de Nantes* (pyramid-shaped boiled sweets) in pretty gift boxes.

To join the wine route leave Nantes heading south, following signs for Poitiers and Bordeaux. You'll cross two bridges spanning the Ile Beaulieu. After the second bridge turn right, off the N149, following signs to Vertou. This is where the marked route begins, and signposted off it you'll soon see directions for the **MAISON DES VINS DE NANTES** in **La Haie-Fouassière** (on the D74).

This is a very good place to start your tour. Financed by the winegrowers' committee, it's full of enthusiastic, multilingual staff who will give you a free tasting (including one of the rare reds made in the region), sell you up to six bottles of wine and a range of tasteful souvenirs, such as a rather nice green *sommelier*'s apron, and hand you more maps, leaflets and stickers than you know what to do with. Perched up on the hill, you have a fine view of the vineyards – a view that may well be improved if their plan to convert an old water-tower into a viewing gallery comes off.

From the Maison du Vin to the first producer is only a short hop; turn right, back onto the D74 in the direction you came, and **BONNETEAU-GUESSLIN** is signposted off to the left. Olivier Bonneteau will show you the floor vats, the *cuve souterrain*, and you'll be offered two wines: a Muscadet de Sèvre-et-Maine, light, fresh and crisp, and the Domaine de la Ferronnière, fuller-bodied and with richer fruit. It's commonly held that Muscadet needs to be drunk young – the most recent vintage for preference. Get away from the commercial products, however, and you'll discover, as I did here, that a couple of years' bottle age can do the wine more good than you'd expect.

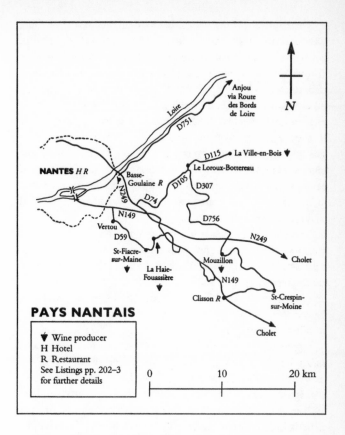

The unassuming M Bonneteau, who speaks excellent English, says: 'I try to make Muscadet, no more no less, with all its typicity and flavour.' His prices are astonishing, ranging from FF19 to FF22.40, and represent really excellent value.

From La Haie turn back onto the wine route and head for **CHÉREAU-CARRÉ**, signposted to the right off the D59 after **St-Fiacre-sur-Maine**. (This means doubling back, but I don't think Chéreau-Carré is the best place to start the tour.)

This is a large operation, comprising six separate estates, with a commercial outlook. English-speaking guides will show you the vineyards and a ruined tower complete with secret passage (inaccessible, alas, although you can climb the tower). The grounds are pretty and the cellars are decorated with grotesque woodcarvings of Rabelais characters. There's a barrel with a glass panel to show you what the lees look like.

They specialize in ageing Muscadet in oak, not something commonly done and not something I particularly warmed to, either, and you're unlikely to meet the winemaker and be able to find out why he does it. Prices here are nearly double those at Bonneteau-Guesslin, reflecting perhaps the cost of marketing activity. Do you think the wines are nearly twice as good?

If all this prickly, fresh, acidic wine has given you an appetite, then stay on the route as far as **Clisson**; it's very clearly waymarked. (If you're really feeling peckish, avoid the spur signposted off on the right to Aigrefeuille. You'll only have to turn around and come back again.) Clisson is a pretty town full of Italianate architecture with a medieval castle and covered market hall.

La Bonne Auberge is a Michelin-starred restaurant, but friendly and unpretentious, offering good value at lunch-time with a menu for FF95 upwards and an excellent selection of local wines. Smashing scallops. After lunch, stroll through the town, or leave on the N149 in the direction of Cholet and turn right into a villa where you can walk through the grounds and admire the view.

Retrace your steps and pick up the wine route again as it leaves Clisson on the St-Crespin-sur-Moine road. When you reach **Mouzillon**, look out for Xavier Gouraud's **DOMAINE DES RIGOLES DU PIN**. This is another small property run by a husband-and-wife team, and they're totally committed to their winemaking. This is where they won't bottle if it's windy. Here, too, the wines give the lie to the idea that Muscadet can't age; there's an '87 for FF28, and more recent wines ranging from FF16 for the Gros Plant to FF21–25 for Muscadet.

On the first Saturday in July, Mouzillon holds a Nuit du Muscadet which looks like quite a party, judging by the photos on view in various albums in the tasting-room.

Incidentally, there's a biscuit made in Mouzillon which is often served to accompany wine tastings. Some of these are completely sugar-free, which is OK, but avoid the slightly sweet ones; they'll make the wine taste sour.

Onward again, on the route (I defy you to get lost on this one, signs are so insistent) to Le Loroux-Bottereau. Here, if you wish, deviate onto the D115 in the direction of Landemont; the **ABBAYE DE STE-RADEGONDE** is signposted on the left at **La Ville-en-Bois**. I mention this place because they've set up a rather interesting wine museum, full of old implements. There's even a travelling still in the courtyard, its bottom helpfully punched out by the French government just in case anyone gets ideas about putting it into use again. Marvel at the pain endured by the wearer of the chain-mail gloves used to strip the vine-stems of parasites.

Ah yes, the wines. Well, there's a very average Muscadet and a pleasant, light red Gamay. There's also a most peculiar-tasting sparkling wine. You may prefer to see the museum and leave a donation in the collecting-box before making your excuses.

In the tradition of leaving the best until last, here's a restaurant I'd rate as unmissable. You can catch this one at the end of a Muscadet tour, or while following the pretty Route des Bords de Loire towards Angers. Villa Mon Rêve is north of **Basse-Goulaine**, where the wine route finishes. Look out for a right turn off the D751 just after the intersection with the N249.

Chef Gérard Ryngel looks just like Pavarotti, as demonstrated by the remarkably friendly caricature of him by Ralph Steadman (drawn <u>after</u> lunch, apparently, which explains it). He shows no sign of Pavarottian temperament, however, producing instead meals of high quality featuring local produce, notably pike. Watch out for his potato purée – it's 50% butter. He didn't get where he is today by producing lean cuisine. In winter he serves *tarte Muscadet*: 'not using a tart Muscadet'. The wine list, apparently the longest in Nantes, is full of Muscadet, with prices starting at FF70. Here I drank the 1976 vintage which for me finally laid to rest the Muscadet-can't-age notion.

He has a fascinating attitude to menu pricing. In effect, all starters and all main courses cost the same. If you want to eat for a certain price, tell him, and he'll create a menu for exactly that figure with wines to match each course. In the winter, he and his wife host Sunday lunch around a huge table. If ever there was a restaurant operating from the heart, this is it.

From here it's either back to Nantes for a last night, or directly onwards to Anjou and inland to more dramatic country side. If you're heading back into Nantes, watch out for the heavy traffic. Most people live south of the city, where it's cheaper, and the queues leaving Nantes in the evening can be quite horrendous.

Anjou-Saumur

WHAT YOU'LL FIND IN THE CELLAR

You'll find all styles of wine here. The white grape is now the Chenin Blanc, which is used for sparkling wines in Saumur, where its high acidity is very important, and for sweet Coteaux du Layon and the intense, dry Savennières.

Anjou Rouge is made from Gamay or Cabernets Franc and Sauvignon, and varies in quality from basic to rather good. One step up is Anjou-Villages, made exclusively from Cabernet and only in the Layon and Aubance valleys. Saumur-Champigny is often the most intense, deep-coloured of all Anjou's reds. It's currently very popular in Paris, which explains its higher price. Anjou is closely associated with rosés. Fashion has turned against rosé and production is declining, but some producers, notably Didier Richou (qv), offer very fine pink wines without a blush.

EXPLORING ANJOU-SAUMUR

From Nantes, pick up the Route des Bords de Loire at **Basse-Goulaine** (the D751). This is well signposted and indeed forms part of the wine route connecting the Pays Nantais with Anjou, running close to the south bank. You pass first through Muscadet vineyards and those of Coteaux d'Ancenis, light red and pink VDQS wines from Gamay and Cabernet.

If your tour starts in Anjou, the town of **Angers** is a fine place to stop, once you've braced yourself to deal with big-town traffic. One of my favourite hotels in the glamorous-room/fancy food class is here, the Pavillon Le Quéré. The Le Quérés (he cooks, she organizes front-of-house and, particularly, the wine list) opened this operation, set in a beautiful 19th-century town house, only a couple of years ago, after building a reputation for fine cooking elsewhere in the town. Bedrooms are named after Anjou appellations and are elegant-modern in style; mine had the fanciest bathroom I've enjoyed in a long time. Food, served in a conservatory dining-room, is modern and Michelin-starred.

Leave Angers on the N23 in the direction of Nantes, turning off on the right, onto the D106, to **Savennières**. (If you're approaching from Nantes, on the D751, turn left in Rochefort-sur-Loire and cross the river to reach the village.)

Savennières is a small appellation, making dry Chenin Blanc whites. They used to make sweet wines here, requiring low yields. The law changed the wine from sweet to dry in 1952, but didn't increase the permitted yields to match. That means the dry whites from Savennières are very powerful, concentrated, long-lasting wines. Although many experts rate these among the greatest whites in the world, they're hardly known in the UK, and I really think it's worth getting acquainted.

Another quirk of the region is that nearly all the wines are made by women. Mme Joly started it all by buying the entire CLOS DE LA COULÉE DE SERRANT appellation in 1959 (not as daunting as it sounds, it's only 7ha). From Savennières, follow the road to Epiré and you'll see the estate signposted off to the right. Today the wines are made by her son Nicolas, merchant banker turned advocate of biodynamic agriculture – an approach which involves working the land when the astronomical conjunctions are favourable and treating the vines with homeopathic plant sprays.

If this philosophy interests you (and it certainly does me), M Joly will offer you a passionate explanation of it. If you taste the results, you'll understand why he's able to charge so much for them – Coulée de Serrant has the depth and intensity you would expect from such passionate commitment. This is not an estate for casual visits (there's a hefty minimum purchase price of FF300, although a range of wines more modestly priced than the Coulée is available), but for an in-depth exploration of a wine you can't do better. M Joly knows he's way out on a limb compared to current accepted thinking, but points out the fact that some of France's finest estates now grow their grapes biodynamically, so there's more to it than meets the eye.

Do take the opportunity to walk in the vineyards, as the view from high above the river is stunning. The next estate, **DOMAINE AUX MOINES**, also has beautiful vineyard views (retrace your steps along the road to Savennières to reach it). Mme Laroche owns part of the vineyard La Roche-aux-Moines, as do the Jolys; that, and Coulée de Serrant, are the two named *crus,* or growths, you'll find in Savennières.

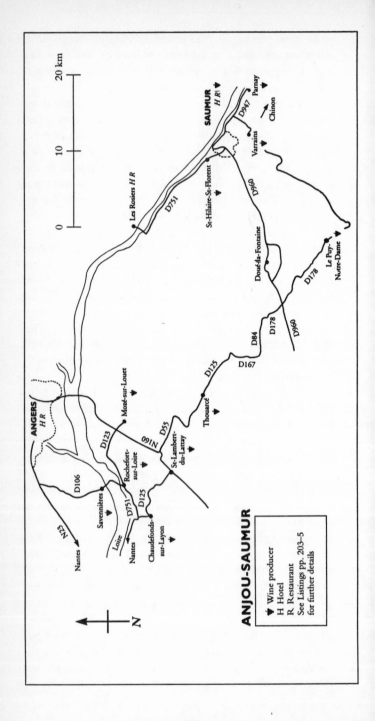

ANJOU-SAUMUR

Wine producer
H Hotel
R Restaurant
See Listings pp. 203–5
for further details

Mme Laroche is bird-like and intense. Her wines have a markedly different character in each vintage and provide an object lesson in how much wines from the same vineyard are influenced by the year's changing weather.

At both these properties you'll notice the elegant formal gardens and expansive architecture, revealing that money has been made from their vineyards for several centuries (La Roche-aux-Moines was planted by monks in the 12th century).

DOMAINE DU CLOSEL also has a fine château setting. Run by Mme de Jessey, tall and with a ready laugh, this property lies near the centre of the village on the banks of the river, and visitors are welcome to walk and picnic in the grounds.

Mme de Jessey plays a major role in promoting the wines of Savennières, lamenting the fact that the local council won't put up signs in the village to guide visitors to winemakers (something every wine explorer suffers for the lack of). In addition to classic Savennières (prices start at just FF50), Mme de Jessey offers good quality, well-priced reds.

For a picture of the younger generation of woman winemaker in action, head back over the bridge to the south bank. Stop first, if you wish, for lunch or a stroll in the pretty village of Béhuard, marooned on a narrow island in the middle of the Loire and accessible from the bridge. Then, in **Rochefort-sur-Loire**, turn left by the church and head out of the village, with the cemetery on your left. After about 800m turn right by a hut and you'll find the **MOULIN DE CHAUVIGNÉ**.

This is a brand-new estate. Sylvie Termeau and her partner Christian Plessis produced their first vintage in 1992. She's proud of the 80-year-old vines planted on her land, with their low, concentrated yields. She makes excellent Savennières, a smooth Coteaux du Layon and an Anjou Rouge.

It's difficult starting up a wine estate from scratch – vineyards are hard to find, the investment in machinery is enormous and the wine ties up your money for years while you wait for it to mature. The Moulin de Chauvigné is about as far from the grand estates north of the river as it's possible to be, but Sylvie draws inspiration from the longer-established women winemakers whose example she follows. Her wines are very fairly priced, good value for money and well worth your support, and you'll receive a friendly welcome here and as full an explanation of the wines as you desire.

Returning to Rochefort, look out for the **DOMAINE DES
BAUMARD** estate on the right just after the cemetery. Here,
young Florent Baumard won't show you the cellars ('no aesthetic attractions') but will take you to an 18th-century tasting-
room, complete with original wall-paintings, and offer a
selection of the estate's range including Savennières (made for
drinking much sooner than the long-lived Joly style) and the
sweet Quarts de Chaume, only made around Rochefort.
(Incidentally, Anjou's other sweet wine, Bonnezeaux, is made
around Thouarcé.) There's also Anjou Rouge, which I bought
here in 1992 for about FF24 a bottle, and it was splendid –
lean, chewy, an ideal summer red.

Newcomers to Loire wines are in safe hands at Baumard.
Florent, who speaks faultless English, said: 'We don't mind
people knowing nothing about wine and are very happy to
help them discover new pleasures. They may help us discover
their pleasures. We don't like people pretending they know
about wine who are just pretenders, but we are afraid there is
nothing we can do about it.'

The tour now heads away from the Loire into sweet wine
territory. If you're convinced you can't stand the stuff, please
don't be put off this part of the route – the road meanders
along the little river Layon, through very attractive scenery.

In the Layon valley, autumn morning mists encourage the
grapes to rot. This is 'noble rot', *Botrytis cinerea*, the same grey
rot that's the scourge of gardeners. Tiny filaments of mould
pierce the grape-skin, then the heat of the afternoon sun allows
the water in the grape juice to evaporate through the holes,
producing a honeyed concentration in the remaining juice
that's absolutely delicious. You need plenty of acidity to balance
such sweetness, and Chenin has an abundance of it. These wines
are little-known in the UK, and deserve closer acquaintance.

First, if you will, a little detour. From Rochefort turn right
onto the D751. In Denée turn right onto the D123 and then
look out for **DOMAINE RICHOU** on your right, before **Mozé-
sur-Louet**. Didier Richou makes a wide range of good wines
at remarkably fair prices. His sweet wine is Coteaux de
l'Aubance, similar in style to Layon wines, from along the river
Aubance which runs parallel to the Layon. He offers a dry
Chenin Blanc called Anjou Sec for FF24, and very well
rounded reds – the Anjou-Villages, from old vines, for FF27, is

the best of these. He has good rosés, too, and even a sparkler. His cellars aren't especially interesting but he has a large, welcoming tasting-room and is very hospitable.

Retrace your steps through Rochefort, along a piece of road by now becoming very familiar, and pick up the wine road on the left where it turns off the D751. This takes you onto one of the prettiest sections of the route, and to one of the finest producers you'll meet in these pages.

DOMAINE GAUDARD is right on the wine route at **Chaudefonds-sur-Layon**. Pierre Aguilas doesn't speak English, but says it doesn't matter a jot and that communication is never a problem with his British visitors. Hardly surprising in a man with such enthusiasm for his product.

He offers various Coteaux du Layon from different villages, showing incredible concentration, most notably the Cuvée Claire, named after the woman who runs the local wine committee. I'm not usually one to rave about the tropical fruit salad tastes I find in my glass but I'm afraid it's unavoidable here. More prosaic, but also good, is the firm red Anjou-Villages.

This is an ideal place to come if you want the very best of the region's sweet wines and to find out more about the subtle differences in flavour between various villages' wines. There's plenty of room to taste, with tables and stools, informative displays and outdoor seating in summer. One to raise the spirits.

The wine route now leads you to **St-Lambert-du-Lattay**. There's a splendid MUSÉE DE LA VIGNE ET DU VIN, which I think is one of the best I've come across. Much more than simply displays of old implements, the exhibits give a real sense of the movement of work with the seasons and the weather. It doesn't take itself too seriously, either – look out for a series of rude wine-related pictures hidden behind screens, which you have to tug a cord to reveal. There's a game involving pulling out drawers full of wine-type smells, and even a tasting-fountain which is filled with Coteaux du Layon on special occasions. Next door a Maison du Vin offers tastings of local wines.

In St-Lambert turn off the wine route onto the N160, heading southwest, and you'll soon see the **DOMAINE DU SAUVEROY** on your right, looking like a ranch house. Pascal Cailleau, who's not yet 30, runs the estate with skill and overwhelming enthusiasm. He offers a wide range of well-priced wines: rosé FF19.50, Anjou-Villages FF23, Coteaux du Layon

FF23 upwards, sparkler FF36. He'll also sell you wines from the pump for ridiculously little. Ask him to point you towards a walk in his vineyards, high above the valley floor.

Now let us take an overview, briefly. For some reason, decent country hotels are hard to find in this region. It's perfectly possible to travel from Nantes to Saumur in a day, if you're linking the two regions, but you won't have much time for vineyard visiting and a first night in Angers is well worth considering (the town also has plenty of architectural and historical interest). But you might prefer instead to be based in Saumur and make a couple of circular trips. Saumur is a lovely place to stay in, which is why I'm mentioning it now rather than waiting until it comes along in the normal course of things.

To continue: head back into St-Lambert to rejoin the wine route, the D55 and then the D125. (Watch out for the narrow bends in St-Lambert. I was staggered by the size of the juggernauts that force their way through the tiny town, and they don't take prisoners.) The wine road meanders through pretty countryside with plenty of picnic opportunities.

After **Thouarcé**, look for a sign on the left to **CHÂTEAU DE FESLES**. It's a beautiful building, in fine, well-kept grounds. One of France's most famous *pâtissiers*, Gaston Lenôtre, is part owner. His image is much in evidence (Quentin Crisp fans will admire his hat), as is his influence, in sugar and chocolate sculptures, displays of local breads, and the inevitable books for sale.

Make an appointment with an English-speaking guide and you'll enter an air-conditioned room full of barrels bought after one year's use from top sweet winemakers Château d'Yquem. See the fermentation cellars, full of stainless steel tanks and controlled by a wonderful electronic console looking exactly like an early computerized theatre lighting board. You can see this console through a glass partition in the tasting-room. Digital read-outs reveal the precise temperature each vat is fermenting at, and you can input new temperatures at will (which is exactly what my guide did. No doubt the cellar-master cursed him). Code: green light = chiller on, red light = heater on. There's also an enormous *tri* table. Every bunch of grapes brought in passes across this table at harvest and is sorted by hand according to quality.

Note the horse's head above the entrance, denoting that the building was formerly stables. Prices are higher than the norm here but the Anjou Rouge, for instance, although FF32, has won several awards and is gorgeous. And if you buy 11 bottles you get a twelfth one free. Is this an offer you can't refuse?

Onward now to Saumur, either following the wine road or, for the impatient, heading for Doué-la-Fontaine and taking the D960 direct to town. Staying on the wine route has the advantage of bringing you into **Le Puy-Notre-Dame**, along the D178, where you'll find the **CHÂTEAU DE BEAUREGARD** if you're lucky (or, like me, phone them from outside the 13th century church after 15 minutes' fruitless searching and they'll come and find you).

Mme Gourdon will show you round the charming, small estate and into the cellar tasting-room. They've only been bottling their own wine since 1989, when her husband took over from his father; previously they sold all the wine to the local co-op. Their Cabernet de Saumur Rosé is bottled in sterilized bottles with an absolute minimum of sulphur: 'So no headache.' Hangover-proof wine must be the coming thing. This is a very attractive wine, as is their Saumur Rouge and, for that matter, their Saumur Blanc. There's one sweetish (*moelleux*) wine for FF50 and all the others sell for FF25, which must make book-keeping easy.

The Gourdons don't get many visitors yet, and they'd like more, so you should get a warm welcome. They have an imaginative way of disposing of the bottles they open for tasting...

There are two hotels I'd recommend in **Saumur**, but neither has a restaurant so you can ring the changes each night; plenty of good places to eat at are within reach. The hotel with the best view is the Anne d'Anjou, restored from ruin a decade or so ago. It faces the Loire and I think the best rooms are those with a river view. There's a splendid staircase with a *trompe-l'oeil* ceiling, and parking at the back. The staff are enormously helpful. To reach it, carry on along the main street even when it appears to be for pedestrians only, and turn right at an improbably tiny roundabout on the banks of the river. It's on the right just after a second roundabout.

Cheaper, but no less considerately-staffed, is the Central (from the main street into town turn left just as the road becomes 'pedestrian priority', then sharp right into a tiny sidestreet). All the rooms are differently decorated and there's a subterranean car park.

The Central has the advantage of being right by what I mentally named Restaurant Street, Rue St-Nicolas. All manner of food is here, plus an excellent picnic shop, Le Traiteur, great for cheese, salads and *rillettes* (potted meats). I enjoyed the cooking at Les Chandelles. Two other reasonably-priced options are near each other on the Rue Maréchal Leclerc, the main road out of town but within easy walking distance of the hotels: L'Escargot and La Croquière.

I also found some very good, simple food in a most unlikely place, the Brasserie Napoléon on the Place de la Bilange, near the tourist information centre. This is a basic bar-brasserie, with banquettes that reminded me of the coffee-bars of my adolescence. I discovered it while recovering from food poisoning, having been told to eat only vegetables – not easy in France. Here, surrounded by the youth of Saumur hunched over a coke, and accompanied by ZZ Top, I had splendid soup and fresh *crudités*, while my husband Ian was surprised by the best grilled lamb chops he'd been offered in a long time. Which just goes to prove the old adage that you can't judge a French eatery by its external appearance.

Saumur is a lively little town with plenty of atmosphere, dominated by the Château de Saumur perched high above it and by the Loire itself. There's a wide mix of architectural styles, particularly between the castle and the river on the tiny twisting streets of the old town (plenty of restaurants here, too). Stroll along the river-bank, it's beautiful at night with the lights beneath the bridge playing on the water.

Saumur makes a good base for touring, and you can easily make the route circular by returning to the Loire at Gennes. Across the river from Gennes, at **Les Rosiers**, the Jeanne de Laval hotel-restaurant is popular with British visitors but manages to keep a high standard of cooking nevertheless.

The town is famous for its cavalry school, the Cadre Noir, and for mushrooms (there's a museum, naturally) which grow in the damp tufa-clay cellars quarried out of the local hillsides. These caves are also crucial to the development of Saumur's famous sparkling wine, providing the constant temperature necessary while wines mature. The founder of local firm Gratien & Meyer (qv) didn't even carve out his own cellars, he simply bought up the land surrounding already-quarried caves – caves that nobody wanted; the price was correspondingly low.

Loire sparkling wines can be pink and even red as well as white. There are various appellations, principally Saumur and the more stringent Crémant de Loire. Still reds are made as Saumur, from Cabernets Sauvignon or Franc, or as classier Saumur-Champigny, from nine villages southeast of the town.

Several large sparkling-wine houses have their headquarters here, making a big play for visitors. I can thoroughly recommend that you visit Gratien & Meyer and Bouvet-Ladubay. **BOUVET-LADUBAY** is located in **St-Hilaire-St-Florent**, just north of Saumur. A guided tour in English costs FF5, and includes the cellars and the process for making traditional method sparkling wine (see Champagne, pages 67–70). Note the old packing hall, with its ornate cast-iron pillars, now used to display a collection of old carriages. Up an awkward spiral staircase there's a library of 6,000 old labels housed on revolving wooden filing cabinets. Very Victorian. It's not included on the general tour, but do ask to see it anyway.

The tour fee includes a tasting, and the wines are of very high quality, with sparklers from FF45 to FF80 and still reds from FF26 to FF39. Across the road the company has opened a museum of modern art, with a recently-renovated old theatre on the first floor.

Just along from Bouvet is **LANGLOIS-CHÂTEAU**. I wasn't so impressed by their wines but I thoroughly enjoyed the walk up into their vineyards which forms part of their longer guided tour. Take your camera: there's a splendid view of the river and across to the château.

GRATIEN & MEYER is on the other side of Saumur. As you head out along the D947 towards Chinon, their imposing buildings are set into the hillside on your right. Tours are free, in English and preceded by a 12-minute video. You'll see a section of their 10km of caves during the half-hour walk – including the Grand Caveau, a subterranean banqueting room – and all parts of the sparkling wine process, before tasting the finished product (also free).

You can take the tasting a stage further by joining one of the English-language classes at Gratien & Meyer's wine school. These cover sparkling wine production and professional tasting technique, moving on to an overview of wines from the whole of the Loire. They cost from FF35 to FF175, run from May to October and need to be booked in advance.

In contrast to the shy style of sister establishment **Alfred Gratien** (qv) in Epernay, the reception here is highly-organized and professional, but the winemaking is equally meticulous and the quality very high. Cuvée Flamme, in particular, is excellent and one of the best examples of sparkling Saumur wine.

The wine road now moves towards the heart of red Loire wine-making, Chinon and Bourgueil. Turning right from Gratien & Meyer, the road hugs the river as you pass through the Saumur-Champigny wine district (along the D947). Here there are several producers to visit. Perched high up on the hill in **Parnay** is **CHÂTEAU DE TARGÉ**. Come for the view, at least; the selection of wine could well be limited to one vintage, which may or may not be to your taste.

Another nearby producer worthy of note is **DOMAINE DES ROCHES-NEUVES** at **Varrains** whose excellent wines were the hit of the Loire stand at the Decanter Wine Fair in 1993.

I mentioned the food-poisoning episode (the restaurant I suspect doesn't appear in this guide). I consulted a doctor in Saumur. You know you're in a winemaking area when the doctor doesn't warn you off alcohol but apologizes instead that your furred tongue will wreck your tasting ability. Naturally he had a hot tip, and here it is: Saumur reds to keep, in a traditional style, from Patrick Vadé at the **DOMAINE ST-VINCENT** in Saumur. Any good? No idea. I couldn't taste a thing that day.

Touraine

WHAT YOU'LL SEE IN THE CELLAR

Touraine is home to the Loire's finest reds: Chinon, Bourgueil and St-Nicolas-de-Bourgueil. These are made from Cabernet Franc, cousin of Cabernet Sauvignon (which is also permitted in small quantities). Known locally as Breton, Cabernet Franc often tastes slightly minty and 'stalky' and is leaner and less overwhelmingly blackcurranty than Sauvignon. The Loire way with red wines is not to aim for a strong, oaky taste, and the number and newness of the barrels you see in the cellar are a fair indication of the producer's attitude to this tradition.

East of Tours, the less fashionable, good-value wines include Gamay de Touraine (light, fruity red) and Sauvignon de Touraine. Sauvignon Blanc makes crisp, dry, high-acidity wines with a grassy, gooseberry taste and smell, best drunk young; and these examples are cheaper than those of Sancerre and Pouilly-sur-Loire. Chenin Blanc is found, too, most famously in Vouvray. Chenin is so malleable that dry, sweet and sparkling Vouvray can be made, so do read the label. You'll also come across some rosé.

EXPLORING TOURAINE

The easiest way of exploring Touraine is to split it down the middle, taking Tours itself as the dividing line. The division into wine regions along the Loire is fairly arbitrary as far as the wine tourist is concerned. We've moved district, to the area controlled by the city of Tours, but in reality Chinon and Bourgueil can just as easily be visited from Saumur, barely half an hour's drive away, as by decamping into the region itself. Any excuse to stay a little longer in Saumur is welcome, and I think the standard of hotels is better there, too.

If you've been following the red wine trail through Saumur-Champigny, keep going along the D947 to Montsoreau and then take the D751 following the river Vienne to Chinon.

Chinon is dominated by the ruins of its imposing castle on the skyline above the town. Narrow old streets run beneath. Just off the main square you'll find one of the strangest wine museums around: it's animated. Accompanied by taped commentary (available in English), life-size puppets act out various processes of winemaking and cooperage from the last century. Halfway through the visit you'll be offered a tasting of Chinon wine (and jam made from the wine, as well). Usually when wine is offered for sale at a venue like this I don't barge it with a touchpole, reasoning that if the wine needs a gimmick like this to help sales it can't be good enough for people to want it in its own right. But this time I was proved completely wrong. The wine at the MUSÉE ANIMÉ DU VIN ET DE LA TONNELLERIE comes from one of the best producers in Chinon, BERNARD BAUDRY, and you can visit his cellars outside the town to taste in more tranquillity.

M Baudry's estate is in **Sonnay**, just before Cravant-les-Coteaux on the D21, right next door to his brothers Jean and Christophe. The visit begins with a tour of the cellars, hewn out of the slope, then you can taste in the cellar, or in the small, comfortable tasting-room if it's cold.

Chinon is simply Chinon – there are no fancy Premiers Crus – but M Baudry subdivides his wine into three. There's Les Granges, from young vines, Domaine, from older vines, matured in stainless steel, and Grezeaux, matured in barriques (small oak barrels), plus an elegant, wood-fermented rosé. This is concentrated Chinon of excellent quality, and one of the three styles (at least) should be to your taste. Prices are fair, too, from FF23 for pink to FF35 for oaked red.

A couple of kilometres on the other side of **Cravant-les-Coteaux** you'll find the **DOMAINE DANIEL CHAUVEAU**, known as Pallus. Daniel's son Christophe is the current wine-maker and both he and his wife Jemma speak excellent English. His preferences lie with using a mixture of oak and stainless steel to mature the wine. Like most of the Loire, the Chauveau estate suffered badly in the frosts of 1991, which left them with a very pale red wine, almost impossible to sell – until people began to drink it with food. Now it's very popular in Paris bistros as a wine light enough to have with lunch. My favourite vintage at Chauveau was the '93, full of concentrated flavour, but it hadn't then been filtered and I hope it's as full afterwards.

In more and more cellars, you taste the wine in cask, express admiration, then buy the same wine once it's been bottled and find all the heart has been taken out by excessive filtration. This often happens when the winemaker employs someone to filter and bottle the wine using portable equipment, a common practice if the estate is too small to be able to invest in the machinery.

Returning to Chinon, make a circuit by turning left in Cravant and taking the riverside road back (the D8). I may be doing the town a disservice in complaining about its hotels, since whenever I've been there it's been the dead of winter, when half of them are shut. The Chinon is on the opposite bank in a kind of industrial park; there are lovely views of the castle but it's a long walk from the old town and the hotel is geared to business travellers rather than tourists. Ignore its restaurant. The Diderot is in traditional-creaky style and in just about every British guidebook. Locals speak well of the Gar'

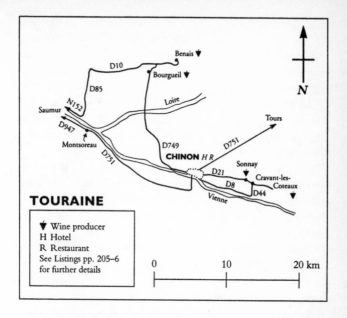

Hôtel and the Hostellerie Gargantua (the latter has a restaurant), and of L'Océanic, offering fish and seafood. You could, however, just as easily use Saumur as a base for touring the area.

Leave Chinon along the Vienne's north bank on the D749 to **Bourgueil**. This isn't a particularly scenic road, but when I reached north of Bourgueil and headed out into the vines, the slope reminded me of the Côte d'Or in Burgundy, and I warmed to it accordingly.

The two producers I'd recommend here make red wines of very good quality, on a small scale; neither speaks English. The first is **YANNICK AMIRAULT**, and his estate is signposted to the north off the D10 above Bourgueil. His house is surrounded by vines, with the cellars just down the road. He'll show you the cellars on request and offer you both Bourgueil and its neighbouring wine St-Nicolas-de-Bourgueil. He practises *pigeage*, the Burgundian technique of plunging down the cap of grape-skins into the fermenting must. As his brochure proves, he does it by hand, or rather foot – standing in the vat, grape juice up to his shorts. He says it's worth the agony for the extra intensity in the wine. No pain, no gain. Prices range from FF31 to FF40.

PIERRE-JACQUES DRUET is based in **Benais**, east of Bourgueil. It isn't easy to get an appointment with him, and even harder to find him (I had to phone and he came to meet me). His cellars are set in old caves outside the village. He uses very low yields and oak casks to produce a wine of enormous structure and concentration which outlives its neighbours. This is definitely an advanced-student visit, an education for fans of the wines of this area who want to know how far you can push winemaking techniques before you reach the limit. Press a coin into the cellar ceiling as a memento; the salt deposits will hold it firm until you return.

From here you can return to Saumur along the edge of the wine slopes on the D10, heading back to the Loire on the D85 and then along the N152. Perhaps take a walk on the gentle vineyard slopes first – there are plenty of paths, but no way-marked routes, so follow your nose.

To move on along the Touraine tour, however, you have to pass **Tours** itself. Since it's unavoidable you may as well turn the traverse to your advantage. Tours has a very attractive old town, a cathedral and various museums, and the hotel I'd recommend, the Royal, is easy to find as it's on the main north–south route through the city. It has modern rooms of fair size and a secure underground car park.

From the Royal, walking to the main sights is easy, and there are several restaurants in the old town, all close to each other so you can poke your nose in the windows, examine the menus and see which suits you best. (See the Listings, page 206.)

Leave Tours on the N152, on the north bank of the Loire and you'll find **Vouvray** a few kilometres outside, signposted on the left. If, however, you'd like to continue along the route by avoiding Tours altogether, here's how: join the D751 Chinon–Tours road, and at Joué-lès-Tours follow signs for the motorway to Blois and Orléans. Join the A10 – this stretch is toll-free – and then leave it immediately after you've crossed the second bridge, via a new exit at Rochecorbon. Now join the N152 in the direction of Blois, and Vouvray is close by.

There's a restaurant here worth trying, Le Grand Vatel. The dining-room is high-ceilinged, the walls covered with murals depicting people eating, drinking and having a good time through several centuries. The excellent food includes regional specialities such as *beuchelle à la tourangelle* (veal kidneys and sweetbreads in mustard sauce with mushrooms). A few rooms in creaky-traditional style are available on half-board terms only.

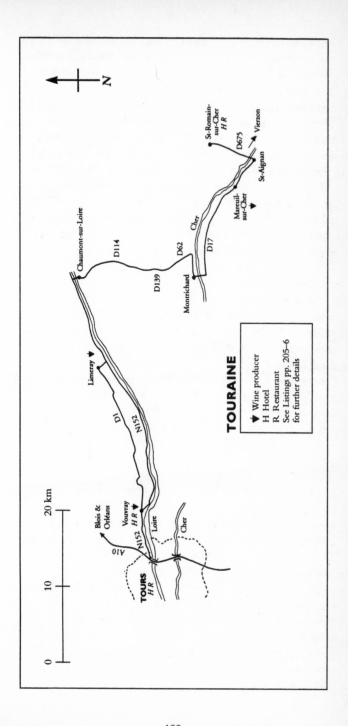

N

TOURAINE

▼ Wine producer
H Hotel
R Restaurant
See Listings pp. 205–6
for further details

0   10   20 km

Blois &
Orléans

A10

N152

Vouvray
H R ▼

Loire

Cher

TOURS
H R

D1

N152

Limeray ▼

Chaumont-sur-Loire

D114

D139

D62

Cher

Montrichard

D17

Marcuil-
sur-Cher ▼

St-Aignan

St-Romain-
sur-Cher
H R

D675

→ Vierzon

Usually I avoid *demi-pension* because I'm always afraid I'll be forced onto a menu I don't fancy, but with this one the rest of the *carte* is accessible by paying supplements. It represents value for money overall, so I'd make an exception here. The staff are very friendly, too. The village also boasts one of France's finest *charcuteries*, Hardouin, located on the main street.

Vouvray is famous for white wines, all made from Chenin Blanc and demonstrates what a versatile grape this is. It produces a range from bone dry to semi-sweet and very sweet via sparkling. There are several big names in the village, but I suggest you visit one of the young rising stars instead. **DIDIER CHAMPALOU**'s small estate is high above Vouvray (take a left turn in the village, signposted Caves de la Bonne Dame, follow signs for Le Grand Ormeau; the estate is signposted in a field on your left). You'll be led into a lovely, damp, musty 300-year-old cellar to taste a dry (*tendre*), a *demi-sec* or medium-dry and a sparkler made at lower pressure than most. Try this one if bubbles usually get up your nose. Try, too, the Champalous' ripe, luscious *moelleux* (mellow) wines. Prices are reasonable for this high quality (sparkler FF37, *demi-sec* FF40, *moelleux* FF60–75). Catherine Champalou offers a warm welcome; she speaks good English and is delighted to explain the region's wines to you.

Wines similar to Vouvray, but less well known and therefore cheaper, are made in Montlouis. Although close as the crow flies, Montlouis is on the opposite bank of the river and involves a detour back into Tours or up to Amboise to find a bridge. It will be interesting to see what the new Touraine wine route does with this little problem.

From Vouvray you have a choice of routes to the next stop, in **Limeray**, and both are scenic. Take either the D1, which is signposted as a *route touristique*, or the main N152 down by the banks of the Loire. Entering Limeray take the left fork up the hill and **DOMAINE DUTERTRE** is on the right. Here you've moved away from the well-known appellations. Local wines are called Touraine-Amboise or just plain Touraine, and because these are little known, prices are lower.

Dutertre's cellars stretch into the rocks; they have a small museum displaying the firm's old implements, and a tasting-room warmed by a log fire in winter. They make reds, mainly from Cabernet Franc although they do also offer a Gamay; avoid the rosé. The whites are mostly Chenin Blanc, plus

Crémant de Loire and Sauvignon de Touraine. The prices? Still wines range from FF20 to FF27, sweet wines are FF46 and Crémant is FF42; *en vrac* wines are available for even less. You can tell you've entered an unfashionable area.

From Limeray join the N152 towards Onzain and cross the river to Chaumont-sur-Loire. Take the D114, which becomes the D139 and then the D62, to reach the river Cher. Cross the river at Montrichard and follow a pretty route (the D17) along the south bank to **Mareuil-sur-Cher**. Just after the village, in the *lieu-dit* of La Méchinière, is **DOMAINE DE LA RENAUDIE**.

Patricia and Bruno Denis are the fourth generation to work this family property and make wines of extremely high quality which age well. They offer three red grape varieties: Gamay, Cabernet and the local speciality, Cot (the 't' isn't pronounced here, unlike further south). There's also a blend of these three in a wine called Tradition. The wines are not perhaps in traditional Touraine style but the results are, I think, really very good.

The domaine has made a big investment in new cellars and equipment over the last couple of years. No romantic rock-hewn caves here, but Patricia brims with enthusiasm and knowledge, speaks excellent English, and will explain the processes, pour the wines and answer all your questions. They sell by the litre (FF6–12) and have a range of empty containers – the largest, 33 litres, costs FF42.50. The Touraine Tradition costs FF20 a bottle and the Cabernet is FF21–28, according to age. Here is some of the best wine-making in the area and a real bargain.

Another bargain is a night's stop at Le St-Romain, at **St-Romain-sur-Cher**. (From Mareuil, head east along the D17, cross the river at St-Aignan and take the D675; the hotel is on the right in the village.) The food here is extremely good value: four excellent courses for FF62, including a dessert selection where everything is made in-house. Rooms cost about FF150 and for that price are clean and very entertaining, eg hand-held shower and no curtain. Bet you can't flood the floor as thoroughly as I did. The double bed was saggy, so book a twin.

If your tour ends here, join the motorway at Blois. For Sancerre, follow the Cher to Vierzon, then the D56 to St-Martin-d'Auxigny. This, I admit, is a dull town, and Menetou-Salon (take the D59 from St-Martin) is little better, but things liven up at **Morogues**. From there keep on the D59 until you join the road into Sancerre.

Listings

When telephoning France from the UK, first dial 00 33 then the number shown. Producers are listed in wine route order, and hotels/restaurants by town or village according to the route. Accommodation prices are per room, meal prices are per head.

THE PAYS NANTAIS

Producers

Maison des Vins de Nantes
Bellevue, 44690 La Haie-Fouassière
Tel 40 36 90 10
Fax 40 36 95 87
Open June–Sept Mon–Sun
8.30–12.30, 13.30–18.30;
Oct–May Mon–Fri to 18.00
Credit cards accepted
Good English

Bonneteau-Guesslin
Domaine de la Juiverie
44690 La Haie-Fouassière
Tel 40 54 80 38
Open Mon–Sat 9–12.30, 14–18;
closed during harvest
Good English

Chéreau-Carré
Château de Chasseloir
44690 St-Fiacre-sur-Maine
Tel 40 54 81 15
Open Mon–Sat 8–18 incl. lunch-time;
visits by appointment Sun
Credit cards accepted
Some English

Domaine des Rigoles du Pin
44330 Mouzillon
Tel 40 36 62 85
Visits by appointment Mon–Sat
9–12, 14.30–18.30; closed Feb and
1–15 Aug
Some English

Abbaye de Ste-Radegonde
44430 Le Loroux-Bottereau
Tel 40 03 74 78
Open Mon–Fri 9–12, 14–17;
visits by appointment Sat and Sun
Some English (by appointment)

Hotels and Restaurants
H Hotel   *R* Restaurant

Nantes
H Amiral
26 rue Scribe, 44000 Nantes
Tel 40 69 20 21, Fax 40 73 98 13
FF269–319

H L'Hôtel
6 rue Henry IV, 44000 Nantes
Tel 40 29 30 31, Fax 40 29 00 95
FF360–400

R L'Océanide
2 rue Paul Bellamy, 44000 Nantes
(Place du Pont Morand)
Tel 40 20 32 28
FF94–260

R La Poissonnerie
4 rue Léon Maitre, 44000 Nantes
Tel 40 47 79 50
Plateaux de fruits de mer FF90/150/220

Clisson
R La Bonne Auberge
1 rue Olivier de Clisson
44190 Clisson
Tel 40 54 01 90
FF98–430

Basse-Goulaine
R Villa Mon Rêve
Route des Bords de Loire
44115 Basse-Goulaine
Tel 40 03 55 50
FF98–225 (or ad lib)

ANJOU-SAUMUR

Producers
Clos de la Coulée de Serrant
Château de la Roche-aux-Moines,
49170 Savennières
Tel 41 72 22 32, Fax 41 72 28 68
Open Mon–Sat 8–12, 14–18
(minimum purchase price FF300
for a tasting)
Credit cards accepted
Good English

Domaine Aux Moines
49170 Savennières
Tel 41 72 21 33, Fax 41 88 59 12
Open Mon–Sat 9.30–12, 14–17;
visits by appointment Sun
(minimum purchase 3 bottles)
Credit cards accepted
Good English

Domaine du Closel
1 place du Mail
49170 Savennières
Tel 41 72 81 00, Fax 41 72 86 00
Open Mon–Sat 9–12.30, 13.30–18,
Sun 9–12.30
(minimum purchase 3 bottles)
Credit cards accepted
Good English

Moulin de Chauvigné
49190 Rochefort-sur-Loire
Tel 41 78 86 56
Open Mon–Sun 9–19 'except
lunch';
appointment preferred
Good English

Domaine des Baumard
49190 Rochefort-sur-Loire
Tel 41 78 70 03, Fax 41 78 83 82
Visits by appointment Mon–Fri
10–12, 14–18
Sterling accepted
Good English (from Florent and
Isabelle)

Domaine Richou
Chauvigné, 49610 Mozé-sur-Louet
Tel 41 78 72 13, Fax 41 78 76 05
Open Mon–Sat 8.30–12, 14.15–19
(minimum purchase 6 bottles
preferred)
Good English

Domaine Gaudard
La Brosse
49290 Chaudefonds-sur-Layon
Tel 41 78 10 68, Fax 41 78 67 72
Open Mon–Sat 9–12, 14–19; visits
by appointment Sun; closed Sun in
winter
Credit cards accepted
English: '3 words'

Musée de la Vigne et du Vin
Place des Vignerons
49750 St-Lambert-du-Lattay
Tel 41 78 41 48
Open April–Oct

Domaine du Sauveroy
49750 St-Lambert-du-Lattay
Tel 41 78 30 59, Fax 41 78 46 43
Open June–Sept Tues–Sat 9–12,
14–19; visits by appointment
Oct–May and all year Sun and Mon
Credit cards accepted
Good English

Château de Fesles
49380 Thouarcé
Tel 41 54 14 32, Fax 41 54 06 10
Open Mon–Sat 9–18 incl lunch-
time; visits by appointment Sun
Credit cards accepted
Good English (by appointment)

Château de Beauregard
4 rue St-Julien
49260 Le Puy-Notre-Dame
Tel 41 52 24 46, Fax 41 52 39 96
Visits by appointment Mon–Sun
(minimum purchase 6 bottles,
3 if sweet)
Some English

Bouvet-Ladubay
1 rue de l'Abbaye
49400 St-Hilaire-St-Florent
Tel 41 50 11 12, Fax 41 50 24 32
Open Mon–Sun 8–12.30, 14–18;
April–Sept incl lunch-time
(admission FF5)
Credit cards accepted
Good English (on request)

Langlois-Château
3 rue Léopold-Palustre
49426 St-Hilaire-St-Florent
Tel 41 50 28 14, Fax 41 50 26 29
Open Mon–Sun 10–12.30,
14–18.30; closed Jan; closed Nov,
Dec, Feb, March on Mon and Tues
(tours FF5–18; the 2-hour FF18 tour
is by appointment or on Thurs at
10.00)
Credit cards accepted
Tours in English (on request)

Gratien & Meyer
Route de Montsoreau
49401 Saumur
Tel 41 51 01 54, Fax 41 51 03 55
Open March–Oct Mon–Sun
9–11.30, 14–17.30; Nov–Feb
Mon–Fri 9–11.15, 14–17.15,
Sat and Sun 10–11.45, 15–17.15
Good English
(For information on wine courses
held at Ch Gratien contact Catherine
Gohier on the above number or
Alfred Gratien (qv) in Epernay.)

Château de Targé
49730 Parnay
Tel 41 38 11 50, Fax 41 38 16 19
Open Mon–Sat 8–12, 14–18;
closes Sat at 16.00

Credit cards accepted
Good English (by appointment
with M Pisani-Ferry)

Domaine des Roches-Neuves
56 boulevard St-Vincent
49400 Varrains
Tel 41 52 94 02, Fax 41 52 49 30
Visits by appointment
Good English

Domaine St-Vincent
49400 Saumur
Tel 41 67 43 19
Visits by appointment
No English

Hotels and Restaurants
H Hotel   **R** Restaurant

Angers
HR Pavillon Le Quéré
3 boulevard Maréchal Foch
49000 Angers
Tel 41 20 00 20, Fax 41 20 06 20
Rooms FF500–800
Meals FF220–450

H St-Julien
9 place Ralliement, 49000 Angers
Tel 41 88 41 62, Fax 41 20 95 19
FF190–360

R La Rose d'Or
21 rue Delâge
Tel 41 88 38 38
FF100–170

Saumur
H Anne d'Anjou
32 quai Mayaud, 49400 Saumur
Tel 41 67 22 42, Fax 41 67 51 00
FF260–640
(There is a fancy restaurant in the
garden, Les Ménestrels.)

H Central
23 rue Daillé, 49400 Saumur
Tel 41 51 05 78, Fax 41 67 82 35
FF210–310

R Brasserie Napoléon
Place de la Bilange
49400 Saumur
FF60–120

R Les Chandelles
71 rue St-Nicolas
49400 Saumur
Tel 41 67 20 40
FF90–194

R La Croquière
42 rue Maréchal Leclerc
49400 Saumur
Tel 41 51 31 45
FF70–157

R L'Escargot
30 rue Maréchal Leclerc
49400 Saumur
Tel 41 51 20 88
FF73–115

Les Rosiers
HR Jean de Laval
Route Nationale, 49350 Les Rosiers
Tel 41 51 80 17, Fax 41 38 04 18
Rooms FF300–580
Meals FF180–420

TOURAINE

Producers
Musée Animé du Vin et
  de la Tonnellerie
12 rue Voltaire
37500 Chinon
Open summer Mon–Sun
10–12.30, 14–19
(25-minute tour; admission FF23)
English commentary

Bernard Baudry
13 Coteau de Sonnay
37500 Cravant-les-Coteaux
Tel 47 93 15 79, Fax 47 98 44 44
Visits by appointment Mon–Sat
9–12, 14–18; closed end Aug and
early Sept
Some English

Domaine Daniel Chauveau, Pallus
37500 Cravant-les-Coteaux
Tel 47 93 06 12, Fax 47 93 93 06
Open Mon–Sat 8–12.30, 14–18.30;
appointment preferred, essential
for Sun
Credit cards accepted
Good English

Yannick Amirault
La Coudraye
37140 Bourgueil
Tel 47 97 78 07, Fax 47 97 94 78
Open Mon–Sat 8–19 incl lunch-
time; appointment preferred
No English

Pierre-Jacques Druet
Le Pied-Fourrier
37140 Benais
Tel 47 97 37 34
Visits by appointment
Credit cards accepted
No English

Catherine and Didier Champalou
Le Portail, 7 rue du Grand Ormeau
37210 Vouvray
Tel 47 52 64 49, Fax 47 52 67 99
Open Mon–Sat 9–12, 14–18;
appointment preferred, essential
for Sun
Good English

Domaine Dutertre
Place du Tertre, 20–21 rue d'Enfer,
Limeray
37530 Amboise
Tel 47 30 10 69, Fax 47 30 06 92
Open Mon–Sat 9–12, 14–18;
visits by appointment Sun
Credit cards accepted
Some English

Domaine de la Renaudie
La Méchinière
41110 Mareuil-sur-Cher
Tel 54 75 18 72, Fax 54 75 27 65
Open Mon–Sat 'all day incl lunch-
time'; visits by appointment Sun;
closed last week Aug
Good English

Hotels and Restaurants
H Hotel *R* Restaurant

Chinon
HR Hostellerie Gargantua
73 rue Haute-St-Maurice,
37500 Chinon
Tel 47 93 04 71
Rooms FF240–600
Meals FF150–200

H Le Chinon
Centre St-Jacques, 37500 Chinon
Tel 47 98 46 46, Fax 47 98 35 44
FF310–380

H Diderot
4 rue Buffon, 37500 Chinon
Tel 47 93 18 87, Fax 47 93 37 10
FF225–380

H Gar'Hôtel
14 avenue Gambetta, 37500 Chinon
Tel 47 93 00 86, Fax 47 93 36 38
FF210–240

R L'Océanic
13 rue Rabelais
Tel 47 93 44 55
FF98–145

Tours
H Le Royal
65 avenue Grammont, 37000 Tours
Tel 47 64 71 78, Fax 47 05 84 62
FF335–398

Tours contd
Old town restaurants:

R La Galette des Rois
Place Plumereau
Tel 47 05 77 17
FF150

R La Poivrière
13 rue Change
Tel 47 20 85 41
FF95–260

R Le Relais des Cigognes
Place Plumereau
Tel 47 20 57 57
FF145

R Zafferano
47 rue Grand-Marché
Tel 47 38 90 77
FF85–150

Vouvray
HR Le Grand Vatel
Avenue Brûlée, 37210 Vouvray
Tel 47 52 70 32, Fax 47 52 74 52
Rooms FF200–260
Meals FF125–220,
half board, FF400–460 for two

HR Le St-Romain
41140 St-Romain-sur-Cher
Tel 54 71 71 10, Fax 54 71 72 89
Rooms FF142–15
Meals FF62–198

The Golden Triangle

Three separate winemaking areas cluster together in northern France, and by accidents of geography they each produce different styles of wine. This means that the intrepid explorer can find wines from Champagne, Burgundy and the Loire valley without the tedium of travelling long distances: you can visit all three regions in one long weekend. The Aube offers the best value and the best scenery in Champagne; Chablis makes fashionable white burgundy, while its satellite villages offer cheaper whites, surprisingly attractive reds and good-quality sparklers; Sancerre's hilltop setting is spectacular and its crisp white wines are prized throughout the world. Pouilly-sur-Loire lends part of its name to the equally sought-after Pouilly-Fuissé.

PLANNING THE ROUTE

This so-called triangle is more of a Golden Straight Line. It takes about four hours to reach the Aube on the A26 from Calais, and not much longer from Zeebrugge. The new Paris–Troyes motorway makes travel via Paris an option and Le Havre an attractive second bet to Calais. For Chablis, you can either travel via Paris and the A6 to Auxerre, or take the A26 as far as Troyes and then D roads via Chaource and Tonnerre. Sancerre has no motorway link at present (although the N7 is to be upgraded to a toll-free motorway). Take the A6 from Paris and turn off onto the N7.

The Aube

This is Champagne's Cinderella, maligned and ignored. So far south of the focus of commerce in Reims, its voice went unheeded until very recently, and the grand houses in Reims looked down their noses at it. No Grandes Marques are found here, and much has been made of the supposed inferior quality of Aube champagne.

The big names like to imply that all the grapes they use to make champagne come from only the very best villages on the Montagne de Reims and the Côte des Blancs, yet these sites account for as little as 15–20% of the total production. They simply won't admit to the fact that nearly all of them buy grapes from the Aube. The region produces the equivalent of about 50M bottles a year, but only about 10M bottles are shipped from the area, in other words are identifiably Aube wines. The rest, 40M bottles' worth, finds its way north, adding its weight to champagne wines made by houses based in Reims and Epernay.

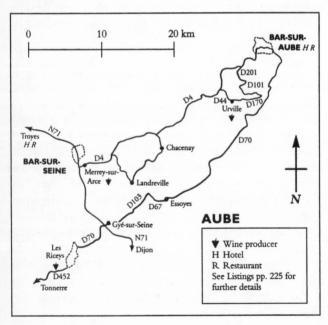

Times are changing, however. As one Aube grower said: 'The big houses are no longer saying the wines are no good in the Aube, because everyone knows they buy here.' The predominant grape in this area is Pinot Noir, which lends structure and depth, and is needed by the big Reims names to enhance their blends.

Nowadays several names are emerging from the Aube to challenge the supposed superiority of Reims and Epernay winemakers. They are gaining a reputation through good results in blind tastings; and as the trend in champagne flavour moves away from light, lemony tastes to heavier, more aromatic blends, Aube wines stand to gain a great deal of ground.

EXPLORING THE AUBE

In an effort to distance themselves from the old days of bad reputations and bulk winemaking, Aube producers have begun to refer to this area as the 'Côte des Bars', taking their cue from the more northerly – and prestigious – Côte des Blancs. It sounds like a good idea to me (well, it worked for Windscale).

The winemaking area is indeed bounded by Bars: Bar-sur-Aube in the east and Bar-sur-Seine in the west. Both these are attractive towns, well worth visiting in their own right; but the best starting-point is **Troyes,** the regional capital and as yet undiscovered by British tourists.

Troyes had the good fortune to be among the first 15 towns and cities singled out for restoration and conservation by the French government in the 1960s. As a result its old town is remarkably intact, with a mixture of half-timbered buildings leaning at eccentric angles and Renaissance architecture which replaced the razed wooden buildings after a fire in the 16th century. Local stonemasons adopted the cabbage as a carving motif – one in the cathedral even includes a chomping snail. Troyes was famous for medieval fairs and markets, and is where Troy weights come from (but not Helen, or the wooden horse).

The city is also famous for its *andouillettes*, sausages of pig intestine stuffed with tripe. (Yum.) Apparently in 1560 the king's army attempted to capture Troyes from the Governor of Champagne. Unfortunately, the king's soldiers dawdled on the outskirts of the city searching for *andouillettes*, whereupon they were surprised and repulsed.

It's the kind of place where you can spend an afternoon wandering around the old town, or days exploring all the museums and churches. The atmosphere is relatively unspoilt by tourism because the city is not on the tour operators' traditional map; no doubt that will slowly change once people begin to take advantage of the new motorway connections, so now is a good time to go.

Right in the centre (but well signposted) is the Hôtel la Poste: smart rooms and glitzy bathrooms, fairly priced, and good breakfasts, less fairly priced. It boasts no fewer than three restaurants, from a pizzeria to *haute cuisine*. The middle restaurant, Bistro de la Mer, decked out like a yacht, offers impressively fresh seafood. Rather easier to find, near the tourist office and station, is the Royal Hôtel.

Leave Troyes on the N71 in the direction of Dijon, and the first port of call is **Bar-sur-Seine**, capital of Auboise Champagne. The town is cut in two by the river Seine and has more attractive half-timbered buildings and churches. Just south of Bar, off the N71 at **Merrey-sur-Arce**, is the first visit, the **UNION AUBOISE**, with its brand, Veuve A Devaux.

The Union Auboise is a super-co-op, a grouping formed 25 years ago by 12 cooperatives to give themselves sufficient financial clout to afford a decent cellar-master and a marketing budget. It's big: 750 producers, 1,200ha of vines, about 3M bottles a year. Quality picked up slowly but the co-op is now winning prizes, especially with its rosé champagnes (a strength in the area as a whole, and based on the use of red wines made from Pinot Noir).

Seven years ago the Union bought itself a slice of history when it acquired the old Epernay champagne house of Devaux, which was one of the first Grandes Marques but had fallen into decline. Buying Devaux enabled the Union to announce that its house was formed in 1846 rather than 1967. (It's common nowadays for cooperatives to use brands rather than to trade under the co-op name: Le Brun de Neuville (qv) in the Sézannais is another example.)

The cooperative's labelling and packaging is glamorous and the champagnes are of very good quality, although dearer than those from small-scale growers. There's a shiny new visitors' centre, where you can taste and buy and see various exhibitions, but there's no opportunity for casual visitors to tour the cellars. For one thing, being situated on the banks of the Seine means that the water-table is just one metre down, making underground cellaring impossible – so there are no romantic *caves* to visit. Romance also flies out of the window when you see the co-op's huge, automated bottling-lines in operation.

If you're interested in watching 4,000 bottles an hour being processed, however, just make an appointment; they will be delighted to show you round and explain the different stages. I love watching mechanical processes, and here there's a fully-automated packing line, from folding the cardboard boxes onwards. The maturation cellars are temperature controlled and even have sensors <u>inside</u> a bottle in each batch; electronic controls display read-outs and bring temperatures into line at the flick of a switch.

Go through Merrey and pick up the D4 to Ville-sur-Arce. Two things immediately become apparent: the scenery here is much more attractive than in the northern part of Champagne, and the sign-posting is much worse. Although there is an official *route du vin* down here, the lack of attention the Aube receives means that it hasn't been given the same investment as the route around Epernay. (Indeed, the big glossy map of the Champagne wine route handed out by tourist offices in Reims and its wine committee ignores the Aube altogether – very supportive.) I do believe this will change. Meanwhile, try this route or just follow your instinct and meander around the very pretty countryside.

From Ville, the route enters Landreville and Chacenay before settling down onto the D4 again. After Bligny, turn right on the D44 into **Urville**, where **ANDRÉ DRAPPIER** is based. You're welcomed in a large, comfortable tasting-room; sit out on the terrace in summer or toast in front of their log fire in winter. Access to the cellars, parts of which were built in 1152 by Cistercian monks, is via a spiral staircase at one end of the tasting-room. There you can hear an explanation of the firm's winemaking processes, delivered in impeccable English.

One of Drappier's specialities is the production of large bottles. Most houses making magnums, jeroboams or what have you will make the champagne in ordinary-sized bottles and simply pour the finished product into bigger ones. It's much harder to complete the second fermentation in larger bottles, as Drappier does. For one thing, the bottles are not machine-made so they are much more likely to explode under the pressure of second fermentation. Michel Drappier says he can lose up to 40% of his bottles this way but believes it's worth it because of the improved quality of the champagne.

This is a family firm, with some of the best vineyards in Urville under its control. The wines are full-flavoured and rich. Michel recognizes the disadvantages of being hidden away in an unknown village at the unfashionable end of Champagne: 'If you want to be at the top, being in Reims is better.' Accordingly, the Drappiers own maturation cellars in the city, which entitles them to put the magic word 'Reims' on the label, but it's clear they're proud of the individual identity of their Côte des Bars wines.

They offer a range starting at FF75, rising to the splendid prestige *cuvée*, Grande Cendrée. If they still have the '85, for FF116, treat yourself (and try the later vintages, too). The bottle is gorgeous: a long-necked, low-slung shape based on an old bottle they found lying in the cellar and copyrighted. The champagne is full of the richness that comes from old vines and from the *tête de cuvée* (the best of the first pressing).

If you're looking for other gift ideas they'll sell you a champagne bottle filled with liqueur chocolates, or a chic black wine cooler. I was impressed by Drappier, both for the quality of the champagne and for the quality of the visit. I believe you'll find a warm welcome here, and every reason to come out afterwards convinced that the Aube has been maligned for far too long. As M Drappier told me: 'It is a pleasure to have the visit of your nice guide buyers when they succeed in reaching us in the middle of nowhere.'

From Urville it's only a short hop to **Bar-sur-Aube**. (D170–D101–D201 and back on the D4.) The journey is shorter than it sounds and worth the complicated route for the scenic pleasures. There's also a splendid view of the Aube valley from the top of a very steep track off to the right of the D4 at Ste-Germaine.

Bar-sur-Aube is the sort of place I always think of as 'undiscovered France': gently-paced, with few tourists, the air heavy with wood-smoke, and full of unannounced architectural pleasures, such as the wooden gallery on the side of the ancient church, which once housed a market.

Sadly, since the Relais des Gouverneurs burned down there's nowhere to suggest you stay: for the time being, it's best to treat the Aube as a circular tour based on Troyes, where there's plenty of choice.

Alternatively, Michel Drappier recommends the Moulin de Landion in Dolancourt (take the N19 north out of Bar-sur-Aube).

A detour if Général de Gaulle interests you; he's buried in the churchyard at Colombey-les-deux-Eglises, near Bar on the N19. A huge cross of Lorraine has been erected in his memory on a nearby hillside. It can be seen for miles.

Leave Bar on the D396 and turn off onto the D70 for Baroville. Follow this road to **Essoyes**, across attractive open countryside. This area isn't particularly strong on restaurants but offers plenty of pretty, unofficial picnic sites. Essoyes, apart from being a pleasant village worth a stroll, is home to a wine museum open during the summer. A clutch of Renoirs is buried here. From Essoyes head back up into the hills towards Gyé-sur-Seine (along the D67 and D103), and from there join the D70 into Les Riceys.

Les Riceys is plural because there are three of them (I found this out the hard way). If you keep turning left when you come into the cluster of villages on the D70 you'll end up on the D17 which climbs steeply; there's a picnic site halfway up the hill on the right, which offers you a commanding view.

Heading back down the D17 and into the villages again, Ricey-Haut is the first Ricey you come to, with Ricey-Bas beyond. Once you've strolled through the winding streets and inspected the three churches, head for Ricey-Bas on the D452 Bar-sur-Seine road. Turn left at the far side of the village, sign-posted D142 Avirey, and **DOMAINE MICHEL NOIROT** is on the right. As you drive through the arch you're met by rose-beds and a slightly decaying château; the Noirots bought the house a decade ago because they fell in love with it, but ever since have sunk their money into the winemaking rather than their home.

I thought Mme Noirot looked a little like Simone Signoret; she's very friendly and laid-back, smokes like a chimney, and is always accompanied by her neighbour's dog. She rescued this dog when it fell behind a bank of maturing champagne bottles and lay trapped for a fortnight; now it follows her everywhere in gratitude, much to the neighbour's annoyance.

To visit here is to discover a champagne house in formation. Until 1993 M Noirot sold part of his harvest by the kilogram, for cash flow, while vinifying the rest himself and slowly building up a good reputation. But in 1993 he cast himself free and vinified all the crop himself. He's used no chemical fertilizers in the vineyard for the past seven years, ploughing and manuring instead.

Things being at an early stage here, you taste standing around a table in one corner of the cellar. They plan something more comfortable, but I think being in the middle of a working cellar is more fun. Unusually for the Aube, where Chardonnay accounts for less than 10% of plantings, the Noirots make a *blanc de blancs* from white grapes (in other words, from Chardonnay only). It's pale and delicate, unlike the more robust character of other Aube wines. Their standard non-vintage is light, too, fresh and lively with lots of fruit. If the vintage 1985, a full, rich champagne, is still available it's well worth trying. A range of elegant, light-bodied wines from a full-bodied couple, unpretentious and friendly.

Before leaving Les Riceys I feel I ought to mention that there's a local wine speciality, Rosé des Riceys, a still pink wine. Try it by all means, but I think it's overpriced.

Les Riceys just about completes the circuit. From here you can head back to Troyes and home or visit Chaource, 22km west of Les Riceys, home of one of my favourite cheeses and also the church of St-John the Baptist, with remarkable art-works. Or you can head directly for Chablis, next stop on the golden-straight-line tour, via the pretty D452 to Tonnerre.

Chablis

Chablis is Burgundy's northern outpost, an isolated wine-making area just about as far north as you can get grapes to ripen. It's famous for its Chardonnay whites, which differ from their southern Burgundy counterparts in their higher acidity (the result of a northern climate) and their minerally taste (the product of a chalky-clay soil).

Naturally, this being France, there's a hierarchy of wines. Generic Chablis is what there's most of – it accounts for 64% of production. Below that there's Petit Chablis, accounting for less than a quarter. This is a relatively new name (cashing in on Chablis' fame, according to some), the vines are planted on poorer slopes and the wines are all too often lacking in decent taste and varietal character. Above generic Chablis there are Premiers Crus (accounting for 11%) and Grands Crus (2%). These are the best the region has to offer and are priced accordingly. Petit Chablis is best drunk young, if at all, Chablis within three years of the vintage, the Premiers Crus at five to eight years and the Grands Crus from eight years.

Being so far north, the angle of the vineyard towards the sun is vital in order to gain every available second of sunshine. The top vineyards occupy the best positions, but these sites also leave the vines highly vulnerable to frost. If you're here in late spring you will see all kinds of measures being taken to protect the delicate buds, from the positioning of braziers to spraying the vines with water (which forms a protective frozen cover over the buds).

The winemakers are deeply divided over what Chablis should taste like – a fairly basic question, you might think. One camp ferments and ages the wine in wood, and believes the extra structure this lends the wine helps it to age well; the other insists that the flavours of wood can overwhelm the natural delicate mineral flavour of proper Chablis, and that the region shouldn't try to imitate its cousins further south. Which is better? I leave that for you to decide. For my part, I find the arguments of each grower, at the moment I hear them in the cellar with a glass in my hand, overwhelmingly persuasive. Then, in the next cellar where I hear the opposing view, I'm equally convinced.

EXPLORING CHABLIS

I've identified three elements to a tour of the area. The first part of the visit is centred on Chablis itself and within walking distance of the hotels – handy for tasting without having to drive. The second part covers 'Chablis satellites' around the village, by car, and the third takes you further afield, visiting the vineyards near the river Yonne.

Chablis the village is surprisingly dull and modern. Not its fault – it was bombed nearly to bits in June 1940 and the rebuild has all the excitement and verve you'd expect of 1950s architecture. Stay either at L'Etoile or Hostellerie des Clos, both of which are in the centre. L'Etoile is cheap, and certain rooms (notably number seven) have been refurbished with some style. At its most basic you can get a very floral room without a bath for just FF140. The cooking is so-so. At the Hostellerie des Clos the food is Michelin-starred (but service is very slow when it's busy) and rooms are expensive and fancy. Restaurant Le Vieux Moulin, close to L'Etoile, has a mill-race rushing beneath and offers good local ham dishes.

Call in at the Maison du Vin for maps and advice; it's in the same building as the tourist information office and well signposted. Then begin your visits to producers at the local cooperative, **LA CHABLISIENNE**. This is a powerful local player, controlling one-third of the Chablis crop. The cellar tastingroom has a long counter with a background of barrels, some of which are glass-fronted and lit so you can see the maturing wine within. It's an easy, relaxed place to taste. The Petit Chablis and especially the Chablis are full of flavour and at fair prices for the area. Basic reds are also available. They'll show you the cellars if time permits, but you may prefer to wait for a cellar visit until you arrive at **JEAN-PAUL DROIN**.

While La Chablisienne, with its enormous production, has one foot in both oak and stainless steel camps, M Droin is firmly on the side of oak. This is a husband-and-wife operation and visits are strictly by appointment – from the outside the elegant villa doesn't look like a winemaker's premises at all. M Droin is the tenth generation to farm the estate ('the eleventh is at school'), which now produces five Grands Crus and seven Premiers Crus. His cellars are proper, romantic, subterranean caves, dimly lit and containing row after row of barrels. Here the advanced student can have a tasting and discuss (in French) the differences between the vineyard sites and the vintages, and the case for and against oak – with the evidence in favour in the glass.

Close by is the domaine of **RENÉ & VINCENT DAUVISSAT**. This is one of the most eccentric visits I've ever had the pleasure of making. The wines are unobtrusively oaked and excellent; this is winemaking of the highest quality. The Dauvissats don't go out of their way to woo the public. You may be able to get an appointment, you may be able to taste

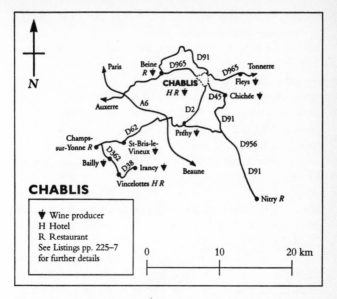

CHABLIS

♥ Wine producer
H Hotel
R Restaurant
See Listings pp. 225–7
for further details

the wines, it may all be terribly vague, but it's definitely worth persevering for the quality of what's on offer.

Some properties based outside the village have shops within and sell to the public from these rather than from the estate. Visit them by all means, but I don't think they are as much fun as a proper cellar visit, and prices can be higher than at the vineyard. If you're pushed for time, however, **LE CELLIER CHABLISIEN** offers a wide selection of local wines. It's run by Bernard Guyot, ex-*sommelier* of the Hostellerie des Clos, and he gives excellent advice in very good English.

The 'Chablis satellites' tour begins with **DOMAINE DES MALANDES** on the Auxerre road, the D965. This is on the out-skirts of the village, but in walking distance of the centre. Lyne and Bernard Marchive, a friendly, unassuming couple, are very firm adherents of the use-no-oak school and make prizewinning wines in their modern cellars.

On to **Beine**, passing a reservoir created by local wine-makers to supply water for spraying vines against frost. There's an excellent lunch stop just off the main road, Le Vaulignot. Enjoy high-quality, modern cooking in its smart, yellow din-ing-room, then head into the village.

ALAIN GEOFFROY's estate is high up in Beine. The wines here are oaked, and I thought them excellent. The Premier

Cru Beauroy, in particular, is a fine wine and FF10 cheaper than the more fashionable Fourchaume. The Geoffroys are very affable hosts (Mme Geoffroy speaks English), and their tasting-room is well-lit and inviting, with table and stools.

Leave Beines on an unnumbered road to La Chapelle-Vaupelteigne, passing through the high Petit Chablis vineyards. Cross the Serein on the D131A and turn right onto the D91. This takes you past all the Grand Cru sites, on your left, and then past Chablis itself, to **Fleys**.

DOMAINE DE LA MEULIÈRE is on your right, and you go straight into an attractive tasting-room in a vaulted cellar. Charming Chantal and Claude Laroche don't speak English although their daughter, who will soon be joining the business, does. Here you'll find well-made wines at fair prices, with Chablis at FF45, and Premiers Crus at FF60.

Return to Chablis and then turn left onto the D45 to **Chichée**. Didier Picq runs the family estate of **GILBERT PICQ**, and will show you the cellar opposite the domaine before offering you a tasting. His tasting-table is cut from a huge slice of elm and the tasting bottles are stored in a fridge inside an old barrel. The family only began to bottle its own wines in 1982, since when it has built up a good reputation. Look out especially for the Chablis *vieilles vignes* at FF48, lying between generic Chablis and a Premier Cru in price and quality.

From Chichée follow signs to **Nitry**. You can either turn off to Préhy first, or continue to Nitry and a rather special restaurant. La Beursaudière is folkloric in decor, with beams, dried flowers and roaring fires, and waiting staff wear regional costume. It may sound artificial but it's carried off with style. The food emphasizes regional dishes and is well cooked and presented with flair. The day I visited, the large dining-room was brim-full of local families having an outing – the place lends itself to a sense of occasion. It's fun without feeling touristy, and worth the detour.

At **Préhy**, seek out the **DOMAINE JEAN-MARC BROCARD** (follow the road behind the church). M Brocard is creating a rapidly expanding operation and offers a wide range of un-oaked wines. Some of the best value lies in his non-Chablis appellations, such as the 'Chardonnay from around Préhy' for FF32. Most tasting takes place in the ground-floor sales area, but do ask to see the stratified wall in his cellar tasting-room.

The exposed rock layers are full of fossils, some of which are still buried in my coat pocket.

From Préhy you can either loop back to Chablis via the D2 or head off to the third circuit by the river Yonne, via Chitry and the D62. **St-Bris-le-Vineux** (lovely name) is the first stop, home to the only VDQS of the area, Sauvignon de St-Bris. Production of this wine is in decline because it doesn't fetch the prices of the local AC wines, but you'll find it at several of the producers I've listed for Chablis.

BOURGOGNES BERSAN boasts some of the most wonderful mouldy cellars I've ever visited. Originally built in the 12th century to garrison soldiers, they contain the remains of a bread oven, a chute in from the street and a stone foot press. One passage runs close to the church; they suspect secret tunnels. The wines are excellent, and excellent value: Sauvignon de St-Bris or Bourgogne Chardonnay for FF29, Bourgogne Côtes d'Auxerre (a relatively new appellation) for FF36. No wine is made in these cellars any more, of course; they're used for a few oak barrels (of which the current winemaker's mother doesn't approve), and for visitors. The winery is on a hill above the village, all gleaming stainless steel and modern technology.

You'll also find good winemaking at **VERRET**, on the Champs-sur-Yonne road on the outskirts of St-Bris. Bruno Verret is the youngest member of the family to join the firm, after studying in Bordeaux and working in Australia. He's full of ideas and happy to explain the local wines and regulations, and to show you round the cellars before offering a tasting that includes the only locally-made sparkling wine apart from the massive local co-op's. There are Irancy reds, too, especially from the tiny Palotte vineyard. Ask him to show you the nearby riverside picnic spot.

Now continue along the D62 to **Champs-sur-Yonne**, where you can have an excellent lunch at Les Rosiers that's very good value. Try the hefty *jarret de porc* (pork knuckle) in the pretty, blue dining-room. Thus fortified, take the D362 along the river towards **Bailly**, following signs for the **CAVES DE BAILLY**. The entrance road runs steeply up the hillside, where you can park if it looks busy, but if it isn't you have the chance to drive right into the cellars, which are cut into the surrounding rock. Deep inside you'll find a huge, subterranean tasting-cavern looking like something out of a James Bond film.

As you can immediately see, this is a big operation. It's a cooperative, but one with an excellent reputation, and the largest producer of Crémant de Bourgogne, producing one-third of all that's made. You can taste for a small sum that's refundable on purchase, and in summer guided tours are available in English. The aim is commercial, certainly, but the visit is fun nonetheless.

Stay on the pretty riverside road to Vincelottes, then turn left onto the D38 to **Irancy**. This place is a little gem, making a tiny amount of red wine that's barely known in France, never mind the UK. It's a Pinot Noir wine, just like its nobler cousins on the Côte d'Or, and although Irancy is so far north, the sheltered valley aspect gives the vines good ripening conditions, so you can expect better colour and intensity than the location might suggest. Vines fight with fruit trees and sunflowers for the best spots. The village is not particularly geared to tourism and few people speak English.

First stop is with the mayor, **LÉON BIENVENU**. He makes wines of good depth and is a passionate advocate for his appellation, petitioning the powers that be to drop 'Bourgogne' as a prefix to the village name, insisting that the quality of the wine should be allowed to speak for itself, and that the wine should not be made to sound generic.

I found passionate commitment too in **JEAN-PIERRE COLINOT**, and you really must visit his cellars. Here is wine-making at its simplest, with open vats set into the cellar floor; some outside in the courtyard date back to the Middle Ages. The wine bubbles away at your feet. *Pigeage*, pushing the cap of grape-skins down into the must, is done with a branch with stumpy twigs at the end. I had a go and found it hard work. He immediately promised to name the vat I'd worked on Cuvée Hilary. Hmm…

Extrovert M Colinot was named Winemaker of the Year in a French magazine a couple of years ago and he's immensely proud of the fact. His wines are lively, juicy and will keep, particularly those from the little Palotte site. You will be warmly welcomed.

An overnight stop with good food that was recommended to me is close by: the Auberge Les Tilleuls at **Vincelottes**. Here you are close to the A6, should you wish to return home, but if you are carrying on down to Sancerre and Pouilly-sur-

Loire there's an extremely pretty route following the canal
along the D100. At Châtel-Censoir this turns into the D21.
Cross the river at Coulanges, then at Clamecy follow signs for
Donzy and from there the directions to Pouilly-sur-Loire. It
will take about a couple of hours.

Sancerre and
Pouilly-sur-Loire

These two towns are close, on opposite banks of the Loire, and
make an obvious touring circuit. West of Sancerre lies another
cluster of wine-producing villages. First there's Menetou-Salon,
then, further west, Quincy and Reuilly. These produce wine
similar in style to Sancerre but cheaper, which makes seeking
them out all the more worthwhile.

While Sancerre the wine is named after Sancerre the town,
Pouilly-sur-Loire has missed the honours by giving its name to
a rather netural wine made from the Chasselas grape. Avoid this
trap: the good stuff, made from Sauvignon, is called Pouilly-
Fumé. 'Fumé' means 'smoked' and some people believe the
name came about because the wine has a gun-flint character.
An alternative explanation is that the powdery deposits which
form on the Sauvignon Blanc grapes look rather like smoke.
Pick the romantic notion you prefer.

EXPLORING SANCERRE AND
POUILLY-SUR-LOIRE

Sancerre perches high on a hill and has an old town full of
meandering streets (a little like Chinon). The hotels themselves
seem to be stuck in a time warp. The Panoramic, for instance,
generally held to be the best of the bunch, has a gorgeous view
of the vineyards but is rather dilapidated and has a breakfast to
ignore (buy coffee and a croissant in one of the local cafés,
instead). Book twin beds to avoid a sagging double.

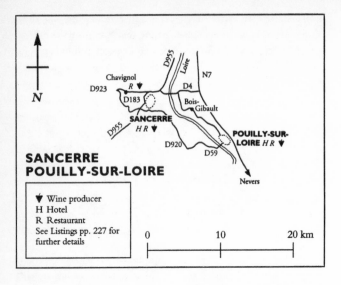

On the other hand, food is excellent in two of the town's restaurants. La Pomme d'Or, not long open, is a hot tip among the locals (do book; it's small and extremely good value). The chef is a veteran of some fine restaurants, fulfilling an ambition to set up on his own, and his cooking is irreproachable. Grander and longer-established, but with an equally good reputation, is La Tour.

For a short, scenic trip leave Sancerre on the D955 towards Bourges, and turn right onto the D923 to Menetou-Râtel. Turn right off this road to reach **Chavignol**, where you can stop after the church at the tasting-room of **HENRI BOURGEOIS**. This is a fairly large family firm (there's also a négociant arm, Laporte, run by a nephew-in-law) making reliable, good-quality wines including a Sancerre Rouge with plenty of depth.

The family seems to be taking over the village; tenth-generation Bourgeois, Jean-Marc, has just opened a restaurant called La Côte des Monts-Damnés. The Monts-Damnés are local vineyard sites, damned because of how steep they are and difficult to work. Jean-Marc has served his apprenticeship in top French restaurants and puts his considerable expertise to good use. Don't miss the tagliatelle with the famous local goat's milk cheese, Crottins de Chavignol. (Another hot tip – remember, you read it here first.)

In the village square pick up signs proclaiming: 'Sancerre par les vignes – Panorama' and follow them up high through the vineyards along a narrow road (apparently one-way) overlooking spectacular views. This road brings you out on the D183. Head into Sancerre and turn right onto the D955, away from the river.

If you're interested in exploring the cheaper wines from the outlying villages, stay on the D955 and retrace the route mentioned at the end of the Loire valley chapter (page 201) as far as Quincy. Two producers I'd recommend are **HENRY PELLÉ** in **Morogues** and **DOMAINE MARDON** in **Quincy** (details are given in the Sancerre and Pouilly Listings). Otherwise, take the D920 at the D955 roundabout, up past the Panoramic hotel on the road to Ménétréol. You'll find **DOMAINE JOSEPH MELLOT** on your right as you descend towards the river.

This estate also has a tasting-room on the main square in Sancerre, called the Auberge du Joseph Mellot, which offers a range of wines to taste with local specialities such as Crottins de Chavignol. At the cellars, on the other hand, you can see a forest of stainless steel and some fibreglass maturation tanks with adjustable lids, which sit on top of the wine forming an inflatable airtight seal no matter how much wine is in the vat.

This is a big company, making good wines – for a price. The Sancerre and Pouilly-Fumé cost from FF45 to FF66, but the wines from the outlying villages of Menetou-Salon, Quincy and Reuilly are a more reasonable FF34 each. From here, take the D920 to St-Bouize and then turn left onto the D59 to Pouilly.

Pouilly-sur-Loire was something of a gastronomic Mecca before the bypass was built but since then things have faded somewhat. Locals speak well of Le Coq Hardi (although it lost its Michelin star rating) and it can also provide accommodation. About 3km south of Pouilly, on the right off the N7, lies the Hôtel de Pouilly. Recently built, its well-equipped modern rooms are a real haven, and it serves an excellent breakfast. The hotel also has a restaurant, and when I was there it seemed as though Pouilly's entire work-force had descended for a good night out, with enormous seafood platters and steaks proving very popular.

Local producer **GUY SAGET** is a self-made man. His father, a small-scale winemaker, died suddenly when Guy was just 19, and he broke off his studies to take over the business, knowing at that time next to nothing about it. I don't think he's had a day off since, as he's laboured to build it up into the thriving vineyard holdings and négociant operation he runs today.

There's a small tasting-room on the main street of Pouilly and a larger one on the N7 south of town, where his head-quarters are. Make an appointment to visit Saget's new project, the Moulin de Beauregard, in the next village south. He's restored this old windmill and created an atmospheric tasting-room amid rows of barrels, as well as setting up art exhibition facilities. It's well worth a visit.

Back in Pouilly, between the N7 and the town centre, is the **TINEL-BLONDELET** estate, run by a young couple offering classic Pouilly-Fumé plus the results of various experiments with different styles of winemaking. There's also a good Pouilly-sur-Loire, proving that interesting wine can be made from the dull Chasselas grape.

Here, as so often, you'll find all manner of filtration equipment. Any unfiltered wine is worth seeking out – see for yourself what difference it makes. Just as I was leaving Pouilly, I met an American importer who rejoiced in having discovered a man producing unfiltered Pouilly-Fumé, just down the road from Tinel-Blondelet: Fabien Colin. Was he in when I called? Of course not. I don't know what the wines are like, but I mention the lead for what it's worth and I hope you strike lucky.

To complete the circuit, head north through Pouilly, and when you come to the turning for the N7 keep going instead towards Les Loges. It's a bumpy, potholed road but the view down across the valley is stunning. In Les Loges, follow signs for Sancerre or Cosne-sur-Loire through Bois-Gibault and Tracy-sur-Loire. When the road comes out on the outskirts of Sancerre you can head back into town on the D4 or take the N7 north and home.

Listings

When telephoning France from the UK, first dail 00 33 then the number listed. Producers are listed in wine route order, and hotels/restaurants by town or village according to the route. Accommodation prices are per room, meal prices are per head.

THE AUBE

Producers

Union Auboise
Domaine de Villeneuve
10110 Bar-sur-Seine
Tel 25 38 30 65, Fax 25 29 73 21
Visitors' centre open Mon–Fri 9–12,
14–18 (provisional times);
cellar visits by appointment
Good English

André Drappier
10200 Urville
Tel 25 27 40 15, Fax 25 27 41 19
Open Mon–Sat 8–12, 14–18; closed
lunch-time (definitely); cellar tour by
appointment: 'phoning only half an
hour beforehand will do'
Credit cards accepted
Good English

Domaine Michel Noirot
Clos St-Roch
4 avenue Croix de Mission,
10340 Les Riceys
Tel 25 29 38 46, Fax 25 29 67 22
Visits by appointment Mon–Sun;
if possible book 1–2 days in advance
Some English
(good English from secretary)

Hotels and Restaurants
H Hotel *R* Restaurant

Troyes
HR Hôtel la Poste
1–3 rue R.-Poincaré, 10000 Troyes
Tel 25 73 05 05, Fax 25 73 80 76
Rooms FF370–520, Meals: La Table
Gourmande FF150–240; Bistro de la
Mer FF90–125

HR Royal Hôtel
22 boulevard Carnot, 10000 Troyes
Tel 25 73 19 99, Fax 25 73 47 85
Rooms FF265–500, Meals FF98–185

HR Moulin de Landion
10200 Dolancourt
Tel 25 27 92 17, Fax 25 27 94 44
Rooms FF310–355, Meals FF97–305

CHABLIS

Producers
Cave Coopérative La Chablisienne
8 boulevard Pasteur, 89800 Chablis
Tel 86 42 11 24, Fax 86 42 47 51
Open Mon–Sat 8–12, 14–18
(open in summer to 19.00),
Sun 9.30–12, 14–18
Credit cards accepted
Good English

Jean-Paul Droin
14bis, rue Jean-Jaurès, 89800 Chablis
Tel 86 42 16 78, Fax 86 42 42 09
Visits (strictly) by appointment
Credit cards accepted
No English

Domaine René and Vincent
Dauvissat
8 rue Emile Zola, 89800 Chablis
Tel 86 42 11 58
Visits by appointment;
closed Sun and during harvest
No English

Le Cellier Chablisien
7 rue Jules-Rathier, 89800 Chablis
Tel 86 42 15 64
Open Mon–Sun 9–12, 14–18
Good English

Domaine des Malandes
63 rue Auxerroise, 89800 Chablis
Tel 86 42 41 37, Fax 86 42 41 97
Open Mon–Fri 9–12, 14–19;
visits by appointment Sat
Credit card facilities to be introduced
Good English

Domaine Alain Geoffroy
4 rue de l'Equerre, Beines
89800 Chablis
Tel 86 42 43 76, Fax 86 42 13 30
Open Mon–Sat 9–12, 14–18;
visits by appointment Sun
Credit cards accepted
Some English

Domaine de la Meulière
Fleys, 89800 Chablis
Tel 86 42 13 56, Fax 86 42 19 32
Open Mon–Sat 9–12, 14–18;
visits by appointment Sun
No English

Gilbert Picq et Ses Fils
3 route de Chablis, Chichée
89800 Chablis
Tel 86 42 16 78, Fax 86 42 42 09
Open Mon–Fri 8–12, 14–18;
appointment preferred; visits (strictly)
by appointment Sat and Sun
Good English

Domaine Jean-Marc Brocard
Préhy, 89800 Chablis
Tel 86 42 45 76, Fax 86 41 45 79
Open Mon–Fri 8–18 incl lunch-
time, Sat 10–12, 15–19; closed Sun,
but shop in Chablis open 9–13
Credit cards accepted
Good English (except on Saturday!)

Bourgognes Bersan
20 rue de l'Eglise,
89530 St-Bris-le-Vineux
Tel 86 53 33 73, Fax 86 53 38 45
Visits by appointment
Some English

GAEC du Parc Verret and Ses Fils
7 route des Champs,
89530 St-Bris-le-Vineux
Tel 86 53 31 81, Fax 86 53 89 61
Open Mon–Sat 8–12, 14–19;
cellar visits by appointment
Good English

Caves de Bailly
Bailly, 89530 St-Bris-le-Vineux
Tel 86 53 34 00, Fax 86 53 80 94
Open for sales Mon–Fri 8–12,
14–18, Sat and Sun: Jan and Feb
14.30–18, March– Dec 10–12,
14.30–18; cellar open April–Sept
Mon–Sun 14–17 (small charge for
cellar visits; tastings FF9 per glass,
refundable on purchase)
Cellar tours in English

Léon Bienvenu
Rue Promenade, Irancy
89290 Champs-sur-Yonne
Tel 86 42 22 51, Fax 86 42 37 12
Visits by appointment Mon–Sun
9–12, 14–18 (not Sun pm)
No English

Jean-Pierre Colinot
1 rue des Chariats, Irancy
89290 Champs-sur-Yonne
Tel 86 42 33 25
Open Mon–Fri 9–12, 14–20, Sat
9–20 incl lunch-time, Sun 9–12
Some English

Hotels and Restaurants
H Hotel   **R** Restaurant

Chablis
HR Hostellerie des Clos
Rue Jules-Rathier, 89800 Chablis
Tel 86 42 10 63, Fax 86 42 17 11
Rooms FF230–570, Meals
FF160–400

H Hôtel l'Etoile
4 rue des Moulins, 89800 Chablis
Tel 86 42 10 50, Fax 86 42 81 21
FF140–250

R Le Vieux Moulin
Rue des Moulins, 89800 Chablis
Tel 86 42 17 30
FF69–185

Beine
R Le Vaulignot
30 Route Nationale
89800 Beine
Tel 86 42 48 48
FF98–235

Nitry
R La Beursaudière
Rue Hyacinthe Gautherin
89310 Nitry
Tel 86 33 62 51
FF75–210

Champs-sur-Yonne
R Les Rosiers
7 rue Dr Schweitzer
89290 Champs-sur-Yonne
Tel 86 53 31 11
FF92–130

Vincelottes
HR Auberge Les Tilleuls
12 quai de l'Yonne,
Vincelottes
89290 Champs-sur-Yonne
Tel 96 42 22 13, Fax 86 42 23 51
Rooms FF230–400, Meals
FF110–250

SANCERRE AND POUILLY-SUR-LOIRE

Producers
Henri Bourgeois
Chavignol, 18300 Sancerre
Tel 48 54 21 67, Fax 48 54 14 24
Open Mon–Sat 9–12.30, 14–19, Sun
and public holidays 10.30–12.30,
15–17; closed Jan and Feb on Sun
Credit cards accepted
Some English

Domaine Henry Pellé
18220 Morogues
Tel 48 64 42 48, Fax 48 64 36 88
Open Mon–Sat 9–12, 14–18
Some English

Domaine Mardon
Route de Reuilly
18120 Quincy
Tel 48 51 31 60, Fax 48 51 35 55
Open Mon–Sat 8–12, 14.30–18;
appointment preferred
No English

Domaine Joseph Mellot
Route de Ménétréol
18300 Sancerre
Tel 48 54 21 50, Fax 48 54 15 25
Cellars open Mon–Sat 8–18 incl
lunch-time; shop open March–Oct
Mon and Tues and Thurs–Sun 8–21
Credit cards accepted
Good English

Guy Saget
Route Nationale
58150 Pouilly-sur-Loire
Tel 86 39 16 37, Fax 86 39 08 30
Tasting-rooms open Mon–Sun
8–12, 14–18
Moulin de Beauregard: visits by
appointment
Good English

Domaine Tinel-Blondelet
La Croix Canat
58150 Pouilly-sur-Loire
Tel 86 39 13 83, Fax 86 39 02 94
Open summer Mon–Sun 8.30–12.30,
13.30–20; closes earlier in winter; closed
first week Sept and during harvest; no
appointment
necessary for tasting, appointment preferred for cellar visit
Credit cards accepted
Good English

Hotels and Restaurants
H Hotel   **R** Restaurant

Sancerre
H Le Panoramic
Rempart des Augustins
18300 Sancerre
Tel 48 54 22 44, Fax 48 54 39 55
FF280–330

R La Pomme d'Or
Place Mairie (on Sentier Pédestre)
18300 Sancerre
Tel 48 54 13 30
FF75–220

R La Tour
Nouvelle Place
18300 Sancerre
Tel 48 54 00 81
FF98–280

Chavignol
R La Côte des Monts-Damnés
18300 Sancerre
Tel 48 54 01 72
FF95–140

Pouilly-sur-Loire
HR Hôtel de Pouilly and
Restaurant Le Relais Grillade
(off N7, 3km south of Pouilly)
58150 Pouilly-sur-Loire
Tel 86 69 07 00, Fax 86 69 02 43
Rooms FF240–360
Meals FF82–155

HR Le Relais Fleuri and
Restaurant Le Coq Hardi
42 avenue de la Tuilerie,
58150 Pouilly-sur-Loire
Tel 86 39 12 99, Fax 86 39 14 15
Rooms FF250–270
Meals FF100–240

Bordeaux and Bergerac

It's no coincidence that Bordeaux is the last region to be covered in this book. It's not just because it's the furtherst from Calais; it's also the most challenging, the most difficult to get to grips with of all the wine regions I've visited. Not impossible, by any means, but there are some pitfalls for the unwary which I need to warn you about. So don't make this the first region you visit. I reckon that, to get the most out of Bordeaux, you need to cut your teeth on some more user-friendly regions first; get a few other regions under your belt before you tackle the Big B. Think of it as Everest, and plan your assault accordingly. That way you'll get maximum benefit with minimum aggro.

Buying wine direct from its makers is not easy here. For a start, some châteaux won't deign to sell you a bottle at all. And those that do sell, offer the wines at prices which you can almost certainly beat in the local supermakret. Some are so highly priced you can even buy them cheaper in the UK.

Why should this be? The answer lies in a mixture of history and economics. Until very recently most estates didn't even bottle their wines on the premises, but sold the wine on in cask to the négoce, the merchants based in Bordeaux city or across the river in Libourne, who for centuries have controlled the wine trade here. The patterns of international distribution are so established that there has been no need to think about selling direct.

The dividing line between producer and seller is blurred, though, because many estates are owned by négociants. Names like Moueix, Janoueix and Lurton crop up with increasing regularity as the négociants build up winemaking stables. The wines are often of very high quality – Moueix owns the fabled Château Pétrus, the world's most expensive red wine – but that's not the issue here.

Where the poachers have turned gamekeepers they're even more aware of the desirability of preserving the status quo, often taking a dim view of the erosion of their traditional outlets by sales to direct visitors. They're not going to welcome you if you're likely to reduce their traditional business. Or they'll make it less attractive to buy direct by charging direct customers inflated prices.

Bordeaux is bordered by great stretches of man-made sandy beach, with large concrete seaside resorts much in evidence. This is a favourite summer playground. In addition, hundreds of coach tours whisk trippers around the famous vineyards. The sad truth in Bordeaux is that they have so many visitors that to most estates you're just another tourist. And to a large percentage of the hotels and restaurants, too, many of whom seem to have forgotten what a friendly welcome and value for money means. The Bordelais are so swamped with coaches and chara-bancs that they are, frankly, blasé about their visitors.

This will no doubt come as a surprise to anyone who has heard about the vast unsold wine lake that's sloshing around in the wine merchants' cellars. Bordeaux has had a string of poor vintages – the last good year was 1990 – and that, coupled with the recession, means that there's too much wine around, and not enough of decent quality. This is why, incidentally, you can wander around the local supermarkets, like Leclerc, and find the top clarets on sale – at prices lower than would have been thought possible a few years ago. These glamorous châteaux wouldn't stoop to mass retailing if they could sell their wine any other way. The bargain deals are the attempts of châteaux and merchants alike to liquidize their less-than-liquid assets.

You would think, wouldn't you, that with the public losing interest in their wines, not to mention the international competition they face from all the other wine-producing countries who've been sharpening up their act and offering well-made wines at reasonable prices, the winemakers would welcome you with open arms and do their best to convince you of their wines' quality and sell to you at keen prices.

Not a bit of it. And the reason seems to be an attitude of narrow regionalism which believes that Bordeaux wines are the be-all and end-all of the wine world. Such faith would be touching if it wasn't so dangerously out of touch with what's going on beyond the Gironde – the estuarine reach of the rivers

Dordogne and Garonne. The wines of Bordeaux are under threat from all sides, and applying the ostrich theory and burying their heads isn't going to avert disaster.

'So what's the point of going?' I hear you cry. I'd suggest two reasons. Firstly, because some of the grandest and most expensive wines in the world are made here, and even if you can't buy them cheaper at least you can visit some of the châteaux and pay homage in person. Secondly, by avoiding grand names and equally grand prices you can find genial winemakers and very well-made wines at prices to compete with the keenest in France.

Talking of bargains, you'll have noticed that this chapter has a double heading: not only Bordeaux but also Bergerac. Bergerac is the poor relation of Bordeaux, to the east, just down the river Dordogne, making the same style of wine with the same grapes but relegated to lower status because it's only just beginning to establish an independent reputation, and to raise its quality levels. Pricing is much more competitive here, and because most visitors pass by on a bee-line between the tourist honeypots of St-Emilion and Sarlat-la-Canéda, Bergerac receives disproportionately few visitors. The welcome is correspondingly cordial, and I think it's a region not to be missed. But more of that later.

Who Makes the Wine?

Although there are plenty of small growers, power in Bordeaux is concentrated in the hands of the big owners and the négoce. As in Burgundy, it was only in the 1920s that winemakers began to bottle their own wine; prior to that period it was shipped in cask, using the flow of the rivers to get to the coast. Elsewhere in France the growth of estate-bottling led to the estate also marketing the wine; but in Bordeaux the double-act of maker and seller persists to this day. One of the reasons the top châteaux don't sell wine to the public is that only the owners' private reserves are still in the cellars. All that's for sale has long been delivered to the négoce for selling on.

The English were early players in Bordeaux. Trade began as early as 1152, when Henry II married Eleanor of Aquitaine; and even after the English were vanquished after the end of the

Hundred Years War the trading connections remained. English merchants set up in Bordeaux, many later buying châteaux, and their legacy is still there in the scattering of English – and Irish names – Barton, Lynch and Talbot among them. One old legend even has it that Château Haut-Brion was originally named after an Irishman, O'Brien.

The average size of property is larger, partly because estates, belonging to companies rather then individuals, haven't had to be equally divided among siblings at successive owners' deaths, a system which created the patchwork of vineyard ownership in Burgundy. The Bordelais look down their noses at their cousins in Burgundy who, with their tiny holdings, make much smaller quantities of wine. But let's face it: it ain't what you've got, it's what you do with it that counts. And, alas, many of the big boys are found wanting.

Another factor is who's in charge of winemaking. This is the region of the 'flying oenologists', the wine scientists who advise many estates. Often they're academics. Names like Peynaud and Rolland are among those you'll hear mentioned, and if your French and interest are up to it, detailed discussions can be had with winemakers about the pros and cons of their oenologists' advice.

You many also pick up on a groundswell of opinion against the supremacy of the oenologist. The chief accusation is that the oenologists' techniques lead to wines from different parts of the region tasting exactly alike, so much so that some people claim to be able to identify a wine by who's made it rather than where it comes from (as one prominent winemaker complained, 'I am fed up of drinking the wines of Peynaud').

Techniques like organic and biodynamic cultivation can be seen as a reaction to this growing homogeneity. We are, I believe, in real danger of wines tasting ever more similar, so the winemakers practising these disciplines are standing up for wines tasting of where they come from and when they grew.

It's probably no coincidence that, as far as I can tell, the largest concentration of winemakers using biodynamic techniques is to be found in Bordeaux. I hope this move towards greater individuality – not to mention the increased health of the soil, which underlies these philosophies – will rapidly gain momentum. Meanwhile these producers are generally making good wines at moderate prices, and deserve support.

THE RANGE OF BORDEAUX WINES

Bordeaux is France's largest 'quality' (as opposed to 'basic plonk') wine region, and also aspires to produce the greatest wines. You only have to look at the humblest wine label to see the words 'Grand Vin de Bordeaux' emblazoned across it. Whether it's 'great' is a decision you alone can make. And one rule of thumb, well established in other regions of France, that does hold true here is: beware of big names trading on past glories rather than current performance.

Just about every kind of wine is made here: red, rosé (including a light red speciality called Clairet, from which the English term claret, meaning any Bordeaux red, derives), and dry and sweet whites. Now there is even an appellation for a sparkling called Crémant de Bordeaux, but I'm not convinced it's that successful. This breadth of styles makes this wine region different from any other in France.

Bordeaux is so vast and has so many differences in style that I think it's easier to break it down into regions and give a description of what's available in each. Its vast size means you could devote a whole book to visiting Bordeaux estates (and indeed there are several tomes dealing solely with their wines).

There are three major red grape varieties you'll encounter, and four whites. Instead of being totally dependent on the performance of one variety, as the Burgundians are with their red, the Pinot Noir, the Bordelais can hedge their bets by blending the different varieties according to which has done best on their soil or during that year. The red varieties you'll come across are:

Cabernet Sauvignon. This grape is most popular in the Médoc and Graves, as it does best on their predominantly gravel soil. It's highly coloured, astringent, tannic, ripens late, and has a thick skin which helps it to resist rot.

Cabernet Franc ripens slightly before Cabernet Sauvignon, and is used in small quantities to add complexity and bouquet.

Merlot thrives on clay, so it's more popular on the north bank of the river in St-Emilion and, especially, in Pomerol. It makes round, generous, fleshy wine, high in alcohol. It ripens a week or two before Cabernet Sauvignon but is prone to rot.

Petit Verdot is a fourth red grape variety, used in small quantities. It ripens very late but gives high colour and tannin and high sugar when it gets the chance to ripen fully.

For whites, the usual options are Sauvignon, Sémillon and Muscadelle:

Sauvignon is the great grape of Sancerre, on the Loire, where it's used unblended. It makes wines of very high acidity, so it's usually blended with Sémillon, which is lower in acidity.

Sémillon is very susceptible to botrytis, so is much used in the sweet wine regions.

Muscadelle is also used, in small proportions: it's very susceptible to a host of diseases but offers a perfumed, floral character when healthy and ripe.

WHAT YOU'LL SEE IN THE CELLAR

Lots of barrels, for a start. The red wines of Bordeaux, and a good proportion of the whites, are aged in barrels containing 225 litres known as *pièces* or *barriques bordelaises*. The proportion of new barrels used, and the length of time the wine will spend in them, varies according to the quality of the wine and of the vintage, ie the better the wine, the newer the barrels, and the longer the stay. The idea is that only wine of first-class concentration and ripeness will be able to withstand prolonged exposure to the nearly-overwhelming flavour of newly-toasted wood. The coopers 'toast' or burn the inside of the barrels according to the buyer's instructions. (Talk of medium-toasting here has nothing to do with the breakfast table.) Most estates will use a proportion of new barrels each year: if the vintage is poor the proportion will drop, but a useful yardstick is that a minimum of one-third new barrels is necessary to produce wine of the quality the château might be expected to aspire to.

It's the mark of a rich estate when the cellars, or *chais* (pronounced 'sha', as in 'shame'), are big enough to allow all the barrels to rest directly on the ground runners, single-storey. It makes the cellar work much easier, as the barrels regularly need to be topped up (*ouillage*) to make good the 'ullage' which evaporates through the wood. This happens as often as once a week, using a thing like a watering-can with an bent spout, often with a candle perched on the end so that you can see what you're doing.

Every three or four months, the contents of the barrel are racked (*soutirage*) into a clean barrel, leaving the lees behind. As the solid matter is gradually deposited the wine begins to 'fall bright'. Traditionally, the wine is then fined with egg-white, either fresh or in powdered form, and bottled without filtering (hooray!), though you'll often see filtration machines in cellars. And you're invariably told that they filter 'as lightly as possible' which is about as meaningful as saying Persil washes whiter. Than what?

Appearance-conscious châteaux will use the spent lees, which are a rich purple colour and the consistency of vinyl matt, to paint the middle section of each barrel mauve. This is intended to disguise the mauve stains which appear when wine is spilt from the bung-hole during racking or topping-up. I like the effect of hundreds of barrels all neatly two-tone. One château I visited, Cos d'Estournel, is so style-conscious that it uses a sander to clean off stains, so all barrels in its *chai* look like they've only just been pressed into service.

But I'm getting ahead of myself. Different wine varieties are fermented separately (some varieties ripen sooner than others and are therefore harvested at different times), usually in stainless steel vats, but occasionally you still see open-topped wooden ones (though even these, given the money that was until recently sloshing about in Bordeaux, often have sophisticated temperature-control equipment installed in them). Once fermentation slows down, after a few days, sugar is added to chaptalize the wine. This increases alcoholic strength and prolongs fermentation, thus increasing the colour and tannin extracted from the skins. The wine is also pumped over several times a day to break up the cap of grape skins – up to a foot thick – which forms at the top and prevents oxygen getting to the wine.

After fermentation there's a maceration, or *cuvaison*, lasting several weeks (again depending on how good the vintage is) which also extracts more colour and tannin, then the wine is racked off its lees into barrels. The residue of lees and skins is pressed, often in old-fashioned wood presses. The resulting *vin de presse* will have much higher tannin and acidity. It's matured separately and some will probably be added to the wine at *assemblage*, to give 'backbone', strength and character, depending on what the winemaker wants to achieve. The remaining *vin de presse* is distilled, by law. Blending usually takes place after the wine has finished its maturation. The wine goes back into vats in blended form to 'marry', then the wine is finally bottled.

In poor years the grapes may not have ripened fully, or may be low in colour and tannin. This is remedied by 'bleeding off' some of the juice shortly after fermentation has started. This improves the concentration of what's left, because it will have proportionately more contact with the skins in the vat, but the juice that comes off is very light red, with next to no tannin. It's fermented separately to make the light red Clairet. Some winemakers bleed their wines and make Clairet each year as a matter of course; others do it only as a necessity in bad years. Expect to find a lot of 1992 and 1993 Clairet.

Look out for how the cellar you're visiting matures its white wines: most will be in stainless steel, but some will be in 'old' barrels – after 3 or 4 years' use a barrel yields no more 'wood' taste, but it still benefits the wine by allowing it controlled contact with the maturing qualities of air. Some whites will be in new or 1–3-year-old barrels, and these wines are likely to be something special (and expensive: a new barrel costs over £200). Many estates practise *bâtonnage*, just as in Champagne or Burgundy: stirring the lees up every week or so with a stick or baton, to impart their flavour to the wine.

Sometimes, in the grander establishments, a tour of the cellar will lead you past locked wrought-iron gates protecting stacks of dusty bottles. Many of these won't be from that château, but are evidence of a long-standing tradition of exchanging bottles with other châteaux: to compare, contrast, run down the competition, or delight in their achievements. However they're used, the stocks appear to be both comprehensive and very mature.

You'll occasionally see underground fermentation or storage tanks, used for reasons of lack of space, or to take advantage of stable subterranean temperatures. On stainless-steel tanks you'll often see characteristic helter-skelter bands on the side where the temperature-control coils lie. Cement vats are also common ('well, if it's good enough for Pétrus...', as one user said).

Second Wines

Another difference in Bordeaux is the prevalence of 'second' wines. Many châteaux make their 'grand vin' from a blend of the very best vats, and any vats judged to be not quite good enough are used to make this second wine. Usually they're made from grapes from less favourably-situated parts of the vineyard, or from recently-planted vines. Vines younger than say 15–18 years aren't held to have enough complexity in their fruit to make the great wine. I do like these arguments which favour maturity over youth.

WHEN TO GO

Because of the intensive cellar practices – topping up, racking – there's often cellar activity throughout the year, which makes it more rewarding to visit out of season. Bordeaux has a temperate maritime climate, shielded from sea breezes by the man-made Landes pine forest planted along the coast to prevent erosion. It suffers from rainy, frosty spring weather but amply compensates for this with warm, sunny autumns which have been the last-minute saviour of many a borderline vintage. The period between harvest and Christmas (think of all those fancy gift-packs!) can be a good time to go. Don't go in August, though: remember wine is a business here, and the workers and proprietors take the traditional holiday. If you visit in early summer, you'll often see roses in bloom at the end of each row of vines, a typical feature of Bordeaux vineyard. They often stay in flower until late autumn. Originally grown as an early-warning sign of vine maladies (eg mildew), they're a charming reminder of a time when life was less high-tech and complicated.

Incidentally, geography gives rise to yet another Bordeaux difference: whereas elsewhere in France the rule is that the best vineyards are on the slopes, here there aren't any slopes to speak of. Soil, subsoil and drainage count for a lot more. They have an old saying that the best vines can see the water, and it seems to be true that the best Médoc wines come from the vineyards closest to the estuary.

PLANNING THE ROUTE

It's a two-day slog from Calais: you might consider an overnight stop in the Loire, which also allows an instructive compare-and-contrast on pricing and quality. From St-Malo, on the other hand, it's less than five hours to Royan – with the new motorway sections open south of Nantes the Rennes–Royan route is perfectly feasible in a day. And it's mostly dual carriageway. It's also possible, though harder work, from Cherbourg, Caen or Le Havre. You may prefer the motorway via Paris from the latter. The other delight of the Rennes–Royan route, however, is that – apart from the stretch south of Nantes – the roads are dual carriageway rather than motorway, so you make good speed without having to pay tolls. There's more dual carriageway around La Rochelle, and the countryside around Rochefort is quite attractive even though you're by now on single carriageway.

The route I've mapped out is a one-way circular tour, starting in Royan for the ferry across the Gironde (well, Bordeaux seems like another country, where they do things very differently, so it seems only proper to approach it by ferry). The route heads south through the Médoc, then into the Graves, then Sauternes, and crosses the river into Entre-deux-Mers. From here it moves east into Bergerac, where it crosses the river again and heads back into the Bordeaux region along the north bank of the Dordogne. Passing through Côtes de Castillon and Côtes de Francs, it nips through St-Emilion and Pomerol, rushes through Fronsac and pauses in Bourg and Blaye before landing up on the motorway and all points north.

Phew! A whistle-stop tour, yes, but I think an instructive one. It should allow the chance to decide for yourself who's making good wine, who's trading on their name and/or fleecing the tourists, and, most importantly, which areas make the wine you might actually want to buy. And if you decide none of it does, well, at least the geography makes more sense now and you can go home via another, perhaps more approachable wine region. On the other hand, you might find you're so completely at home with the wines made by one or two of these producers that you'll never shop elsewhere again. And there are people on this itinerary you can really warm to. Well, I did, anyway.

The Médoc

This is where some of the world's greatest full-bodied red wines are made. And they certainly know it. I have to say that this is the most challenging wine area I've ever visited. The first time I travelled to the Médoc, before I became what's loosely called a wine-writer and was just a fan of wine and France, in that order, I felt so intimidated by all these imposing châteaux that, once off the Royan ferry, I started driving through the vineyards, and was simply too overwhelmed to stop. I didn't get out of the car until St-Emilion. And once there I wandered into one of the wine shops on the main square, where you can't taste, and bought a few bottles recommended by the proprietor. And got them home and found they were undrinkable. I had been simply seduced by the name.

That is how not to do wine tourism. It was an experience which proved to me the hard way that you can't judge by appearances, or names. You need to know what's what. And nowhere is this more true than in the Médoc. This is, after all, where they won't even sell you a bottle half the time. And don't even think about turning up unannounced. What you can do is write, or phone, and ask for an appointment to make a visit.

When you arrive at a grand château you're highly unlikely to meet the winemaker. They employ hostesses to deal with the likes of us. Often young multilingual women fresh out of college, they'll be professional, and may even be charming. They'll probably speak good English. But they won't be too clued-up on technical matters, and may even get irritated that you've asked.

Some of them will let you taste the wine in barrel (cheaper than opening a bottle, but possibly less fun for you: it could be a while away from being drinkable.) Some of them may even open a bottle for you – and they may also charge you for it. Some of the grandest, such as Château Mouton-Rothschild, don't let you taste at all, though they admit they may have to bow to public expectation and start pulling the corks out – for a fee.

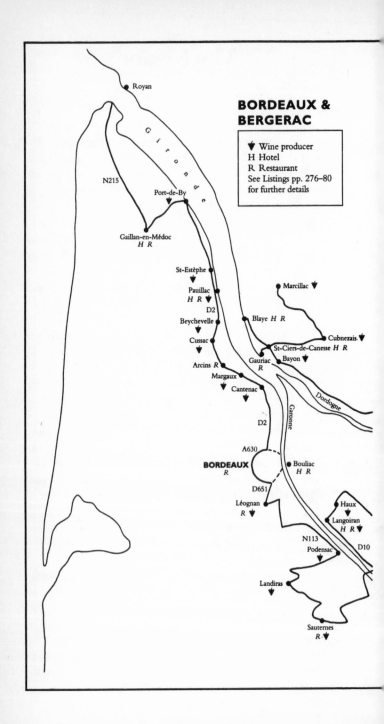

**BORDEAUX &
BERGERAC**

♥ Wine producer
H Hotel
R Restaurant
See Listings pp. 276–80
for further details

Royan

Gironde

N215

Port-de-By ♥

Gaillan-en-Médoc
H R

St-Estèphe ♥

Pauillac
H R ♥
D2

Beychevelle ♥

Cussac ♥

Arcins *R*

Margaux ♥
Cantenac ♥

D2

Marcillac ♥

Blaye *H R*

Cubnezais ♥

St-Ciers-de-Canesse *H R*
Gauriac   Bayon
R

Garonne

Dordogne

A630

BORDEAUX
R

Bouliac
H R

D651

Léognan
R ♥

Haux ♥
Langoiran
H R ♥

N113

D10

Podensac ♥

Landiras ♥

Sauternes
R ♥

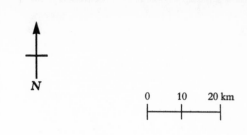

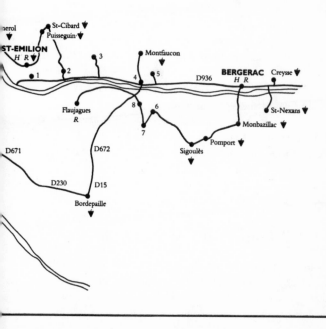

1 St-Etienne-de-Lisse
2 Belvès-de-Castillon
3 St-Michel-de-Montaigne
4 Pont-Ste-Foy
5 St-Avit
6 Saussignac *H R*
7 Monestier
8 Razac-de-Saussignac

Will they take you seriously? That rather depends on you. Jeans, trainers, a 10-year-old car? Probably not. Much judging-by-appearances goes on here, and you really have to front it out. Jackets and ties, skirts and heels, if you can face it on your hols. Drive the poshest, shiniest car you can lay your hands on. A letter of introduction from your wine merchant helps. Don't expect the supermarkets to do this, but a good independent merchant who sells you the wine in the UK can often be prevailed upon to write saying you're an important customer.

Some producers admit they'll be sizing you up by careful observation of your tasting technique. It can be a dead give-away if you swallow the lot rather than spitting, for instance, so you might want to check out the tasting technique described in the Introduction. And making notes looks impressive even if they're gibberish.

One thing you can't help noticing in the Médoc is that it's the land of the big establishment: both in terms of the size of vineyard holdings and the grandeur of the châteaux. Sadly, very few estate owners actually live on the property (legend has it that if you see the tricolour flying it means the owner's in residence, but who's going to give such a clear signal to burglars by not flying it?) Few owners are in residence because few estates remain in family hands: in a number of cases the owners are now insurance companies or multinational businesses.

As a result, complained one estate-worker who was echoed on all sides, the Médoc is dead at night. That's why the few decent restaurants are packed at lunchtime and deserted at the end of the day. It also accounts for the fearsome rush-hour traffic, as estate-workers undertake mass migration after break-fast and again after lunch, from the suburbs of Bordeaux to their château of employment. It's a sad fact that decent hotel accommodation is hard to find in the Médoc, and often woe-fully overpriced and erratic. The local use simply isn't there to support it. (Better news follows, however, in other districts.)

HOW THE WINES ARE CLASSIFIED

Let's start at the top. In 1855 the top wines of Bordeaux were ranked in order of the prices they were achieving at auction, the theory being that the most expensive wines would be the best. It turned out that all but one of these top wines (Château

Haut-Brion in the Graves) came from the Médoc. They were grouped into five categories, from first growths (Premiers Crus) to fifth.

If you're interested in historical documents, you can check this list out. To me, it seems pretty hollow: in 150 years there has been just one sole amendment, moving Château Mouton-Rothschild up from second to first growth in 1973. Now what classification can possibly hold good for that length of time? Properties change hands, amalgamate and disappear, quality rises and falls. Many châteaux print the 1855 classification on their label but sometimes the quality within does absolutely nothing to justify it. If you're a serious buyer of Bordeaux you'll be making it your business to know precisely who's over- and under-valued. For the rest of us, the properties listed here will give you a good insight into what's happening right now.

Below the crus classés you'll find a separate rating system, the crus bourgeois. This was introduced in 1978, and châteaux can be Cru Bourgeois, Cru Grand Bourgeois and Cru Grand Bourgeois Exceptionnel. You won't see these last two names on labels, however, as they're now forbidden under EC rules.

However, if a château isn't in this classification it doesn't mean it isn't any good; some châteaux declined to be involved because they feared it would prejudice their position if the 1855 classification were ever revised. And some weren't included because they declined to join the local syndicate, which then decided that syndicate membership was a prerequisite for classification. So there's no way you can take either of these ratings systems as a reliable indicator of quality. The only thing that matters, here more than ever, is whether you think the wine is worth the asking price.

These lower-classified and unclassified establishments are often patronizingly referred to as 'petits châteaux'. These so-called little estates can often offer some of the best value around, precisely because nobody thinks they're sufficiently important to bother about.

So those are the quality levels. Then you need to add geographical area (who said this was going to be easy?). Bottom of the scale, of course, is generic AC Bordeaux, which is a kind of bottom-line for any red or white within the delimited wine producing area of Bordeaux, not just the Médoc. All of the following ACs refer to red wines only.

The Médoc is divided into two, helpfully called Médoc and Haut-Médoc. Médoc was originally called Bas- or lower, but vanity prevailed and the 'lower' is generally dropped. The upper (Haut) Médoc is south of the lower Médoc.

Then there are the four famous communes: from north to south come St-Estèphe, Pauillac, St-Julien and Margaux. These, plus the lesser Listrac and Moulis, are the only specific communal names you'll see as ACs. Aficionados will discuss the differences in taste and style from these communes, and indeed some have devoted a lifetime to the study of these wines. But we're here to enjoy ourselves...

EXPLORING THE MÉDOC

Once in Royan, follow the 'Bac' signs painted on the road to guide you to the car ferry. The crossing takes half an hour, but runs infrequently out of season; be more efficient than me and check timings (telephone 56 09 60 84), or be prepared for a longish wait (three hours over lunch.) The crossing takes half an hour, and on landing take the main road, the N215. The landscape here is bleak and windswept: reclaimed by Dutch engineers several hundred years ago, it looks decidedly Flemish.

Eventually vineyards start to appear, and soon after you reach the outskirts of **Gaillan-en-Médoc**. If you've been driving all day this is a good point to make an overnight stop at the hotel Château Layauga, easy to spot on the right on the N215. It's less a château than a chartreuse, a Bordelais bungalow. (But on two storeys. Don't ask me.) The restaurant here has a well-deserved Michelin star; there's a cordial welcome and comfortable rooms, though maybe the beds are a little past their best-before date.

Setting out on the wine route, you soon discover one of the aspects of touristic welcome in Bordeaux: there is no sign-posted route. Except for some old signposts in Sauternes and Graves, there is no attempt in Bordeaux to guide the motorized visitor through the vineyards. Remember, there are enough tourists here anyway, so no need to encourage them.

Instead, use the local road D2 as an unofficial route through the Médoc. It has the advantage that most of the châteaux are more or less clearly signposted from it, making it a reasonably useful introduction to the region. The first visit on my route is in **Port-de-By**, in the Médoc classification area, so from Château Layauga take the D3 in Lesparre-Médoc. If you're coming directly from the ferry you can pick up the D2 further north, at St-Vivien-de-Médoc. **CHÂTEAU LA TOUR DE BY** is well-signposted from either direction.

This is a really welcoming visit, with plenty to see. Marc Pages, joint owner and manager, has been making wine here for 29 years, since leaving Algeria at the time of independence (you'll come across a fair number of ex-Algerians in Bordeaux and Bergerac). M Pages receives many visitors himself, a rarity in the Médoc, although in season there's also a hostess to share the workload.

A tour through the *chai* reveals many unusual things. The old open wooden vats are still used, a rarity nowadays, and if you look up as you pass them you'll notice they're festooned with netting at the top; a safety-net as used at a circus ring to catch workers who slip while working on the open vat tops. M Paget collects old winemaking tools, with an eye for the off-beat. Ask for an explanation of their function – there's some unusual stuff here, and his enthusiasm makes past eras spring to life.

He's keen on old oxen harnesses, relics from when beasts of burden formed the vineyard power unit. There's a training harness, for a young ox to be strapped in between two more experienced beasts; a two-size harness for combining ox and donkey power; and a curious double harness with cupped pads to fit on the animals' foreheads. The span is extra-wide so the oxen could pass between the rows of vines. (You can flesh this information out further at the splendid museum of Libournais life in Montagne: see page 269.)

La Tour de By's wines, classified Cru Bourgeois, offer some of the best winemaking in the area: medium bodied, elegant and very good value. In addition to La Tour de By they also offer a second wine, and even a Cuvée de Prestige in the best vintages (which means they haven't made one recently). The wines aren't filtered, and the use of traditional methods produces here a high-quality product. And you're welcome to taste whatever interests you.

Don't leave without visiting the tower which gives the estate its name. A former lighthouse marooned in a sea of vines, it's still a local landmark. Climb the 55 steps for superb views of the estuary and surrounding vineyards.

Pick up the D2 as it runs south, scenically, along the coast. The road eventually brings you into the commune of **St-Estèphe**, the largest of the four great communes. These are solid, full, tannic wines, and the best of the commune is **COS D'ESTOURNEL**. Cos originally meant 'hill of pebbles', as the vineyards prove.

This estate offers you a classic Médoc visit: in many ways it's a classic Médoc establishment. You must visit strictly by appointment; no mass tourism here. The hostess, Catherine di Costanzo, who speaks excellent English, is very charming, and seems to know more about winemaking than many of her counterparts at other establishments. She says she likes to adapt her presentation according to visitors' level of interest and knowledge.

Cos d'Estournel, with its three pagoda-style turrets, has some of the most stylish looks of the Médoc. The oriental style stems from the original owner's trade with the Raj, but there are Arabian, Chinese and Japanese influences too. The huge, ornately-carved doors apparently once guarded the entrance to the sultan of Zanzibar's harem. Good photo-opportunity.

The visit opens with a ten-minute slide-show. Though the commentary is studded with purple prose (grapes are 'black pearls', for example) the photography is stunning and there's a coup de théâtre at the show's climax.

The tour then takes you past dimly-lit bottle stores and through elegant barrel cellars (watch out for those sanders). Note the lampshades, made from halved baby barrels. To finish you're taken into the modern tasting-room and offered a recent vintage of Cos and also the second wine, Château de Marbuzet. They'll give you a special passport as a parting gift.

The car park at Cos was festooned with signs warning tourists to leave nothing of value in their cars as a spate of thefts had been reported. Can't happen to me, I thought. Foolish woman. My purse disappeared the very next day.

Moving south from Cos, you cross a slight valley with a stream running through it, which forms the boundary between St-Estèphe and Pauillac. Shortly before the town you'll see **MOUTON-ROTHSCHILD** signed off on the right. Subsequent signs modestly refer to the estate simply as 'Mouton'.

In charge of visits here is James Stewart ('not as in the American actor; as in the Scottish king'). While on the subject of names, please note that the French pronunciation of Rothschild follows its German origins (meaning 'red shield') and is thus more like 'rot-shild'. I'm told that if you encounter the proprietor, Baroness Philippine, she will correct you if you get it wrong. Unlikely your paths will cross, I know, but I always think it best to get these little matters sorted out in advance.

This is the only first-growth estate prepared to sell wine to you at the property, but don't imagine they'll let you taste it first, even for money. The tour of the property, after the obligatory slide-show, takes you into the splendid 100m-long barrel cellar. Here, all the barrels are laid out single-storey, evidence of serious investment. At the end is a large reproduction of the family coat of arms, including two sheep rampant which look incredibly camp close to. (The use of a sheep is a joke: Baron Rothschild was an Aries.) Don't miss the display of labels, which since 1945 have featured commissioned paintings by artists such as Picasso and Chagall.

This love of art found its apogee in the Musée du Vin et de l'Art, a stunning collection of art and artefacts which has turned this château into the most-visited in the Médoc, if not the whole of Bordeaux. James Stewart is a mine of impressively detailed information on all the exhibits, though if you visit at peak times his attention is likely to be divided throughout a fairly big group. If you only see one museum, see this one – though the one in Montagne is pretty ace, too.

The D2 now takes you into **Pauillac** itself, a dull town blighted by an old oil refinery. On the river-front, however, is a large tree-lined parking area where you can picnic on the banks of the estuary, with appropriately scenic views. As you leave town you'll pass the Maison du Vin, which doubles as a tourist information office and can help with accommodation. Maisons du Vin are plentiful in the Médoc, and their staff are generally helpful and worth calling in on. This one has a wide range of wines on sale from all the Médoc, and can advise you on how to make further châteaux visits. In the car park there's one of those big press-a-button-and-the-route-lights-up displays, very useful for finding your way to your next appointment.

No problems with finding the next stop, however: leave Pauillac heading south on the D2 and it's a couple of hundred

metres on the right. **CHÂTEAU LYNCH-BAGES** is another grand
name, ranked fifth growth in 1855 but held to be rather better
than that these days. Again you're greeted by a hostess (having,
of course, made an appointment) – although mine didn't seem
to know too much about what went on. It seemed like just
another trot through the fermentation and maturation cellars,
and was beginning to get rather tedious, when suddenly everything changed.

Climbing a flight of stairs, I found myself on a platform
above the old open vats. This old pressing and fermentation
area has been preserved to show how things were done a century ago. Grapes were hoisted up onto a large mobile platform
on the first floor, where they were crushed by foot. The juice
was channelled off into different vats by moving the crushing
platform along on rails. (Those who have visited Champy's
fascinating installation in Beaune will find the contrast in
methods particularly interesting.)

It was dangerous: the wooden floor is slatted, to allow the
lethal carbon dioxide given off from the open fermenting vats
to sink down to the ground floor, out of the workers' way.
Candles were used to detect the presence of safe levels of oxygen. It's worth visiting just to see all this, although they will
also pour a young vintage for you free of charge. Lynch-Bages
1988 is FF195 a bottle.

Practically next door, and related, is one of the best hotels
I've stayed in anywhere, certainly the best bet in the Médoc.
Château Cordeillan-Bages is a 17th-century château, complete
with wings originally used for wine production, now converted
into a really welcoming hotel. Food is starred, the staff are
relaxed yet very alert to what needs doing, and bedrooms are
large and comfortable, giving onto a quiet inner courtyard.
Huge buffet breakfasts.

If making all these appointments is getting too much, ask
the hotel to take over. There's a wine school attached to the
hotel which can organize guided tours of vineyards and cellars.
Use them shamelessly if you want any particularly grand doors
to be opened to you. Or take their photography course, which
involves taking a mental picture of various wines during a
pre-dinner tasting, then having them served to you blind over
dinner to identify/guess which is which. Speaking as someone who prefers to drink for pleasure come dinner-time it

sounds a bit too much like hard work for my liking, but it's apparently very popular.

Southbound again, pass through St-Julien-Beychevelle and, in **Beychevelle** itself – the next village down, and still in the St-Julien appellation – turn right, following the signposts to **CHÂTEAU LAGRANGE**, a couple of kilometres out in the countryside. This is an interesting visit to make – by appointment, of course. (I think it's best to assume you have to make an appointment unless it specifically says otherwise.) You'll be greeted by the cellarmaster or other senior technical person rather than a professional hostess. This means you can ask as much as you need to know about the winemaking, and the considerable investment you'll see all around you.

Lagrange had experienced a severe decline in the middle years of this century, but was rescued by the Japanese drinks giant Suntory in 1983. Their multi-million-pound investment has turned things around completely. Lagrange make two wines: their second, Les Fiefs de Lagrange, made from the high proportion of young vines planted since Suntory's takeover, is in great demand in its own right. I can exclusively reveal that the marketing director of a well-known high street wine chain once spent most of his free time going round all the branches he could reach, snapping up every bottle of Les Fiefs before the punters got wind of how good it was.

Although you can taste here from the barrel (check your technique – they'll be observing you closely!) you can't buy. The wines are all sold the old-fashioned way, through the Bordeaux merchants. I include Lagrange because it's a good example of the kind of welcome and time and effort the high-quality, but lesser-known, establishments will devote to you. I felt I'd got a little closer to the winemaking process here than I had in some other classed-growth châteaux, and there was a very honest feel to the place. They reckon to get few visitors because the name isn't so well-known, and want to make it memorable for those who do come. This isn't really a touristic-type visit, but if you're serious about their wines you'll be made very welcome.

The D2 goes ever on and on, this time as far as **Cussac**. **CHÂTEAU BEAUMONT** is, just for a change, signposted off on the right. It's well-signed until the driveway to the château, where all help deserts you: when the road bends sharply left and you can see a likely-looking building straight ahead down a chalky track, you're right – that's it. If you don't trust your instincts, however, I can guarantee there's a good turning place a short way down the road.

Château Beaumont is also part-owned by Suntory, and has benefited from considerable investment, though on a lesser scale than its classed-growth cousin. The château, built in 1854, is of particular interest to wine tourists because it offers simple but elegant bed-and-breakfast accommodation. No dinner, but the locals' favourite hangout, the Lion d'Or at Arcins, is just a few minutes down the road, and given that next to no-one actually lives in the Médoc it shouldn't be packed out at night. (Book ahead for lunch there, though.)

The appellation here is Haut-Médoc; being just outside St-Julien and Margaux, the wine is much more competitively-priced. The technical manager will show you round and he clearly takes a lot of pride in his installation. The vinification is traditional: 'we put the grapes in the vat and wait!' The resulting wine, deeply coloured, tannic and with good fruit, is mostly sold to the merchants but some is kept for direct sales – around FF40 a bottle. It's often bought by other Beaumonts, who travel from all over the world to visit their namesake, though nobody appears to be directly related. You can taste barrel samples free, but they'll make a charge if they open bottles for you. No great pretensions here, but honest winemaking in elegant surroundings, and fair prices.

Back on the D2, though Lamarque and Arcins (the Lion d'Or restaurant is on the left, on a bend, and hard to spot from this direction until you've driven past it), and as you enter **Margaux** you can't miss signs for **CHÂTEAU PRIEURÉ-LICHINE**. This proudly proclaims that it's open without appointment 365 days a year, which is great, and it's a classed growth, but I warn you, it's very touristy. They charge FF30, and for that you get to browse in its shop/reception area, watch a video (if it's working; it wasn't when I dropped in) and be guided through some of the more scenic cellar areas. Then you can taste two vintages. As a gentle introduction, this is a very low-stress place to visit: but it's so geared up for tourists, including large groups, that you're not going to find out too much or experience any personal touches. The price for the 1990 Lichine is FF169.

Just after Lichine, having turned right onto the D2 of course, you'll see signs on the right for **CHÂTEAU D'ANGLUDET**. This is not an imposing château, more a comfortable chartreuse: it's a family home, unusual for the Médoc. British wine merchant Peter Sichel, provider of a great deal of the generic Bordeaux found on British shelves, took over this property in the 1960s and made it the success it is today. Visits are now conducted by his son, Benjamin. This is a Cru Bourgeois, but the wine is certainly of classed-growth quality. Talking of classed growths, the Sichels have a share in illustrious Château Palmer and can also arrange an English-language visit for you there. The second wine, la Ferme d'Angludet, is also of very good quality, and the dismal harvest in 1992 prompted them to produce a very refreshing Clairet. This is a relaxed, enjoyable visit; it's heartening to find somewhere so unstuffy. And the wines are very good value. Prices: FF54–110.

The D2 continues into the northern suburbs of Bordeaux and alas, there's now nothing for it: you have to join the motorway. I'd really like to avoid routing you this way, because the Bordeaux *rocade* (bypass) was the scene of the most terrifyingly bad driving I've ever seen in my life – and that includes Paris. Unfortunately there's no way of avoiding it but whatever you do don't venture on during rush-hours.

Traffic, and parking, in Bordeaux itself can be bedlam and requires a good deal of courage. If you do hazard it in, there are two museums of interest: the Musée d'Aquitaine, which is devoted to wine history from 1750 to 1950; and the Musée des Chartrons, which depicts the life of the Bordeaux wine merchant. For lunch, try the Bistro du Sommelier, where you can buy reasonably-priced wines by the glass to accompany traditional dishes.

Otherwise press on round the bypass, following the airport signs and ignoring the chaos all around you, and leave at junction 18. Take the D651 towards **Léognan**: you're now in the Graves region.

The Graves

The Graves, as the name suggests, has gravelly soil. The countryside is hillier and more interesting than the Médoc, and as you
drive south you'll notice how agricultural land fights for space
with the pine trees of the Landes forest. This enormous woodland was planted to stop the coastal erosion, and if you get
bored with the wine route head west for the sea: you'll hit
splendid sands and the chance for some bracing bathing.

Although red wine is in the majority here (the ratio is about
55:45) Graves is still thought of as a white wine region – one of
my first vinous memories is of my grandfather uncorking a
sweet white Graves at Christmas. Graves Supérieur is how the
sweet or semi-sweet whites are labelled, bottled in clear glass.
Wines labelled simply Graves are dry, frequently bottled in
green glass. They're often of very good concentration and aged
in wood.

There is a classification, but it was last revised in 1959 and is
long overdue an overhaul. In the north, Graves wines from
certain areas in the north of the region can label their wines
Pessac-Léognan. The wines aren't generally held to have the
quality of the top Médocs, but here's some very good winemaking going on here and some good value to be found. And
some pretension too, of course – we're not yet far enough
away from Bordeaux to have escaped that.

EXPLORING THE GRAVES

Head south from the bypass towards **Léognan**. The original
winemaking area extended right into the city of Bordeaux and
now the suburbs have encircled some of the top châteaux. In
Léognan itself the restaurant La Forge is good for a budget
lunch; otherwise keep heading south and just as you leave the
village take a sharp left to **CHÂTEAU LA LOUVIÈRE**. You may
see the sign in time.

La Louvière is one of several properties belonging to négociant André Lurton. Château Bonnet, another Lurton estate, is
quite well-known in the UK, but discourages visitors. Here, on
the other hand, you're welcome. The château was declared an

ancient monument in 1946 and is beautifully-proportioned. The cellars run down either side of the courtyard and a new tasting-room in the château itself is decorated with murals of the various Lurton properties. You can taste three wines for FF20, which is refundable on purchase. I found these wines to be of high quality, but prices are steep – and you can only buy in units of three, for up to FF1220. They're cheaper in the local Leclerc supermarket. Louvière produces red and white Pessac-Léognan, but wines from the rest of the empire are also on sale.

Turn left out of La Louvière, and continue along the D651 even when it becomes the D111. Turn right in Cadaujac, taking the D111E4 to Martillac. This route takes you past some of the big names so you know where they are without going through all the hassle of actually trying to get an appointment. Pick up the D214 and head south for a short stretch on the N113.

When you get to **Podensac**, look out for signs on your right to **CHÂTEAU DE CHANTEGRIVE** – it's on the road to St-Michel-de-Rieufret. A *chantegrive* is a song-thrush, a bird which competes with grape-pickers for the annual harvest and which apparently makes a bee-line for this estate's best vineyards.

You'll be received by a hostess who may or may not speak English (depending on who they hire). Wines are indeed well-made, notably Cuvée Caroline, a dry white aged in new wood, for a hefty FF60. More basic whites are around FF40, and the red Graves FF40–60. All very efficient, and I recommend it for quality, but maybe not for friendliness.

The contrast with the next property couldn't be more marked. From Chantegrive head into St-Michel then turn left onto the D117/D109 to Illats. There turn right onto the D11, and **DOMAINE DU MOULIN À VENT** is on your left on the outskirts of **Landiras**.

This is a small family business which has tended its vines organically since the 1960s. Dogs and chickens roam the yard and vegetable patch. A tour of the winery reveals it to be pretty chaotic. The maturation cellar has an earthen floor, for greater humidity, but the dirt seems to have seeped next door into the fermenting cellar. Upstairs is the oldest labelling machine I've yet come across, a very satisfying and well-oiled piece of machinery.

Tasting takes place in what is possibly the dining-room; all very relaxed and casual. Prices are reasonable (FF28–40), but doubts about quality crept into my mind. At first I put this down to the tasting-glasses which had sat for too long in a cupboard, and the fact that the samples poured came from already-opened bottles.

I tried the wines back in the UK, and found the white was oxidized. The welcome at the domaine was very friendly, and after so many cold-hearted wine estates I really wanted to find somewhere which offered both a genuinely warm welcome and good wines: I sincerely hope I was just unlucky.

From Landiras take the D116 towards **Sauternes**, noticing how the Landes pine forest is now dominating the landscape, with occasional clearings for vines. Turn right onto the D114, which is signposted as a touristic circuit for the Sauternais. Viticulture is once more king, with rolling hillsides and immaculately-tended vines. Sauternes is the world's most famous and expensive producer of sweet wines. The dearest, Château Yquem, claims that one vine produces enough grapes to make just one glass of its wine. (Wonder how big the glass is?) Sauternes and neighbouring, not-quite-so-fashionable Barsac are near the river Garonne, well-located to benefit from the damp morning mists which allow the rot to set in. Sauternes village is well-organized for wine tourists, with several wine shops and a Maison du Vin, which should be able to help with arranging visits.

The wines are expensive partly because of their labour-intensive nature. Noble rot (see page 188) gradually shrivels the grapes, and pickers must pass through the vineyard several times, harvesting only the fully-shrivelled berries yet leaving sufficient infected berries on the vine to spread the rot to their neighbours. It's a skilled job, and one which continues dangerously late into the autumn, risking rain, frost and the loss of what remains on the vine.

Many of the big names will see you by appointment, if you can stomach the prices they'll charge (though not forgetting that not all will allow you to buy anyway). I had made arrangements to visit Château Rieussec, but the difficulties I encountered sum up the kind of problems you can face in Bordeaux. The château is run corporately from Paris, and you have to make your appointment through them. Unfortunately they're not always in during office hours, and the last message I left on their answering-machine wasn't relayed to the château. Result: confusion, and nobody able to show me round when I arrived.

Following the marked wine route will take you past most of the big names. Showpiece of the region is **CHÂTEAU DE MALLE**, in Preignac (signposted off the route). It's a beautiful 17th-century château, Sauternes' only historic monument, which can be visited from Easter to October. You can enjoy visiting the château, but if you're looking for value rather than a posh name, you might like to hide your wallet until you get to Bergerac.

From Preignac take the N113 north through **Barsac**, which also has its share of wine shops, and turn right onto the D11 to **Cadillac**, across the river Garonne.

Entre-deux-Mers

We've moved wine region again. As the name implies, this is the area bordered by the 'two seas' – in fact rivers – Garonne and Dordogne. Entre-deux-Mers is an appellation solely for white wines, but along the north bank of the Garonne you'll find a red appellation, Premières Côtes de Bordeaux. And of course anyone in the region can make generic red AC Bordeaux if they wish.

EXPLORING ENTRE-DEUX-MERS

Follow the D11 north along the river bank: you could almost be in the Loire. Just before **Langoiran,** turn right up the hill towards the **CHÂTEAU LANGOIRAN**. The visit isn't in the castle, which has ruins dating back to the 12th century and which you can visit, but just beneath it – quite literally, as far as the cellars are concerned, tunnelling deep into the rock. The property makes two wines: Château Langoiran and Château Tour de Langoiran. The latter is darker, deeper and matured in oak.

This is hardly a great discovery on my part – the estate sold 14,000 bottles to Threshers last year – and nor is it incredibly cheap (FF30–42, or from the pump at FF22/litre) but it's a good example of what you can find by following your nose. I was served this wine at dinner the night before, on the waiter's recommendation, and it was so good I just phoned on spec the following morning to arrange a visit.

In Langoiran itself is one of the most convivial hotels I've stayed in, and also one of the cheapest. The Hotel St-Martin has welcomed guests for over a century, as sepia photos on the restaurant walls testify. The downstairs bar-restaurant, popular with locals, offers stunning views directly across the river. The food is good value, particularly at lunch, and the rooms are plainly decorated but with some style. New owners took over in 1993, and so far it hasn't hit the guide books. All the more reason to visit now.

Your alternative is to head up the pretty coast road as far as Bouliac, high on the hill, to the Hostellerie St-James. This is the best restaurant in Bordeaux and frankly some of the best food I've eaten anywhere. Although the food gets two stars the wine list is a lesson to more pretentious places: mark-ups on top growths are low, and there's a good choice of bottles under FF100, featuring many of the less fashionable appellations (and including several of the small producers featured in this chapter.) Exemplary restaurant staff, relaxed and unpretentious.

You can stay here, too, in the most futuristic bedrooms I've ever encountered. Like the restaurant they have panoramic views of the city. Warning: don't do what I did, and arrive late and exhausted after one visit too many. You need to pay close attention to what the young man who carries your bags wants to tell you about how the room works. Inattention will end in tears as you try to fathom out how the lighting works, or how that aesthetic but impenetrable Bang & Olufson sound system functions.

There's no separate bathroom, just a bath between the sleeping area (beds on high plinths) and the sitting area, screened off by glass panels. People either love or hate it, apparently: I started by hating it but grew to love it as I unwound after a particularly frustrating day, and found out how it all worked.

The route moves inland at Langoiran. Take the D239 to Haux, and 500 metres after the Cellier du Graman take a right turn signposted to **Haux**. After a short drive you enter **Les Faures**. CHÂTEAU DE HAUX is signposted off on the right.

This is a curious place. It's run by an aristocratic Dane, a former wine importer in Copenhagen, with an incomer's zeal about the superiority of Bordeaux over all other wines. (He believes, for instance, that his rivals in Burgundy are very inconsistent – 'one year it's good, the next year it's vinegar'. Not what you'll find from the producers in this book!)

Not surprisingly, good English is spoken here and good wine is made, too. They don't want to be overrun with visitors and prefer you to come on Tuesdays at 2pm, when they make up a multilingual party and take you round for a couple of hours. They know a lot about the château's history – how, for instance, a daughter of the house married a missionary against her father's wishes. The father recorded that the young man then went to Africa and 'had the misfortune to allow himself to be eaten'.

Peter Jørgenson cheerfully admits that the number of bottles opened for you to taste very much depends on how you look and how you taste, so be warned – best behaviour! Prices range from FF26 for their Entre-deux-Mers, Clairet and lesser years of Premières Côtes, to FF50 for their top Premières Côtes, a barrique-aged red.

Head back to the main D20 and follow signs to Créon, a fortified town dating back to 1313 with a splendid town square. Take the D671 to Sauveterre, through pleasant rolling country-side and mixed agriculture. This is the prettiest part of the region for me, and also one of the least pretentious. Nowhere more so than at the next visit.

After Sauveterre take the D230 (off the D670) towards Monségur, and as you enter Le Puy pick up the D15 and drive to the village of **Bordepaille**. CHÂTEAU LA TUILERIE DU PUY is signposted on the left. If in doubt, head for the massive green hangar-like building on the skyline – it's their new winery.

This was one of the best visits in all Bordeaux. It's a beautiful spot for starters, with views right across the valley. Jean-Pierre Regaud combines modern and traditional winemaking methods to produce wines of exemplary quality, at startlingly low prices. His Entre-deux-Mers is just FF20, for example, while his reds range from FF24–32. Far from the shores of the Garonne and the Premières Côtes, these wines have the simple appellation 'Bordeaux Supérieur.' M Regaud vinifies each parcel of vines separately, making a total of up to 20 vats. To make the blend, he says, he and his wife sit down at the kitchen table one evening with a bottle drawn from each vat but unidentifiable. They drink from each, take a note of their reactions, then go to bed. The next day he creates a blend from the best vats, regardless of variety. The rejected vats he sells off in bulk, which eases cash-flow but also means he can put his name only to those wines he wholeheartedly approves of.

Another case of unpretentious winemaking can be found at **CHÂTEAU DU BRU**. Take the D15 to Pellegrue then the D672 to **Ste-Foy-la-Grande**. Join the D936, an extremely over-burdened, tedious trunk road towards Bergerac until the hamlet of Les Briands. Look out for signs to the château on the left.

This château makes extremely good-quality basic appellation red, pink and white wines. Prices are remarkable – even the barrique-aged reds, which have to include in their price calculations the cost of all that wood, mostly come in under FF30. If you buy from the pump the dry white is a mere FF8 a litre. Josette Duchant, joint owner, exhibits paintings in the maturation cellar each summer. I was shown round by the secretary. As is so common in Bordeaux I didn't meet the owner, but this time for a different reason: many small proprietors market their wines themselves, and much of their time is spent on the road, exhibiting at fairs or visiting larger clients. One last point: the property offers two of the best-appointed gîtes I've ever seen.

Château du Bru just squeezes into the Bordeaux appellation; properties north and south of it are in Bergerac. It's in the eastern-most corner of Bordeaux, and we now switch regions to check out the 'poor relation'.

Bergerac

Geography worked against this ancient winemaking area from the moment the Bordelais gained the upper hand in controlling trade. All the winemaking areas of the southwest (known, cow-boy-fashion, as the 'High Country') fell foul of the Bordeaux merchants' desire to give themselves competitive advantage.

Such regions as Cahors and Duras found that using the main communications artery, the river Garonne, meant they fell under the power of Bordeaux. And the merchants there refused to allow 'High Country' wines to pass out of port to the lucrative English and Dutch markets until after their own wines had been sold. Other free-market rulings included levying duty by barrel, not by volume, and insisting that non-Bordeaux wines be shipped in 200-litre barrels as opposed to the 225-litre Bordeaux size, thus sneakily increasing their competitors' taxation.

Geography did offer Bergerac one advantage over the other competing regions, however. Whereas the only waterway available to Duras or Cahors was the Garonne, Bergerac was on the Dordogne. (Still is, actually.) Shipping on that river was controlled by Libourne, which, although run by merchants, was less strictly under the thumb of Bordeaux, so Bergerac had better access to international markets.

Another reason for including Bergerac in this chapter rather than Cahors or Duras is its close geological relationship with Bordeaux. There was even talk, at the time the appellations were being laid down, of grouping the Médoc and Graves into one region, and lumping together all the areas on the northern bank – St-Emilion, Pomerol, Castillon and Bergerac – as one distinct region, because their soils and geological structure are so similar.

It didn't happen, and gradually the Bergeracois themselves assimilated the idea that their wines weren't as good as Bordeaux. Before the days of strict control of origin one local cooperative, whose members had vineyards in both Bordeaux and Bergerac, didn't vinify these two areas separately. Instead, so I heard, they used to vinify all the grapes from different areas together, just as they happened to arrive, and then simply go round, taste the finished wines, and label the best ones Bordeaux and the less good Bergerac.

And of course if your wine has a lesser reputation you can't get as much for it. What's the point of making heavy investment in equipment, and keeping yields low, to make better wine if you can't get a decent return on your investment? Or any return at all?

These were the issues conspiring against the emergence of Bergerac as a quality wine region. Happily things look a great deal brighter for the region than they did twenty or thirty years ago. You'll find in this section a series of small- to medium-sized producers who are making very good wine and only want maybe FF20–30 a bottle for it. And who actually seem pleased to see you, provided you've let them know in advance.

Another real plus is that the local wine committee is working hard with local growers to create a comprehensive wine route. This doesn't just mean big new shiny signs. You will occasionally come across old red-painted wine route signs in the region, but they're not particularly comprehensive. This new route goes the whole hog. They're producing a brochure giving exact details of each recognized producer on the route, together with local amenities such as picnic areas and swimming pools. Theoretically, to be 'recognized', producers will have to fulfil very stringent criteria in terms of the wines offered, welcome and tasting facilities. It'll be interesting to see how it works in practice.

CLASSIFICATION

Red, pink, and dry and sweet whites are on offer. Red can be plain Bergerac or fancier Côtes de Bergerac (higher alcohol by law, better quality depending on who's made it – rather like Bordeaux Supérieur). Whereas Bergerac Rouge can be drunk young, so the official line goes, Côtes de Bergerac Rouge is selected from the best the vintner has to offer and must be matured for a year before being offered for sale.

Then there are a couple of specific local red appellations, Pécharmant (held to be the longest-lived the region makes) and Montravel. Montravel can also be a dry white. Then there are Côtes de Montravel and Haut-Montravel, both semi-sweet whites. All this complication for an area of just a few square kilometres. I know full well that this differentiation is very important to those who live there and make the stuff, but as a consumer I was first taken aback and, in the end, overwhelmed by the number of appellations in such a small region. I think we might find it easier to get a grip of the region, and for it to grow in popularity, if we could be confident of a few names rather than vague about many. (This is probably just the polemic of a befuddled hack – anything for a quiet life!)

The sweet wines, as you'll have gathered, come in two grades, semi-sweet (*moelleux*) and sweet (*liquoreux*). In theory only Monbazillac produces the true sweet wine, but other parts of the region have their eyes on this prize too. See below. Other semi-sweet areas are Saussignac and Rosette (which is practically extinct.) And anyone not in a named village can call their *moelleux* wines Côtes de Bergerac Moelleux.

Simple, eh?

EXPLORING BERGERAC

If you're coming from Château du Bru, go back as far as Les Briands and cross that dreaded trunk road the D936 to St-Philippe-du-Seignal. Then pick up the D18 as far as **Monestier**. Head towards Saussignac and you'll find **CHÂTEAU RICHARD** on your left.

The eponymous winemaker's surname is Doughty, a fact that made my heart sink. Brits in Bergerac, toying with the vine? Great. All of which only served to demonstrate that I should leave my prejudices at the door. Richard Doughty is half-French, half-English and pursued a successful career in off-shore oil exploration until a broken leg gave him time to think. He chucked it all in to study winemaking, and harvested his first vintage in 1988.

Richard has a real feeling for his vines. He talks about them the way I talk about my cats – as if they're almost human. His white wines are noticeably lower in acidity than his neighbours', which I appreciated. He says that's what the vines want to do, and who is he to stop them? As he tells it, his learning curve has consisted of gradually developing the confidence to throw away the rule book and let his wines speak for themselves. And as you taste succeeding vintages you'll notice how the wines develop in concentration and depth, even through all those supposedly 'difficult' vintages.

One thing I noticed in Bergerac, as well as in the outlying parts of Bordeaux, is that many places call themselves château when there isn't a grand building in sight. Someone tried to tell me it was part of the AC rules, legally enforceable, but the truth is much more plausible – pretension. Growers are encouraged by professional buyers to exploit the commercial advantages the word 'château' has over the more humble 'domaine'. And while the law certainly states that a property making humble table wine or *vin de pays* can't call itself château so-and-so, there's no law to say that AC producers must. Richard originally called his property a domaine, but says that when he made a barrel-aged wine he labelled it 'château' instead, and liked it so much he went out and built himself a tower.

He grows his grapes organically, though it doesn't say so on the label (he doesn't like the sticker the organic growers' association provides, and reckons the French associate the organic term 'biologique' with laboratories and white coats). He doesn't filter his reds, and for that matter he also offers an unfiltered white, which is gorgeous. If you want to fool your friends, pour this with a dish that needs a dry white wine – its colour is so deep gold you'll be certain it must taste sweet. It fooled me twice.

Not content with that, he's been stirring things up in the appellation. Currently president of the local committee, he's been petitioning the powers-that-be to allow the makers of *moelleux* Saussignac to be allowed to produce a fully sweet wine to rival Monbazillac. Yet another appellation on the cards? It may take some time, but look out for (probably) Premières Côtes de Saussignac. Richard's will certainly be worth trying.

Next you could experiment with the One That Got Away. There's one on every trip that I can't find or is shut or it's too late to get to. In Bergerac it was **CHÂTEAU DE PANISSEAU**. From Monestier take the D16 towards **Cunèges**, and it's signed on the right. Allegedly.

There's an attractive building which could legitimately be called a (small) château, a young couple farming their grapes organically, and wine of international reputation. And English spoken. The top price is FF31 for an oak-aged Côtes de Bergerac red.

Now head for **Saussignac**. As you enter the village there's a sign on the left for a Salon de Thé: turn down here, and after a hundred metres or so there's a track on the left leading to **CHÂTEAU LES MIAUDOUX**. Gérard Cuisset is another young producer, pal of Richard Doughty – they each own a quarter share in a travelling bottling and labelling line syndicate, an admirable idea which gives small growers flexibility and control without tying up too much capital. He'll sell you basic red and white for just FF20, and an extraordinary Saussignac *liquoreux* (pre-empting Richard's new appellation) with a deep golden colour, a luxuriant honey/beeswax nose, good acidity and a finish which lasts for ever. Excellent quality, for FF60. Try buying for this quality–price rapport in Bordeaux.

In the village you'll find Hôtel le Saussignac. Rooms are basic but cheap. Arriving on a damp November night the room was cold and I couldn't make the heating work, so I phoned down for advice. I learned that they weren't going to switch the heating on as they were closing for the winter in a couple of days! Great. Opinion is divided over the food, so you may find yourself better catered for in Bergerac town instead.

Leaving Saussignac on the D4 towards Gardonne, turn left onto the D14. CHÂTEAU COURT-LES-MÛTS is second on the left, on the hillside with far-reaching views. The winemaker here, Pierre-Jean Sadoux, is a big cheese locally, as his oenology lab does all the sampling and testing for 40 local growers. His wife, who receives you (pull the bell-rope with vigour to gain attention) feels that all these controls and tests have greatly improved awareness among growers and overall wine quality. Well, I suppose she would, wouldn't she, but it's a fact that quality in the region has markedly improved over less than a generation.

Wines are dearer here – FF30 for dry white or rosé, FF36–42 for reds, with 1989 and 1990 still on sale. Plenty of magnums available, too. The tasting-room is attractive, in the barrel cellar. Mme Sadoux will tell you every bit as much as you want to know about the wines and the region.

Turning back along the D14, take a right on the D15 for Cunèges and then the D16 to **Pomport**. From here follow signs to Bergerac, and CHÂTEAU BÉLINGARD is off on the left. This is a splendid spot; from in front of the house the proprietor, Laurent de Bosredon, can point out the sites of the first and last battles of the Hundred Years War. On a clear day you can see as far as the nuclear plant in Blaye, 150km away.

He has evidence of the antiquity of winemaking on this site. 'Bélingard' comes from the Celtic 'Garden of Bélin', the sun god. In the garden you can see a seat of sacrifice, complete with thoughtfully-provided runnels round the back to channel the beheadee's blood. It's oriented to face the rising sun at the summer solstice.

More modern techniques are in evidence in the cellars, giving rise to an elegant range of wines. M Bosredon has a special selection range named after his late grandmother, Blanche de Bosredon; the Monbazillac is superb, a rich sweet wine, for FF75–90 (whereas his Château Bélingard label is just FF40). Dry whites and reds range from FF23–38. An interesting visit, conducted with charm in faultless English.

More charm at the next visit, too. To find **CHÂTEAU HAUT BERNASSE**, take the D17 towards Bergerac, then once you've turned left on to the main D933 take the first right, signposted **CHÂTEAU DE MONBAZILLAC** (which is where, incidentally, the local co-op which owns it sell their wines, and there's also a well-regarded restaurant serving Périgord products). When you reach a T-junction turn right; the property's on your left after the woods.

Jacques Blais is a passionately-committed winemaker and, he says, indifferent cellist (which I doubt). He produces very well-made, underpriced reds and dry whites (FF22–38) but he lives for his Monbazillac, which is a thing of beauty, approaching Sauternes in quality for maybe a fifth of the price. Don't miss him if you're in the market for serious stickies, but he's well worth a visit too for the rest of his range. Ignore the cats.

Bergerac the town is next on the agenda; retrace your steps to the main road, brace yourself for the inevitable confusions of the one-way system on the outskirts, cross the river and head uphill to the upper town. There's a gaggle of hotels here, around the tree-lined square used for the twice-weekly market. Serious picnickers can also make use of the daily covered market halfway down the hill.

The best food in town is at Le Cyrano – after all, where else could you eat in Bergerac? Rooms here are cheap but very basic. For more comfort try the Bordeaux or the France. These three are a stone's throw from one another. Other eateries include La Treille, perfect in summer out on the magnificent terrace with its views across the Dordogne. Or L'Imparfait, run by a Breton jazz fan, which has good shellfish and an open fire for grills. I think a base in Bergerac town centre is the best bet for exploring the region – the first time is the worst with that one-way system.

Near the quayside the Maison du Vin is housed in an exquisite old cloister, and is renovating and expanding its exhibition facilities to coincide with the launch of the new wine route. Well worth a visit, as is the old town which you'll walk through en route from your hotel.

Back on the wine trail, cross the river again and take the N21 towards Agen, then turn left on the D19 to **St-Nexans**. **VIGNOBLE LA GRANDE BORIE** is off on the right just before the entrance sign to the village, by some ugly concrete pillars. Signposting is poor – you need to know that the owners' names are Lafon and Lafaye in order to find the place.

Notice that, for once, the title is 'Vignoble' (in the sense of estate, not vineyard) rather than 'Château'. No pretensions in the name, and no pretensions in the winemaking either, just solid good quality and some of the lowest prices in this chapter. Just FF17.50 for the dry white, FF18–19 for the reds. It's very much a family business; I visited them after lunch on a public holiday, and the entire family came on the tour of the cellars with me, keen to show me everything and for me to like it. No problems there. M Lafaye will sell to you *en vrac*, too, and is keen to expand his direct sales. You'll find a warm welcome here and, if you speak French, a great willingness to explain the winemaking and the area.

From St-Nexans you can either return to Bergerac and cross the river there, heading for Sarlat, or go to Cours-de-Pile and cross there. Either way, take the D660 and at the entrance sign to **Creysse** turn left under a railway bridge. Follow signs to **CHÂTEAU DE TIREGAND**.

This is a property in the old, grand, style, with a genuine château for once (though mostly closed up at present). It's run by the St-Exupéry brothers, distantly related to the writer. The estate, dating from the 17th century, includes formally-laid out woodlands which visitors are welcome to stroll and picnic in. The winery itself is the last building you come to: keep going past the château and neighbouring courtyards. You're now in the subregion of Pécharmant, where the longest-lived reds of the region are made. Wines here aren't the cheapest of the region (FF39 for the 1992) but they're of excellent quality and will keep well if you're looking for wines to lay down.

The visit is currently guided, but there are plans to create a self-guided visit which will include more information on the many old artefacts on view. François-Xavier, the younger brother, is heavily involved in the creation of the new wine route and you can expect Château de Tiregand to feature prominently in it. His sister-in-law produces a range of tinned duck products (you know the sort of thing: *foie gras, paté, confit, rillettes*) which are also on sale.

Go back through Bergerac (it gets easier every time) and leave on the D32. This is an attractive back road to Ste-Foy, a more relaxing alternative to joining the HGVs on the D936. In Le Fleix turn right on the D20 to **Mussidan**; CHÂTEAU DE LA MALLEVIEILLE is about 4km along on the left. Hélène and Philippe Biau are a charming, friendly couple who offer a warm welcome, with explanations of the wines in English. The wines are very fairly priced: FF17 for the rosé, up to FF33 for their top oak-aged cuvée.

The Biaus are friends of the couple who run the next establishment, which is how I met them. Jean and Evelyne Reybeyrolle run CHÂTEAU LA RESSAUDIE in **Porte-Ste-Foy**, which is close by: head back towards Ste-Foy and in Porte-Ste-Foy turn right on to the D708, Montpon. You'll see a bunch of signposts off to the right: if you've time to read them all you'll find La Ressaudie among them (if not, as usual, I know there's somewhere close where you can turn round).

Not only will you find good wine here, and a relaxed, warm welcome, but also gîtes and comfortable chambres d'hôte. Great hospitality. If you stay to breakfast don't miss the intricate clockwork turning mechanism for the spit roast in the kitchen's open hearth. Heath-Robinson would have been proud.

From Ste-Foy take the D672 and turn right along the riverside, the D130. I know this brings you back south of the river, but it's pretty, and the only other option is the ghastly D936. Cross the river again at Pessac; or continue along as far as Flaujagues. It's a detour, but if you need a hearty lunch go to the Café des Sports there. This is one of those places where you can believe in the FF50 menu again. For that price you get a carafe of wine and a jug of water plonked down on the table, then in quick succession vegetable soup (a whole tureen, serve yourself), a plate of charcuterie, turkey casserole with a mound of chips, cheese (self-service again), and choice of puds. Coffee's the only extra. You can often see this kind of deal advertised in small village cafés, and it does pay to trust your instincts and just dive in if the signals are right. You could have a bumper meal, and if it's no good, well, it didn't cost that much.

So, go back to Pessac, cross the river, and take the D9 north. Where it intersects with the D936 go straight over, to St-Michel-de-Montaigne. Keep going until you see the **DOMAINE DE PERREAU** on the left.

Jean-Yves Reynou is the fourth generation of winemakers on site, and he'll sell you crisp dry whites for FF17, well-structured reds for FF19 and brilliant semi-sweet Montravel for FF35. Excellent winemaking, yet again; how come it's so much more expensive just up the road?

And with that we pass seamlessly out of Bergerac, back into the north-eastern corner of Bordeaux. Only the prices will change...

The Côtes de Castillon and Côtes de Francs

Côtes de Castillon derives its name from the local town, Castillon-la-Bataille. This was the scene of the last battle of the Hundred Years War, in 1453. In 1953 they added the suffix in commemoration. Côtes de Francs is to the north. It was removed from the St-Emilion appellation in the 1920s and took quite a while to recover from the shock. It got its own appellation in 1976.

EXPLORING THE CÔTES

From St-Michel-de-Montaigne, join the D936 briefly, into **Castillon**, where you turn right on to the D17. **CHÂTEAU CÔTE-MONTPEZAT** is about 3km along on the right. This is a young estate making deeply-coloured, concentrated and long-lasting red wines (FF40–45). They also sell wines from **CHÂTEAU HAUT-BERNAT**, in Puisseguin-St-Emilion, which is the proprietor's other property. Estate-manager Stephane Toutoundji speaks good English and expresses some forthright opinions on the region and its wines.

Moving from the Côtes de Castillon appellation to that of the Côtes de Francs (just across the road), turn right back on to the D17 and fork right on the D123. **CHÂTEAU PUYGUERAUD** is (barely) signposted on the right. From the château itself you'll be directed down a narrow track to the estate office, where you can be received in French by Nicolas Thienpoint or in English by his brother. Or their secretary.

The Thienpoint family is Belgian, and has developed extensive holdings in Bordeaux – Nicolas has just taken over the directorship of Pavie-Macquin in St-Emilion, for example. The family's wines are characterized by very high quality and attention to detail which has been rewarded by international recognition. The best in the area, I'd say, yet the estates and the people who run them are refreshingly down-to-earth and unpretentious.

At Château Puygueraud you can taste and buy Puygueraud itself, a rich, supple red; Château Laclaverie, rounded and elegant; and Château Charmes-Godard, a deep, oaky dry white. All of really excellent quality, at prices from FF50–60. This is winemaking to compete on equal footing with its western neighbours, at much more modest prices.

Prices are even more modest across the road. If you can find the place – there were no signposts at all when I visited, but the young winery worker who receives you has promised to rectify that. (Diagonally opposite Puygueraud, by the bus stop, then first on the right. Look for three brown-fronted single-storey buildings, then holler for attention.) Owned by a Champagne house, **CHÂTEAU CANTEGRIVE** offers very deeply-coloured reds, including a terrific prestige range named 1453, after the battle.

Turn right onto the D123 and left on the D244, then take the D17 to St-Genès-de-Castillon. From St-Genès, take the D243 towards St-Emilion, and then turn right to St-Etienne-de-Lisse. Drive through the village, still heading towards St-Emilion, and **CHÂTEAU JACQUES BLANC** is on your left.

But before making the visit, a few words about the change of district, because we're now in St-Emilion.

St-Emilion

These wines are very different in character from those of the Médoc, because the grape blend is different. Whereas the Médoc leans to Cabernet Sauvignon, in St-Emilion the fleshier, richer Merlot dominates, making rounder and more approachable wines than their more austere Médoc rivals. This makes St-Emilion a better place for beginners, as you can drink something which gives more immediate, accessible pleasure.

THE CLASSIFICATION

St-Emilion was a late starter, not coming out with a classification until 1954. It's based on a mixture of taste tests, soil analysis and reputation, and thus should offer a more accurate guide to who's who, particularly as the intention was to revise it regularly. However, this is another good intention which bit the dust, and the most recent 'revision' in 1985 neither promoted ambitious rising stars nor demoted the underachievers. So, in descending order, you'll find wines labelled Premier Grand Cru Classé, Grand Cru Classé, Grand Cru, and then at the bottom plain St-Emilion. (This was what the undrinkable stuff I bought first time round was labelled. Just thought I'd mention that.)

This is an area of small estates, reflecting the fact that winemaking on the right bank of the river got off to a relatively late start – it wasn't until after the Second World War that prices began to take on Médoc proportions. Neither are there many grand châteaux, which doesn't, of course, stop people from calling their properties 'château' anyway.

EXPLORING ST-EMILION

There are a number of 'satellite' villages which make wine in the St-Emilion style. You can take a very scenic tour of these by taking the D122 north from St-Emilion to Montagne, where I would like to insist you stop to visit the outstanding Ecomusée/Musée du Vigneron. This is one of those splendid exhibitions which gives a social context to life in the vineyards a hundred or so years ago. Fascinating stuff on childhood, marriage, health and death flesh out the descriptions of the viti-cultural year. And if you've ever wanted to stick your nose into all those phials which are supposed to give you a whiff of the olfactory components of wine, this is your chance. Then continue through Lussac and Puisseguin... to end up back in **St-Etienne-de-Lisse**. Which is where we came in.

CHÂTEAU JACQUES BLANC is run by Pierre Chouet, who has cultivated his grapes biodynamically since 1989 after years of organic cultivation. These methods have certainly resulted in ex-cellent wines: his top-level Cuvée du Maitre in particular has great depth. Prices, around FF50–80, are very fair for the quality.

Turn left onto the D245, and in **St-Hippolyte** turn right onto the D243E2. Take a left onto the D243 then fork left onto the D243E1. **CHÂTEAU PAVIE-MACQUIN** is on the left, on the hill known as 'Côte Pavie' with pretty views of the town of St-Emilion. Pavie-Macquin is one of those happy finds, an undervalued wine. It's rich and ripe, not unlike a Burgundy, which means it's a great pleasure to drink. The *chai* is unpretentious, with a charming touch – all the fermenting vats have names on the front ('Brunhilde's fermentation is stuck'). As Nicolas Thienpoint, its new director, pointed out, you don't need a very modern *chai* to make great wine – if you know what you're doing. Clearly they do. Prices: FF90–110.

I've been putting this off for as long as possible, but there's nothing else for it – it's time to visit **St-Emilion**, the town. Brace yourself. This is mass tourism in action. St-Emilion is the Beaune of Bordeaux, a town so exquisitely pretty that the whole place has been declared a national monument. But unlike Beaune, which although very attractive and popular with tourists is still a thriving economic hub, St-Emilion seems to have surrendered itself completely to the tourist industry. Restaurants and wine shops abound, but you try finding an ironmongers. Rather like living in Blackheath.

And of course this relentless onslaught of tourists by the coachload has taken its toll on the hotel and catering trade. Prices are high, welcomes are scarce. The Plaisance is the best hotel in town, with comfortable rooms but frosty staff. In its starred restaurant you can sample the outer reaches of French cuisine, such as warm bird (eg sparrow) with avocado. I've also stayed at the Logis des Remparts (offhand staff; they also denied all knowledge of an exchange of faxes, and tried to sell me a room at a much higher price). At the restaurant Logis de la Cadène, on the other hand, the friendly staff will offer you enormous helpings of simple grills or the bordelais speciality *lamproie* (lampreys), cooked in red wine and their own blood. St-Emilion is one of the few French towns which imposes a 'tourist tax' on its visitors. Well, I suppose they have to pay for all those street sweepers somehow. The best advice is to get up early and stroll round the town before the coaches arrive, or leave it until after dinner, by which time the worst crush is over. Even in winter it's busy, but in summer it can be so crowded as to be absolutely unbearable.

The Maison du Vin will sell you a wide selection of local wines. They also have on offer, uniquely in Bordeaux in my experience, a list of all the properties which accept visitors, including opening hours, languages spoken, tasting fees, and whether you need an appointment. If only the rest of the region were so user-friendly.

The grandest hotel by far is about 3km outside the town, on the D243 towards Libourne. Hôtel Château Grand Barrail is surrounded by vines, a turn-of-the-century building on which money has been lavished to transform it into a luxury hotel. Unfortunately it has experienced severe staffing problems, as the new manger cheerfully admits; she has ambitious plans to raise standards, including the recruitment of a dynamic young chef, so I hope things will go her way.

Just a hundred metres up the road in each direction from the Grand-Barrail are two more visits, chalk and cheese in status but not in attention to quality. CHÂTEAU FIGEAC is one of St-Emilion's top estates: and, like many of the top estates in Bordeaux, they won't sell to you direct. It's all sold straight to the merchants, and you can buy it in the St-Emilion wine shops. You'll be met by an English-speaking hostess (the owners live on the property but were nowhere in sight; you can only visit in the week so they can have some privacy at weekends).

They're not interested in the casual visitor, but will spend an hour or so with someone who's specifically interested in Figeac, usually gathered into small groups. Uniquely in St-Emilion they used the old open-topped wooden vats, with a grille set into them beneath the surface of the fermenting wine to hold back the grape skins, preventing them from forming a stifling cap at the top of the vat. Old hydraulic presses are used, too.

The Grand Vin matures in 100% new oak, the second wine in one-third. In the dimly-lit cellars (lampshades are made from trios of empty bottles bound together) the second wine is stored in bottle, as are the 'proprietor's reserves'. They'll open a bottle for you to taste in a tapestry-hung tasting room; it could well be an older vintage, too, which makes a pleasant change.

Back on the D243 towards the town, **CHÂTEAU HAUT-SEGOTTES** is just past Grand-Barrail, on the right. I was told the proprietor, Mme André, would be in her wellingtons, and indeed she was. Birdlike and active, she's very much a hands-on winemaker – and the results are very appealing, and very good value. You'll taste from the barrel in her attractive small cellar, surrounded by bottles and barrels. If you visit when things are quiet she'll have time to explain to you all you wish to know, in French. After so many grand estates it's heartening to see someone making wines of such good quality – and for such modest prices – on a small property.

Pomerol

Close at hand, but very unlike St-Emilion in its attitude to visitors, Pomerol isn't even a place. Although you see signposts to Pomerol centre, that's just the town hall, the church and a few scattered buildings. No shops, no bar, no Maison du Vin. Without a physical focus for visitors the scattered properties aren't generally so geared up to receive them. It's as if they simply want to be left to get on with making their wine undisturbed.

A notable exception is **LA CROIX DE GAY**. It's on the D245, going towards the N89, and you can turn up without appointment, even on a Sunday. The cellars are the most immaculately clean I've ever seen. One of the maturation cellars is built from stone taken from an old church.

Two wines are made here, La Croix de Gay and La Fleur de Gay. Fleur is the top wine, from very old vines and aged in 100% new wood. Some rate it as a rival to Pétrus. If that's the case, FF300 a bottle is a steal.

From here you can either dice with death on the Libourne ring road or take a scenic route into Fronsac, the neighbouring wine region. Cross the N89 and continue until you reach the D910. Turn right on to this until you get to Les Billaux, where you take the D18. On the outskirts of Galgon turn left onto the D18E1 towards Saillans. You're now in Fronsac, some of the prettiest countryside of the region, with mixed agriculture and small farms.

Fronsac

My big tip in the region was Château Vieille Cure. Excellent quality, American-owned, so English spoken — just the job. Or so I thought. The courteous fax I received from the owner, replying to my request for an appointment, sums up the situation in Bordeaux so neatly I feel moved to quote it at length.

'First, the good news. Château la Vieille Cure is by far the best-known and most widely sold Fronsac in England. Thus the name will be familiar to many of your readers. Our facilities are among the most modern in all the Bordeaux region, and Fronsac the prettiest vineyard area.

'Next, the bad news. While we occasionally sell the odd case of wine to a visitor, we rather discourage this type of business. Further, our price ex-cellars to individuals is slightly higher than what the wine sells for in Sainsbury's in England and substantially higher than the price at Sainsbury's shop in Calais. Château la Vieille Cure is American-owned, but fluency in English is not an attribute of our staff.

'You might want to make a note of the Maison du Vin in the village of Fronsac, where Château la Vieille Cure and many other Fronsac wines are sold, at the same price in our case as ex-cellars, and where there is an English-speaking staff.'

I should point out that the fax did indicate that they would be happy to have me visit the château nonetheless, but invitations like this are 'professional' visits; extended to the trade and wine-writers, but not available to the general public. That's

why in so many articles about Bordeaux you'll read about the
fascinating experience of meeting the owner which the
writer enjoyed, but which you are highly unlikely to be able to
replicate when turning up as a member of the public. I feel
reasonably confident that I've managed to establish at these
properties exactly who you'll meet, as I hate reading those
gushing articles or wine-merchant reports in wine lists about
intriguing Monsieur so-and-so and then turn up to be met by
the hired help.

So I suggest you follow that advice: call in at the Maison du
Vin (it's on a sharp bend in the centre of Fronsac) taste some
wines and see if the owners of those which take your fancy will
accept visitors.

So from Fronsac take the D246 on the right; turn left onto
the D137 and join the D670 towards St-André-de-Cubzac for
the final leg of the Bordeaux region. From here take the D600
towards Bourg. It's a very pretty road. After Bourg you head
towards **Bayon**; look out for **CHÂTEAU FALFAS**, which is off
on your right.

Bourg and Blaye

Bourg and Blaye are two up-and-coming appellations on the
opposite side of the Gironde to the Médoc, known more for
red than white wines. Many new estates are developing a
reputation, including Château Falfas which was bought by
American lawyer John Cochran and his French wife Véronique
in 1988. Véronique's father is a consultant who helps vineyards
wishing to cultivate biodynamically, so not unnaturally Château
Falfas moved in this direction. John was unconvinced at first,
until the quality won him over. That quality was recognized by
a wider audience when their first vintage in 1989 won a blind
tasting organized by the local Maison du Vin. Now he works
part-time as a lawyer, part-time on the estate. And the wines
are really excellent, with great depth and concentration of rich,
ripe fruit, even in the so-called difficult vintages. Prices are
around FF40 – a bargain.

There's a good value hotel nearby, La Closerie des Vignes. Turn right out of Falfas and follow signs for **St-Ciers-de-Canesse**. From there you'll pick up little green signs to the hotel. It's small and tranquil, surrounded by vines, with good-value modern rooms. The food isn't so hot, though, so stick to basic dishes or try the Falfas recommendation, La Filadière, at Furt, a hamlet near Gauriac (head back towards Bayon, and it's on the 'route verte'). It's right by the river, with lovely views.

Continue on the coast road to Blaye, where the old-town citadel is worth a visit, then take the N137 towards Bordeaux as far as Pugnac. Take the D249 to Cézac then the D248 **Cubnezais**. **CHÂTEAU LA BERTINERIE** is signposted in the village, but you can spot their vineyards well in advance – they're the only ones in the area to be trained in the 'lyre' system, which involves taking two main stems up from the vine in a sort of curved Y-shape.

Château Bertinerie is a Premières Côtes de Blaye, which is Blaye's most important appellation. This is certainly excellent quality, with the reds in particular being made to withstand considerable ageing. Whites from FF30, reds up to FF50. These are wines with big aspirations. And visits without appointment!

No appointment needed at the final visit either. From Cézac head to St-Savin, then up the D115 and then the D132 to Reignac. By now, signs for the motorway have appeared, but resist the temptation to start the journey home if you have any room left in the car. Head on up to **Marcillac**, where in the middle of the village you'll find the **CAVES DES HAUTS DE GIRONDE**. This cooperative, as well as making very well-priced *vrac* wines, also offers many good-quality wines at around the FF25–50 mark, including the oak-aged Duc du Tutiac, a Premières Côtes de Blaye. I just thought it might be useful to have somewhere reasonably-priced up your sleeve in case one thing or another prevented you from buying as much wine as you'd intended…

And so it's back to the motorway and all points north: the A26 junction is just minutes from the co-op. Congratulations! You've made it though France's toughest wine region. I think you really deserve a pat on the back after this.

Listings

When telephoning France from the UK, first dial 00 33 then the number shown here. Producers are listed in wine route order, and hotels/restaurants by town or village according to the route. Accommodation prices are per room, meal prices are per head.

Producers

Médoc

Château La Tour de By
33340 Bégadan
Tel 56 41 50 03 , Fax 56 41 36 10
Open Mon–Fri 8–12, 14–18,
Sat and Sun in July and August
Credit cards accepted
Good English

Château Cos d'Estournel
33180 St-Estèphe
Tel 56 73 15 50, Fax 56 59 72 59
Open by appointment only
Mon–Fri 9–12, 14–17
Credit cards accepted
Good English

Château Mouton-Rothschild
33250 Pauillac
Tel 56 59 22 22, Fax 56 73 20 44
Open Mon–Thur 9.30–11, 14–16
Fri 9.30–11, 14–15
Open Sat and Sun 15 April–30 Oct.
Appointment preferred
Credit cards accepted
Good English

Château Lynch-Bages
33250 Pauillac
Tel 56 73 24 00, Fax 56 59 26 42
Open 1 Nov–1 April Mon–Fri 9–11,
13.30–16.30, 1 April–31 Oct
Mon–Sun 9–11, 14–17.30 (Fri 17)
Appointment preferred but will
welcome casual visitors if they can
Credit cards accepted
Good English

Château Lagrange
33250 St–Julien-Beychevelle
Tel 56 59 23 63, Fax 56 59 26 09
Open by appointment only
Good English
No Sales

Château Beaumont
Cussac-Fort-Médoc, 33460 Margaux
Tel 56 58 92 29, Fax 56 58 90 94
Open Mon–Fri 9–12, 2–6
Appointment preferred for a
visit in English
Chambres d'Hôte FF300 for two,
Breakfast FF50 per person

Château Prieuré-Lichine
33460 Margaux
Tel 56 88 36 28, Fax 56 88 78 93

Château d'Angludet
33460 Cantenac
Tel 57 88 71 41, Fax 57 88 72 52
Open Mon–Fri 9–12, 14–17
By appointment
Visits to Château Palmer in
English can be arranged
Good English

Graves

Château La Louvière
33850 Léognan
Tel 56 64 75 87
Open Mon–Fri 8–12, 13.30–17.30,
Sat and Sun by appointment
Some English

Château de Chantegrive
33720 Podensac
Tel 56 27 17 38, Fax 56 27 29 42
Open Mon–Fri 8–12, 14–18, Sat
8–12
Credit cards accepted
Some English

Domaine du Moulin à Vent
33720 Landiras
Tel 56 62 50 66, Fax 56 62 41 22
Open Mon–Sun by appointment,
closed during Ascension week
Good English, by appointment

Entre-deux-Mers
Château Langoiran
33550 Langoiran
Tel 56 67 08 55, Fax 56 67 32 87
Open Mon–Sun 9–12, 14–18
Appointment preferred
Good English

Château de Haux
33550 Haux
Tel 56 23 35 07, Fax 56 23 25 29
Open Mon–Fri 9–12, 14–17
by appointment but
Tuesday 1400 preferred
Credit cards accepted
Good English

Château La Tuilerie du Puy
Bordepaille, 33580 Le Puy
Tel 56 61 61 92, Fax 56 61 86 90
Mon–Sun 8–12, 14–18
Appointment preferred
Good English

Château du Bru
St-Avit-St-Nazaire,
33220 Ste-Foy-la-Grande
Tel 57 46 12 71 Fax 57 46 10 64
Mon–Fri 9–17 (Fri 1600) Sat and
Sun by appointment
No English
Gîtes from FF1560–3000 per week

Bergerac
Château Richard
La Croix Blanche, 24240 Monestier
Tel 53 58 49 13 or 53 58 48 94
Fax 53 61 17 28
Open 9–12, 14–19
English like a native

Château de Panisseau
Thénac, 24240 Sigoules
Tel 53 58 40 03, Fax 53 58 94 46
Open Mon–Sat 8–12, 14–18
Good English

Château Les Miaudoux
Les Miaudoux
24240 Saussignac
Tel 53 27 92 31
Fax 53 27 96 60
Open Mon–Sat 8–12, 14–18
Appointment preferred
No English

Château Court-Les-Mûts
24240 Razac-de-Saussignac
Tel 53 27 92 17, Fax 53 23 77 21
Open Mon–Fri 9–11.30, 14–18
Sat by appointment
Good English

Château Bélingard
24240 Pomport
Tel 53 58 28 03, Fax 53 58 38 39
Open Mon–Sat 8–18
Appointment preferred
Good English

Château Haut Bernasse
24240 Monbazillac
Tel 53 58 36 62, Fax 53 61 26 40
Open Mon–Sun by appointment
No English

Vignoble La Grande Borie
St-Nexans, 24520 Mouleydier
Tel 53 24 33 21 or 53 24 35 65
Fax 53 24 97 74
Open Mon–Sat by appointment
No English

Château de Tiregrand
24100 Creysse
Tel 53 23 21 08, Fax 53 22 58 49
Open Mon–Sat 8–12, 14–18
Good English

Château de la Mallevieille
24130 Monfaucon
Tel 53 24 64 66, Fax 53 58 69 91
Open Mon–Sun 9–19
Credit cards accepted
Good English

Château La Ressaudie
Port-Ste-Foy
33220 Ste-Foy-la-Grande
Tel 53 24 71 48, Fax 53 58 52 29
Open Mon–Sun 8–12, 14–18
Good English
Chambres d'Hôte FF210 for two,
Breakfast FF25 per person

Domaine de Perreau
24230 St-Michel-de-Montaigne
Tel 53 58 67 31
Open Mon–Sun 9–12, 14–19
Appointment preferred
No English

Côtes de Castillon, Côtes de Francs

Château Côte-Montpezat
33350 Belvès-de-Castillon
Tel 57 47 96 04, Fax 57 47 90 82
Open Mon–Fri 9–18; by appointment Sat and Sun and lunchtime (if
you must)
Good English

Château Puygueraud (also for
Château Laclaverie and Les
Charmes-Godard
Lauriol, 33570 St-Cibard
Tel 57 40 61 04, Fax 57 40 66 08
Open Mon–Fri 8–18, Sat & Sun by
appointment
Appointment preferred
Credit cards accepted
No English

Château Cantegrive
Terrason-Montbadon
33370 Puisseguin
Tel 26 52 14 74, Fax 26 52 24 02
Open Mon–Sun 9–18
No English

St-Emilion

Château Pavie-Macquin
33330 St-Emilion
Tel 57 24 74 23, Fax 57 51 26 44
Open Mon–Fri 9–12, 14–17
Appointment preferred, Sat and Sun
possible
No English

Château Jacques Blanc
St-Etienne-de-Lisse
33330 St-Emilion
Tel 57 40 18 01, Fax 57 40 01 98
Open Mon–Fri 8.30–12,
13.30–17.30 (1700 Fri)
Sat by appointment
Some English

Château Figeac
33330 St-Emilion
Tel 57 24 72 26, Fax 57 74 45 74
Open Mon–Fri 9–12, 14–18 by
appointment (phone the day before)
Good English
No sales

Château Haut-Segottes
33330 St-Emilion
Tel 57 24 60 98
Open Mon–Sun 9–12, 14–19
No English

Pomerol

Châteaux la Croix de Gay/
La Fleur de Gay
33500 Pomerol
Tel 57 51 19 05, Fax 57 74 15 62
Open Mon–Sun 9–12, 13.30–18
No English

Bourg and Blaye
Château Falfas
33710 Bayon
Tel 57 64 80 41, Fax 57 64 93 24
Open Mon–Sat 10–12, 14–18 by
appointment
Good English

Château Haut-Bertinerie
33620 Cubnezais
Tel 57 68 70 74, Fax 57 68 01 03
Open Mon–Fri 9–12, 14–18
Good English by appointment

Cave des Hauts de Gironde
La Cafourche, 33860 Marcillac
Tel 57 32 48 33, Fax 57 42 49 63
Open Mon–Sat 8.30–12, 14–18.30
No English

Hotels and Restaurants
H Hotel *R* Restaurant

Gaillan-en-Médoc
HR Château Layauga
33340 Gaillan-en-Médoc
Tel 56 41 26 83, Fax 56 41 19 52
Rooms FF495, Meals FF195–345

Pauillac
HR Château Cordeillan Bages
33250 Pauillac
Tel 56 59 24 24, Fax 56 59 01 89
Rooms FF800–870, Meals
FF180–380
Member of Relais & Châteaux

Arcins
R Lion d'Or
33460 Arcins
Tel 56 58 96 79
FF60–210

Bordeaux
R Bistro du Sommelier
167, rue G-Bonnac, 33000 Bordeaux
Tel 56 96 71 78, Fax 56 24 52 36
FF116–200

Léognan
R La Forge
67 cours Maréchal Leclerc
33850 Léognan
Tel 56 64 11 58
FF82–250

Langoiran
HR Le St-Martin
En Bordure de la Garonne
33550 Langoiran
Tel 56 67 02 67, Fax 56 67 15 75
Rooms FF240–280, Meals FF42–200

Bouliac
HR Le St-James
3, place Camille Hostein
33270 Bouillac
Tel 57 97 06 00, Fax 56 20 92 58
Rooms FF600–850, Meals
FF160–400
(cheaper meals in Le Bistroy next
door, same phone no.)
Member of Relais & Châteaux

Sauternes
R Les Vignes
place Eglise, 33210 Sauternes
Tel 56 76 60 06, Fax 56 76 69 97
FF60–130

Saussignac
HR Le Saussignac
24240 Saussignac
Tel 53 27 92 08, Fax 53 27 96 57
Rooms FF170–250, Meals FF65–160

Bergerac
HR Bordeaux
38, place Gambetta, 24100 Bergerac
Tel 53 57 12 83, Fax 53 57 72 14
Rooms FF290–420, Meals FF93–220

H France
18, place Gambetta, 24100 Bergerac
Tel 53 57 11 61, Fax 53 61 25 70
Rooms FF230–325

HR Le Cyrano
2, bd Montaigne, 24100 Bergerac
Tel 53 57 02 76, Fax 53 57 78 15
Rooms FF220–240, Meals FF90–200

BUYING WINE IN FRANCE

R La Treille
12, quai Salvette, 24100 Bergerac
Tel 53 57 60 11
FF80–150

R L'Imparfait
8, rue Fontaines, 24100 Bergerac
Tel 53 57 47 92
FF65–150

Monbazillac
R Le Restaurant du Château de
Monbazillac
24240 Monbazillac
Tel 53 58 38 93
FF150–250

Flaujagues
R Café des Sports
33350 Flaujagues
Tel 57 40 11 24
FF50 and 90

St-Emilion
HR Hostellerie de Plaisance
Place Clocher, 33330 St-Emilion
Tel 57 24 72 32, Fax 57 74 41 11
Rooms FF495–790, Meals
FF136–270

H Logis des Remparts
Rue Guadet
Tel 57 24 70 43, Fax 57 74 47 44
Rooms FF360–650

R Le Logis de la Cadène
Place du Marché-aux-Bois
33330 St-Emilion
Tel 57 24 71 40, Fax 57 74 42 23
FF90–180

HR Château Grand Barrail
33330 St-Emilion
Tel 57 55 37 00, Fax 57 55 37 49
Rooms FF1000–1200, Meals
FF160–380

St-Ciers-de-Canesse
HR La Closerie des Vignes
Village des Arnauds
33710 St-Ciers-de-Canesse
Tel 57 64 81 90, Fax 57 64 94 44
Rooms FF350, Meals FF120–160
Member of Relais du Silence

Gauriac
R La Filadière
Lieu-dit 'Furt', 33710 Gauriac
Tel 57 64 94 05, Fax 57 64 94 06
FF85–160

Blaye
HR La Citadelle
Place d'Armes, 33390 Blaye
Tel 57 42 17 10, Fax 57 42 10 34
Rooms FF270–370
Meals FF98–260

Ferry Factfile

Of all the ways you can get across the Channel, which one is right for you? Sometimes it's clear that only one route is feasible. At other times there's a choice, for which you need more information. In the course of researching this guide I've travelled on most of the available crossings and the following is one woman's subjective response to her experiences. I hope this information will help you make up your mind how to travel.

The crossings divide into three groups: those that deposit you at or near Calais, those that drop you in Holland or Belgium, and those that set you down somewhere along the Normandy coast. The short crossings operate frequently, the longer crossings perhaps only twice a day. Bear in mind with the longer routes that they may only let you on the ship an hour before sailing; at night it could be better to eat before you embark.

First, the crossing to **Calais**. This is easily the best of the shorter routes as far as roads are concerned on both sides of the Channel. The new M20/A20 dual carriageway takes you right up to the roundabout outside the port of **Dover**, and the computerized check-in takes a matter of minutes. You'll be given a lane number to follow; you park in that lane and board usually within 20 minutes. At Calais, the motorway again extends right up to the port – there's no quicker getaway.

Both P&O and Stena Sealink offer a service as frequent as every 45 minutes at peak times of the day, even in winter. Sealink ferries take 90 minutes to cross, P&O only 75. P&O has extra lounges, accessible on payment of a £7 supplement, where you can retire to if the ship is very full. Sealink, alas, is phasing out its free motorists' lounges; apparently it's too hard to keep out non-motorists.

Then there are the catamaran and hovercraft services run by Hoverspeed. These also cover the Dover to Calais route, with an additional SeaCat service from **Folkestone** to **Boulogne** (a much more pleasant option for a day trip, but less use if you need to put in any distance after landing as you have to cut across country to join the A26). The SeaCats are quicker than the ferries, taking 50 minutes, and the hovercraft claims just 35, although when I last travelled on the hovercraft, in a brisk Force 6, the crossing took nearly an hour. The stuffy craft heaved and banged about (the noise level is almost overwhelming) and people looked more than a little green.

The SeaCat, too, has an unnerving tendency to roll in even moderate seas, and it takes practice for those without good sealegs. Sit right by a window and don't take your eyes off the horizon. I always have a bottle of Bach Rescue Remedy to hand, whatever means of crossing I'm using – even planes. It helps me to keep my equilibrium (and breakfast) when all around are losing theirs.

Sally Line also covers the same section of the Channel, but I don't think it's a contender. Access to **Ramsgate** is via a much slower road than the one to Dover, and from **Dunkerque** you either have to drive south to pick up the A26 at Calais or join it south of Lille. Although the motorway to Lille is toll-free, it's badly-surfaced and very congested with local traffic. And since the crossing time (2½ hours) is at least an hour longer than the Dover route, it's clear that the timings just don't compare.

In addition – and I know it was only one journey – when I travelled with Sally Line the outward boat was cancelled altogether (wait another couple of hours for the next one or drive to Dover) and the return boat was delayed for 20 minutes. I also found port direction signs poor, check-in staff very fierce and the ship lacking in quiet, smoke-free areas for passengers to sit in. All in all, it's not to be recommended.

What about the **Channel Tunnel**, running from **Folkestone** to just outside **Calais**? The idea is that the check-in is like a French *péage* or tollbooth: turn up, pay your money, join the queue for the next train. Although you can buy tickets in advance you can't book a particular train. They'd like (at present) to discourage advance booking, so there is no separate queue for ticket-holders; those with pre-paid tickets simply get in line with those buying tickets on arrival.

Then you have the choice of stopping to eat or buy duty-free goods (there's no shop or buffet on the train) or of going straight into the holding area to join the queue for the next train. Once you're in the holding area there's no escaping the queue and heading back to the service area (perhaps with one of those handy numbered tickets you get at delicatessen counters to keep your place). This, it is hoped, will not be a problem, with a crossing anticipated every 15 minutes in peak hours. The possibility of delays shouldn't be ruled out, however, until the system has become fully operational and trains reach maximum frequency.

The Tunnel offers a revolutionary way of crossing the Channel. It's fast and those with less than cast-iron stomachs don't need to worry about rough seas. Motorway connections are good at both ends – on the French side you are five minutes from the A26 just outside Calais.

Whether or not you fancy travelling this way, I believe the Tunnel has one enormous advantage over every other means of crossing – courtesy of Customs and Excise. When you cross by train, all Customs formalities are completed on the departure side. This doesn't make a great deal of difference when you're heading towards France, as French Customs officials don't seem to mind too much what we bring in. But anyone who's zoomed off the ferry in the UK port in double-quick time only to be brought to a standstill by a queue inching past stern-looking Customs officers will have cause to be thankful. With the Tunnel, this is an experience you undergo while you're waiting for the next train under the Channel and have nothing better to do, rather than after landing when you're itching to get onto the motorway and home.

For crossing to Holland and Belgium, the Olau Line operates in some style between **Sheerness** and **Vlissingen**. The only disadvantage to this route is not of the company's making – it's the approach roads. From the M2 to Sheerness is half an hour of single-carriageway tedium, while from Vlissingen it's all motorway, but never the same one for very long.

Then there's **Harwich** to **Hook** (Sealink) and **Felixstowe** to **Zeebrugge** (P&O). These are handy crossings for avoiding the M25. Zeebrugge lies closer to the crossings to France but either is feasible, particularly if you're planning a longer holiday with an 'open-jaw' route.

North Sea Ferries, operating out of **Hull**, offers motorists from the north of England and Scotland the chance to avoid the long slog south – at a price. When costing the trip, however, bear in mind that, unique among ferry operators, dinner and breakfast are included in the fare. This leads to enormous pressure on the restaurant and my timing tip is to go in late for dinner. The ships sail at 6pm and arrive in **Zeebrugge** or **Rotterdam** at about 8am, so these are the only crossings which allow you to eat at a reasonable hour <u>and</u> get a decent night's sleep. Dinner service starts at 6pm, for families, and soon after it's bedlam; but hang on until 7.30 or, even better, 8pm, and the queues have usually subsided.

The other irritant for rugged individualists like me is that stewards herd you onto tables of eight to eat communally. I'm told by the PR people that individuals and couples can request separate tables, but to be on the safe side I'd have a strategy up your sleeve, such as friends about to join you or an unappealing personal habit. Breakfast queues are even worse, so hang back until 7.30am or so.

Of North Sea Ferries' two routes, the ships sailing to Rotterdam are bigger and newer and don't have those cabin-speakers through which to pump incredibly loud good-morning-campers messages as the Zeebrugge ships do. The crews are unfailingly friendly and the stabilizers, particularly on the boats to Rotterdam, are excellent. Although this port seems a long way north it can offer a very useful route through to Alsace, Burgundy and the Rhône.

Of the crossings for the Loire Valley, **Portsmouth** to **St-Malo** (taking nearly nine hours) is the best for getting a proper night's sleep. Brittany Ferries' boats are smart, the staff are sharp and the food is good. Brittany's crossings from **Portsmouth** to **Caen** (taking six hours) leave you bleary-eyed the next morning if taken overnight, and are better by day. The ship in fact docks at Ouistreham, 15km or so from Caen. (The company has a fiddly loading policy, which always seems to leave me hanging around on the quayside while cars on my right and left sweep on board. It's all about achieving the right balance, apparently.)

Le Havre is better-placed for motorway connections than Caen, and the routes to Le Havre often give you a longer overnight crossing.

The ferry routes I like least for getting to the wine regions are the ones to **Cherbourg**. The roads from Cherbourg are single-carriageway unless you drive round to Caen – in which case, why not take that crossing? It takes hours to get from Cherbourg to Angers or Tours, far longer than a motorway run would take. This is fine if you intend to pootle gently through the countryside from the moment you dock, but not if you want to get to your chosen area quickly.

Then there's the **Newhaven–Dieppe** crossing. Newhaven is now easy to get to thanks to the Brighton bypass, and Dieppe is by far the prettiest Channel port. If your schedule allows, you can spend a very pleasant first or last night here. Roads inland are not the fastest but you can still be on the outskirts of Paris in a couple of hours. This route is now served by conventional ferries and by Sea Lynx – a fast multi-hulled vessel which cuts the crossing time by almost half. They've also built new port facilities at Dieppe which allow you a much faster getaway. Good to see this kind of investment in ports away from the Dover–Calais axis.

A couple of final notes: Brittany Ferries crosses from **Plymouth** to **Roscoff**, which is handy for reaching the Loire if you live in southwest England, but a long slog otherwise; and Sally Line also runs a service from **Ramsgate** to **Ostend**.

Further Exploration

DIY VISITS

After following the wine routes described above, you may feel inspired to branch out and arrange your own visits. Perhaps you've enjoyed a particular wine bought in the UK and would like to trace it to its source. There are several ways in which you can go about this.

The traditional method of making contact with a wine-grower is to ask your local wine merchant for an introduction. I did this when I first began to buy wine in France. My local merchant contacted several producers on my behalf. The results in France ranged from the distinctly off-hand to a VIP-style reception, proving that this method is no guarantee of a warm welcome but can be a good starting-point.

Most of us buy wine from the supermarket, so what would happen if you contacted Tesco, say, for an introduction to one of its suppliers? I asked all the major supermarkets and high-street chains what their reaction would be if you asked for help. Most said that they would at least supply you with the grower's name and address, although few would go so far as to contact them on your behalf.

This is one area where the independent merchant can probably offer you more help than the high street wine shop or supermarket, but in most cases you are on your own in your investigations. You can also write to the address shown on a wine label; even if it's simply a name and a town, it should get through. Or you can write to the local wine committees. Some of them provide lists or even books of producers who sell direct to the public.

When you're in the region itself you'll drive past plenty of wine estates but how can you spot one worth visiting from the roadside? The first thing to check is that it does sell direct. Without signs such as *dégustation-vente* (tasting-sales), *vente directe* (direct sales) or *dégustation gratuite* (free tasting) you can't be sure that the public is welcome. A lack of these signs doesn't mean the producer definitely won't see you, but proceed with caution. The property may only receive visitors by appointment, and the winemaker may be busy; ask when it would be convenient to come back.

Next, size up the way the estate presents itself. I fight shy of places that proclaim themselves too loudly, with signs and displays such as barrels with bottles on top that shout at you from the roadside. This is pure prejudice on my part, but I prefer an estate which makes a more modest display. If you see a symbol on the display boards which looks like a person in a smock with a barrel for a head, it's a good sign. It means that this is a grower producing and bottling his or her own wine, not a négociant selling other people's produce.

After that, it's down to instinct, gut feeling, call it what you will. Is there a friendly welcome from whoever is on duty? Is the place clean? Are you offered a wine to taste in a decent-sized tasting-glass (shaped like an elongated tulip, called an ISO or INAO glass) or in little ones you can't get your nose into for a proper sniff? Is the winemaker showing you the wines you want or pushing something dearer? You can walk out at any time if the place doesn't look or feel right.

If you find yourself becoming totally hooked and want to brush up your French to have esoteric discussions with producers on the finer points of winemaking, I recommend you buy *Lexivin/Lexiwine* by Paul Cadiau. This is a handy, pocket-sized dictionary giving translations between English and French of useful wine terms. If you want to know the French for crusher-destemmer, this book is for you.

When planning your own routes, the Michelin atlas gives the distances and journey times between major towns. If you devise a route following scenic back roads, remember to allow for the slow progress you'll make at, say, 50–55km per hour. You also need to watch out for the 'same-surname' problem among producers; there are often several winemakers with the same surname in one village, all scions of a single family. First names count. Watch out, too, for *lieux-dits*, 'named villages'; tiny hamlets outside a village with blue roadside signs, shown on the atlas (if at all) in tiny type. Lieu-dit names often sound like house names: if in doubt, get the producer to send you a map (often helpfully included in their brochure).

If you want to stay longer than a few days in a region, consider self-catering accommodation. *Gîtes* are available in all the wine regions, but unfortunately the organizations in the UK which act as agents for them tend not to have much on offer amid the vines. Get round this by writing to the tourist information office in your chosen region and asking it to send you a list of what's available; then book direct. Many towns also offer a list of *gîtes* available locally.

You will also occasionally see signs advertising *chambres d'hôtes*. These offer bed and breakfast, and sometimes evening meals as well, usually eaten around a big table with the family – fine if your French is up to it. A few winemakers also offer bed and breakfast; the local tourist information office or Maison du Vin should be able to help you find them.

I believe you will enjoy the trip no matter what happens or how the visit is arranged. There's so much to discover in wine country, not only bargains bottles but also friendly people, beautiful countryside, good food... Remember *la politesse*, have confidence and, above all, have fun!

Lexivin/Lexiwine by Paul Cadiau; self-published by Paul Cadiau in 1988, ISBN 2 907080 01 06; available from bookshops in the wine regions, Maisons du Vin, etc.

Index

Abbaye de Ste-Radegonde 182-3, 202
Accad, Guy 90
accommodation 15, 16-18, 288
Aligoté 88, 97, 99, 106, 110, 154, 169
Aloxe-Corton 89, 101
Alsace 13, 18, 20, 24, 36-61, *43*, 72, 284
Ambonnay 72, 77, 82
Ambroise, Dom Bertrand 99-100, 114
Amiens 42
Amirault, Yannick 197, 205
Ammerschwihr 39, 54, 60
Ampuis 158-9, 173
Andlau 46-7, 60
Angers 175, 177, 184, 190, 204, 285
Angludet, Ch d' 251, 276
Anjou 175, 184
Anjou Rouge 184, 187, 188, 191
Anjou-Saumur 177, 179, 184-94, *186*, 203-5
Anjou Sec 188
Anjou-Villages 184, 188-9
appellation contrôlée (AC) 32-3
   Alsace 38, 39
   Burgundy 87
   communale 88
Arcelain, Virely 106
Arcins 279
Arnould, Michel 76, 80
Aubance 184, 188
Aube 66-7, 73, 79, 207, 208-14, *208*, 225
autolysis 69
Autoroutes (A roads) 14
Auxerrois 50
Auxey-Duresses 108
Avize 82
Ay 78, 82
Ayala 68, 78, 80

Bailly 219-20
ban de vendange 34
Barge, Dom Gilles 159, 172
Barr 46
Barraques, Les 171
Barraud, Dom Daniel 127, 130
barrel fermentation 68, 76
Barsac 254, 255
Bar-sur-Aube 209, 212-13
Bar-sur-Seine 209, 210
Bas-Rhin 44
Basse-Goulaine 183, 184, 203
bâtonnage 48, 236
Baubigny 108
Baudry, Bernard 195-6, 205
Baumard, Dom des 188, 203
Bayon 274
Beaujeu 143, 149
Beaujolais 84, 132-49, *136*
Beaujolais Blanc 133, 146, 147
Beaujolais, Maison des 145
Beaujolais Nouveau 133, 134, 140
Beaujolais Supérieur 133
Beaujolais-Villages 133, 137, 143
Beaumont, Ch 249-50, 276
Beaune 85, 88, 91, 101-5, 108, 110, 117
Beauregard, Ch de 191, 204
Becker, Jean/Beck, Gaston 51, 58
beer 29
Béhuard 187
Beine 217-18, 227
Bélingard, Ch 263-4, 277
Belleville 144-5, 149
Benais 197-8
Bennwihr 52
Bergerac 231, 238, 258-7, 260, 277-8, 279-80
Bergères-lès-Vertus 79, 83
Bergheim 50, 60
Bethon 79
Beychevelle 249

Bienvenu, Léon 220, 226
Biguet 166
biodynamics 232, 270, 274
blanc de blancs (champagne) 65
blanc de noirs (champagne) 65
Blanche de Bosredon 264
Blanck, Paul, & Fils 53, 58
Blaye 238, 274-5, 279, 280
Bollinger 82
Bon Gran, Dom de la 123
Bonhomme, Dom André 122, 130
Bonnes Mares 97
Bonnet, Ch 252
Bonneteau-Guesslin 180-1, 202
Bonnezeaux 188
Bordeaux 10, 12, 13, 19, 229-80
Bordeaux Supérieur 258
Bordepaille 257-8
Botrytis cinerea see noble rot
'bottle sickness' 133
Bouilland 101, 117
Bouliac 256, 279
Boulogne 282
Bourg 238, 274-5, 279
Bourgeois, Henri 222, 227
Bourgogne Aligoté 88
Bourgogne Aligoté de Bouzeron 110
Bourgogne Blanc 88
Bourgogne Chardonnay 97, 219
Bourgogne Côtes d'Auxerre 219
Bourgogne Grand Ordinaire 87
Bourgogne Passetoutgrains 88
Bourgogne Rouge 88, 99, 111, 119
Bourgognes Bersan 219, 226
Bourgueil 175, 194, 195, 197-8
Bouvet-Ladubay 193, 204
Bouzeron 88, 110
Bouzy 66, 77
Bouzy Rouge 77
Braillon, Guy 138, 148
Breton 194
Briday, Dom Michel 111, 116
Brocard, Dom Jean-Marc 218-19, 226
Brouilly 135, 143, 144
Bru, Ch du 258, 277
Brun de Neuville, Le 79, 80, 210

Burgundy 13, 33, 72, 84-117, *94*, 118, 207, 284
Bussières 125-6
Buxy 85, 111-12

Cabernet Franc 21, 175, 184, 194, 200, 201, 234
Cabernet de Saumur Rosé 191
Cabernet Sauvignon 21, 184, 194, 233
Cadillac 255
Caen 284, 285
Cahors 259
Calais 13, 14, 281-3
Cantegrive, Ch 268, 278
carbonic maceration 132
Castellane, De 81
Castillon 259, 267
Cave Coopérative La Chablisienne 216, 225
Cave Coopérative Clairette de Die 168-9, 173
Cave des Producteurs des Grands Vins de Fleurie 141, 148
Cave de Tain l'Hermitage 162-3, 172
Cave des Vignerons d'Igé 124, 130
Cave Vinicole de Kientzheim/ Kaysersberg 53-4, 58-9
Cave Yves Cuilleron 160-1, 172
Caveau l'Eglise de Domange 130
Caves de Bailly 219-20, 226
Caves de Cheilly 109, 115
Caves des Hautes-Côtes 105, 115
Caves des Hautes de Gironde 275
Caves des Vignerons de Buxy 111, 116
Cellier Chablisien, Le 217, 226
Centre Oenologique des Côtes du Rhône 165
Cercié 144
Chablis 16, 33, 84, 207, 214-21, *217*, 225-7
Chagny 108, 109, 117
Chaintré 129, 137
Chambertin 89, 93, 95, 96
Chambertin Clos de Bèze 93
Chambolle-Musigny 97

Chamirey, Ch de 112, 116

Champagne 13, 21, 34, 35, 42, 45, 62-83, *74*, 93, 207, 208-14, *208*

Champalou, Catherine and Didier 200, 205

Champs-sur-Yonne 219, 227

Champy Père & Cie 103-4, 115

Channel tunnel 282-3

Chanos-Curson 167

Chantegrive, Ch de 253, 277

Chaource 214

Chapelle-de-Guinchay, La 138

Chapoutier, M 162, 164, 173

chaptalization 68-9

Chardonnay 21, 65, 76, 79, 85, 88, 119, 133, 154, 155, 214, 219

Chardonnay (village) 122

Charmes-Chambertin 89, 93

Charmes-Godard, Ch 268

Charnay 127

Chassagne-Montrachet 89, 107

Chasselas 38, 41, 221, 224

Chassey-le-Camp 109, 117

Château-Grillet 151, 152, 160

Château-Thierry 79, 83

Châtillon-en-Diois 169, 170

Chaudefonds-sur-Layon 189

Chauveau, Dom Daniel 196, 205

Chavanay 161, 173

Chavignol 222, 228

Cheilly-lès-Maranges 108, 109

Chénas 134, 138

Chenin Blanc 21, 175, 184, 185, 188, 195, 200

Cherbourg 285

Chéreau-Carré 181-2, 202

Chevalier de Sterimberg 166

Chiche 218

Chinon 175, 194, 195-6, 206

Chiroubles 135, 141-2, 149

Chorey-lès-Beaune 100-1

Clairet 233, 236, 251, 257

Clairette Brut 169

Clairette de Die 168-9

Clape, Auguste 165, 173

claret 151, 233

Clessé 119

Clevner 40

Clisson 182, 202

cloning vines 33

Clos de la Coulée de Serrant 185, 203

Clos du Fief, Dom du 137, 148

Clos Rousseau 108

Clos St-Landelin 57

Clos St-Marc, Dom du 155, 172

Clos de Tart 97

Clos de Vougeot 84, 87, 97-8

Clos de Vougeot, Ch du 97, 98, 103, 114

Clos Windsbühl 55

Closel, Dom du 187, 203

Clouet, André 77, 80

Clusel-Roch, Dom 158, 172

Colin, Fabien 224

Colinot, Jean-Pierre 220, 226

Colmar 37, 55-6, 60-1

Colombey-les-deux-Eglises 213

Colombo, Jean-Luc 165-6, 173

colour 20

Condrieu 151, 152, 155, 158, 160-1, 173

Confrérie des Chevaliers du Tastevin 97

Confrérie de St-Etienne 53

Coopérative de Manipulation (CM) 65

Cormatin 120

Cornas 153, 163-4, 165-6, 174

Corsin, Dom 127, 130

Corton 100

Corton-Charlemagne 100, 101

Cos d'Estournel, Ch 235, 246, 276

Cot 201

Côte des Bars 209-14

Côte de Beaune 91, 100

Côte de Beaune-Villages 88

Côte des Blancs 66, 79, 209

Côte Blonde 153

Côte de Brouilly 135, 144

Côte Brune 153

Côte Chalonnaise 84, 85, 88, 91, 93, 109-13

Côte-Montpezat, Ch 267, 278

Côte de Nuits 85, 91, 93, 100
Côte de Nuits-Villages 88
Côte d'Or 84, 85, 88, 90, 92, 93–109
Côte-Rôtie 153, 158, 159, 161
Côtes de Bergerac 260, 262
Côtes de Bergerac Moelleux 261
Côtes de Castillon 238, 267-8, 278
Côtes de Francs 238, 267-8, 278
Côtes de Montravel 260
Côtes du Rhône 151-2, 155, 158, 160, 165-6
Côtes du Rhône Parallèle 45 166
Coteaux de l'Aubance 188
Coteaux d'Ancenis 184
Coteaux Champenois 66
Coteaux du Layon 184, 187, 189
Coteaux du Lyonnais 146-7, 154-5
Court-les-Mûts, Ch 263, 277
Cravant-les-Coteaux 195, 196
Cray 123
Crémant d'Alsace 41, 52, 54
Crémant de Bordeaux 233
Crémant de Bourgogne 88, 120, 123, 220
Crémant de Die 169
Crémant de Loire 193, 200-1
crème de cassis 88, 147
Créon 257
Creysse 265-6
Croix Blanche, La 125, 131
Croix de Gay, Ch La 272, 278
Crozes-Hermitage 151, 154, 161, 162-3, 166, 167
Cru Bourgeois 243, 245, 251
Cubnezais 275
Cussac 249
cuvaison 235
cuvée 68
cuve égoutteuse 163
Cuvée Prestige 111
Cuvée de Prestige (champagne) 66
Cuvée Spéciale 39

Dambach-la-Ville 48
Dauvissat, René & Vincent 216-17, 225

Davayé 127
Deiss, Marcel 50, 58
Delbeck 75, 80
Départmentale (D) roads 14
Desmures, Anne-Marie and Armand 142, 148
Deux Roches, Dom des 127, 131
Die 167-70, 174
Dieppe 285
Dijon 85
Dom Pérignon 62-3, 66
Domptin 83
Dopff & Irion 52, 58
dosage 63, 70
Dover 281-2
Drappier, André 211-12, 225
Droin, Jean-Paul 216, 225
Drouhin 87
Druet, Pierre-Jacques 197-8, 205
Duboeuf, Georges 137, 138, 139-40, 141, 142, 148, 154
Duboeuf, Roger 129, 131
Dujac, Dom 95-7, 114
Dunkerque 282
Duras 259
Dutertre, Dom 200-1, 205

Echelle des Crus 67
Ecomusée 269
Echézeaux 98
Edelzwicker 41, 52
Eguisheim 56, 61
élevage 86
Emeringes 149
Entre-deux-Mers 238, 255-8, 277
Entrefaux, Dom des 167, 173
en vrac 28
Epernay 66, 72-3, 78, 81, 82
Epfig 48
Epiré 185
Essoyes 213
Euroroutes (E roads) 14

facture 26
Falfas, Ch 274-5, 279
Faures, Les 257
Fayolle, Dom 161, 172

Felixstowe 283
Ferme d'Angludet, La 251
fermentation 23-4, 89-90, 132-3
ferries 10, 13-14, 281-5
Ferronnière, Dom de la 180
Fesles, Ch de 190-1
Fiefs de Lagrange, Les 249
Figeac, Ch 271-2, 278
filtration 23, 24-5, 125
Fine de Bourgogne 122
fining 24, 95, 235
Fixin 93, 116
Flagey-Echézeaux 98, 116
Flaujagues 266-7, 280
Fleur de Gay, Ch La 272, 278
Fleurie 135, 141, 149
Fleys 218
Folie, Dom de la 110, 115
Folkestone 282
Froehn 51
Fronsac 238, 273-4
Fuissé 119, 128-9, 131
Fuissé, Ch de 128-9, 131

Gaillan-en-Médoc 244, 279
Gamay 87, 119, 123, 124, 126, 132,
    133, 154, 155, 183, 184, 200,
    201
Gamay (village) 107
Gamay de Touraine 195
Garaudet, Jean 106
Gaudard, Dom 189, 203
Gauriac 280
Geoffroy, Alain 217-18, 226
Gerin, Dom 158, 172
Germain, Dom Jacques 100-1, 114
Germain, Maison Jean 106, 115
Gervans 161
Gevrey-Chambertin 89, 91, 93, 95,
    99, 116
Gewurztraminer 21, 38, 40, 48, 49,
    55
Gillet, Dom Emilian 123
gîtes 288
Givry 110, 111, 113, 117
Golden Triangle 67, 79, 176, 207-
    28, 208, 217, 222

Grand Cru
    Alsace 38, 39, 52, 53
    Burgundy 88-9
    Chablis 215
    St-Emilion 269
Grand Cru Classé 269
Grand Ordinaire 99
Grands Goulets 171
Grand Vin de Bourgogne 89
Grandes Marques 65, 81-3
Grands Echézeaux 98
Granges-lès-Beaumont 167, 174
grape varieties 33
Gratien & Meyer 78, 192, 193-4,
    204
Gratien, Alfred 68, 78, 80
Graves 238, 251, 252-5, 259, 276-7
Graves Supérieur 252
Gresser, Dom 47, 58
Gresser, Rémy 34
Gros Plant 177, 182
Gros Plant du Pays Nantais 177
Gueux 75

Haie-Fouassière, La 180
Hameau du Vin 118, 129, 139-40,
    141
harvesting 34-5
Harwich 283
Haut Bernasse, Ch 264, 277
Haut-Bernat, Ch 267
Haut-Bertinerie, Ch la 275, 279
Haut-Brion, Ch 232, 243
Haut-Koenigsbourg 50
Haut-Médoc 244, 250
Haut-Montravel 260
Haut-Rhin 44, 48
Haut-Segottes, Ch 272, 278
Hautes Côtes 92
Hautes Côtes de Beaune 85, 88, 99,
    101
Hautes Côtes de Nuits 88
Haux 256-7
Haux, Ch de 257, 277
Hermitage 151, 154, 161-4, 166
Hermitage La Chapelle 162, 166
Hinsingen 45-6, 59

Hook 283
Hospices de Beaune 102-3
Hôtel-Dieu (Beaune) 102
hovercraft 282
Hull 13, 284
Husseren-les-Châteaux 56

Igé 124
insurance 15
Irancy 90, 220
Itterswiller 37, 47-8, 60

Jaboulet Ainé, Paul 162, 163, 166-7, 173
Jacques Blanc, Ch 268, 270, 278
Jadot, Louis 87, 104
Jambles 111
Janoueix 229
Jasmin, E.A.R.L. 158-9, 172
Jouy-lès-Reims 76
Juillot, Michel 112
Juliénas 134, 137-8, 149

Kaefferkopf 39, 54
Kaysersberg 37, 53-4
Kientzheim 52-4, 60
Kir 88
Kir Royal 88, 120
Klein aux Vieux Remparts 48-9, 58
Klevner 40
Klevner de Heiligenstein 40, 46
Klipfel, Dom 40, 46, 58
Krug 68
Kuentz-Bas 56, 59

Laclaverie, Ch 268
Lacondemine, Vincent 143, 148
Lagrange, Ch 249-50, 276
Landiras 253-4
Langlois-Château 193, 204
Langoiran 255-6, 279
Langoiran, Ch 255-6, 277
Lapierre, Hubert 138, 148
Laporte 222
Latour 87
Layon 184, 188
Le-Bois-d'Oingt 146

Le Havre 13, 284
Léognan 251, 252, 279
lieux-dit 39, 49, 288
Limeray 200-1
liquoreux 261
Listrac 244
Loché 119
Loire valley 13-14, 35, 175-206, 181, 186, 197, 199, 207, 284, 285
Louvière, Ch la 252-3, 276
Louvois 77
Lugny 119
Lurton, André 229, 252-3
Lynch-Bages, Ch 248, 276

Mâcon 127-8, 131
Mâcon Blanc 119
Mâcon Blanc Supérieur 119
Mâcon Chardonnay 122, 143
Mâcon Rouge 119
Mâcon Supérieur 119
Mâcon-Villages 119, 126, 127
Mâcon-Viré 122
Mâconnais 84, 118-31, 121
Mâconnaise des Vins, Maison 127-8
Malandes, Dom des 217, 226
Malle, Ch de 255
Mallevieille, Ch de la 266, 278
malolactic fermentation 24, 69, 133
Maranges 109
Marbuzet, Ch de 246
Marc de Bourgogne 122
Marcillac 275
Mardon, Dom 223, 227
Maréchal, Dom Jean 111, 116
Mareuil-sur-Cher 201
Margaux 244, 250-1
Marlenheim 46
Marne 66
Marque d'Acheteur (MA) 65
Marsanne 151, 153
Médoc 237, 238, 239-52, 240-1, 259, 276
Médoc AC 244
Mellot, Dom Joseph 223, 227
Melon de Bourgogne 177

Menetou-Salon 201, 221, 223
Mercier 81
Mercurey 110, 111, 117
Merlot 233, 269
Merrey-sur-Arce 210
Mesnil-sur-Oger, Le 79, 83
Meulière, Dom de la 218, 226
Meursault 103, 106, 107, 108, 117
Meursault, Ch de 106, 115
Meyer, Jos 55, 59
Miaudoux, Ch Les 262–3, 277
Michel, Dom Ren 123, 130
Michelin maps and guides 14–15, 30, 31
Mittelbergheim 46
Mittelwihr 52
moelleux 261, 262
Moët & Chandon 65, 66, 78, 81
Moines, Dom aux 185, 187, 203
Monbazillac 261, 264, 280
Monbazillac, Ch de 264
Monestier 261-2
Montagne 269-70
Montagne de Reims 66, 75-6, 77
Montagny 111
Monthélie 99, 108
Montlouis 175, 200
Montrachet 107
Montravel 260
Mont-Ste-Odile 46
Morey-St-Denis 95-7
Morgon 135, 142-3
Morogues 201, 223
Morot, Dom Albert 104-5, 115
Mortet, Dom Denis 93-4, 114
Moueix 229-30
Moulin à Vent 134, 138
Moulin à Vent, Dom du 253-4, 277
Moulin de Beauregard 224
Moulin de Chauvigné 187
Moulis 244
Mouton-Rothschild, Ch 239, 243, 247, 276
Mouzillon 182
Mozé-sur-Louet 188
Mulhouse 42

Muré, René 57, 59
Muscadelle 234
Muscadet 13, 20, 175, 177-9, 180-3, 184
Muscadet des Coteaux de la Loire 178
Muscadet Côtes de Grand Lieu 178
Muscadet de Sèvre et Maine 178, 180
Muscat 38, 40, 168
Musée Animé du Vin et de la Tonnellerie 195, 205
Musée d'Aquitaine 251
Musée des Chartrons 251
Musée de la Vigne et du Vin 189, 203
Musée du Vigneron 269
Musée du Vin de Bourgogne 103
Mussidan 266
Mussy, Dom André 105-6, 115
must 68

Nancy 57
Nantes 177, 179-80, 183, 202
Nantes, Maison des Vins de 180, 202
négociant 86-7, 103-4, 229
Négociant-Distributeur (ND) 64
Négociant-Manipulant (NM) 65
Newhaven 285
Nitry 218, 227
noble rot 38, 188, 254
Noirot, Dom Michel 213-14, 225
non-vintage (NV) 66, 70
Nuits-St-Georges 93, 99, 116

oak barrels 23-4, 68, 90, 96, 120, 126, 138, 165, 216
Obernai 46
Oingt 146
Orches 108
organic cultivation 47, 253, 262
Orléans 176
Ostend 285
Ostertag, Dom 48, 58
Ottrott 46
ouillage 234

Pallus 196, 205
Palmer, Ch 251
Palotte 219, 220
Panisseau, Ch de 262, 277
paperwork 26, 96
Parnay 194
Patriarche Père & Fils 103, 106, 115
Pauillac 244, 247-8, 279
Pavie-Macquin, Ch 270, 278
payment, methods of 26
Pays Nantais 175, 177-83, *181*, 202-3
Pécharmant 260, 266
Pellé, Henry 223, 227
Pernand-Vergelesses 101
Perreau, Dom de 267, 278
Perrier-Jouët 81
Pessac-Léognan 252-3
Peters, Pierre 79, 80
Petit Chablis 215, 216, 218
Petit-Pierre, La 45, 59
Petit Verdot 234
Pétrus, Ch 229, 236
Peynaud 232
Phylloxera vastatrix 86
Picq, Gilbert, et Ses Fils 218, 226
Pierreclos 126
Pierres Dorées 145
pigeage 89-90, 105, 112, 197, 220
Pineau de la Loire 175
Pinot Auxerrois 38, 40, 41
Pinot Blanc 38, 40, 41, 48, 50, 55, 88
Pinot Gris 38, 40, 48
Pinot Meunier 65, 66
Pinot Noir 21, 38, 41, 65, 76, 77, 85, 88, 89, 119, 124, 209, 210, 220
Piper-Heidsieck 81
Piron, Dominique 142-3, 148
Pizay 144, 149
Plymouth 285
Podensac 253
Pomerol 233, 238, 259, 272-3, 278
Pommard 105, 108
Pommard, Ch de 105, 115
Pommery 81
Pomport 263
Port-de-By 245
Porte-Ste-Foy 266
Portsmouth 13, 284
Pouilly 119, 126
Pouilly-Fuissé 127-9
Pouilly-Fumé 221, 223, 224
Pouilly-sur-Loire 176, 195, 221-4, *222*, 227-8
Préhy 218-19
Preignac 255
Premeaux-Prissey 99-100
Premier Cru
    Bordeaux 243
    Burgundy 88-9
    Chablis 215
Premières Côtes 257
Premières Côtes de Blaye 275
Premier Grand Cru Classé 269
press 23
Prieur, Dom Jacques 106-7, 112, 116
Prieur-Brunet, Dom 108, 115
Prieuré-Lichine, Ch 250-1, 276
Prissé 119
Prudhon, Dom Henri, & Fils 107, 115
pruning vines 34
Puligny 107
Puligny-Montrachet 89, 107
pupitre 63
Puygueraud, Ch 268, 278
Puy-Notre-Dame, La 191

Quarts de Chaume 188
Quincy 221, 223
Quintaine 123
QWPSR 32

Ramsgate 282, 285
Récoltant (R) 64
Récoltant-Coopérateur (RC) 64
Récoltant-Manipulant (RM) 64
Régnié 135
Reims 42, 66, 72-3, 75, 77, 81, 82
remuage 63, 70
Renaudie, Dom de la 201, 205
Réserve 39

Ressaudie, Ch la 266, 278
Reuilly 221, 223
Rhône 12, 13, 150-74, *156-7*, *168*, 284
Ribeauvillé 51, 60
Riceys, Les 66, 213-14
Richard, Ch 261-2, 277
Richou, Dom 184, 188-9, 203
Riesling 18, 21, 36, 38, 39, 47, 48, 55
Riesling Schlossreben 49
Rieussec, Ch 254-5
Rigoles du Pin, Dom des 182, 202
Rilly-la-Montagne 76
Rion, Dom Armelle & Bernard 98-9, 114
Riquewihr 52
Robert, Alain 79, 80
Roche-aux-Moines, La 185
Rochebonne, Ch de 145-6
Rochebonne, Dom de 146, 148
Rochefort-sur-Loire 187-8, 189
Roche de Glun, La 166
Rochepot, La 107
Roches-Neuves, Dom des 194, 204
Roche-Vineuse, La 124-5
Rodet, Antonin 106-7, 111, 112, 116
Roederer, Louis 81
Rolland 232
Rolly Gassmann 40, 50, 58
Romanèche-Thorins 118, 139-40, 149
Romanée-Conti 98
Romanée-Conti, Dom de la 110
Rorschwihr 50
Roscoff 285
Rosé des Riceys 66, 214
Rosette 261
Rosiers, Les 192, 205
Rotterdam 284
Rouge de St-Hippolyte 49
Roussanne 151
Route des Crêtes 44
Routes Nationales (N roads) 14
Rully 109-10, 111, 117
Rully, Ch de 111, 112, 116
Saget, Guy 223-4, 227

St-Amour 134, 137
St-Aubin 107
St-Bris-le-Vineux 219
St-Ciers-de-Canesse 275, 280
St-Emilion 231, 238, 259, 268, 269-72, 278, 280
St-Estèphe 244, 246
St-Etienne-de-Lisse 268, 270
St-Fiacre-sur-Maine 181
Ste-Foy-la-Grande 258
St-Gengoux-le-National 113
Ste-Germaine 212
St-Hilaire-St-Florent 193
St-Hippolyte 48-9, 60, 270
St-Jean 111
St-Joseph 151, 153, 161
St-Julien 244, 249
St-Lambert-du-Lattay 189-90
St-Laurent-d'Oingt 146
St-Malo 13, 284
St-Martin 111
St-Martin-d'Auxigny 201
St-Nexans 265
St-Nicolas-de-Bourgueil 194, 197
St-Péray 153, 166
St-Romain 108
St-Romain-sur-Cher 201
St-Véran 120, 126, 127
St-Verand 146
St-Vincent, Dom 194, 204
Sancerre 18, 176, 177, 195, 207, 221-4, *222*, 227-8
Sancerre Rouge 222
Santenay 85, 108
Sarazinère, Dom de la 126, 130
Saumur 175, 177, 184, 190, 191-3, 194, 195, 196, 198, 204-5
Saumur-Champigny 184, 194, 195
Saussignac 261, 262, 263, 279
Sauternes 238, 254, 279
Sauveroy, Dom du 189, 203
Sauveterre 257
Sauvignon 184, 234
Sauvignon Blanc 18, 21, 176, 195, 221
Sauvignon de St-Bris 32, 219
Sauvignon de Touraine 195, 200

Savagnin 40
Savennières 184, 185, 186, 187, 189
Savigny-lès-Beaune 101, 116-17
Schlossreben 49
Schoffit, Robert 59
SeaCat 282
Sea Lynx 283
Sélection des Grains Nobles 38, 40
Sélestat 49, 60
self-catering accommodation 288
Sémillon 234
semi-maceration 133
Sennecé-lès-Mâcon 128, 131
Serrières 161, 173
Sézannais 66
Sézanne 79
Sheerness 283
Sick-Dreyer 54, 59
Société de Récoltant (SR) 65
Sonnay 195-6
Sorrel, Marc 163-4, 173
soutirage 235
spirits 29
Strasbourg 42, 45, 59-60
sur lie 177-8
Sylvaner 38, 41, 51, 55
Syrah 151, 152, 153, 160

taille 68
Tain l'Hermitage 154, 162-5, 166,
    167, 173-4
Taluyers 155
Targé, Ch de 194, 204
tastevin 103
tasting 20-2
    glasses 287
terroir 32, 33, 42, 47
tête de cuvée 212
Thalabert, Dom 166
Thann 42
Thannenkirch 49-50, 60
Theizé 145-6
Thénard, Dom 113, 116
Thévenet, Dom Jean 123-4, 130
Thévenet, Jean-Claude 126, 130
Thiers, Jean-Louis 166, 173
Thouarcé 188, 190

Tinel-Blondelet 224, 227
Tiregand, Ch de 265-6, 278
Tokay Geisberg 49
Tokay Pinot Gris 38, 40
Tollot-Beaut & Fils, Dom 100, 114
Tonnerre 214
Tour, Ch de la 98, 101, 114
Touraine 175, 176, 177, 194-201,
    197, 199, 205-6
Touraine-Amboise 200
Tour de By, Ch la 245-6, 276
Tour de Langoiran, Ch 255-6
Tournus 120, 122, 131
Tours 177, 195, 198, 206, 285
Tradition 168, 201
traditional methods 41, 67
training vines 34
'Trois Glorieuses' 103
Troyes 209-10, 213, 225
Tuilerie du Puy, Ch la 257-8, 277
Tupin 159-60
Turckheim 54-5

Union Auboise 210-11, 225
Urville 211-12

Vallée de la Marne 66, 78
Varrains 194
Vassieux-en-Vercors 171
Vaux-en-Beaujolais 145
VDQS 32
Vendange Tardive 38, 39, 49
vendange verte 34
vente directe 44-5, 287
Vercors 170-1
Vérenay 155, 158
Vergisson 127
Verlieu 160-1
Vernay, Georges 159-60, 172
Verret et Ses Fils, GAEC du Parc
    219, 226
Vertus 79, 83
Verzenay 76
Veuve A Devaux 210
Veuve Clicquot 62-3
Vieille Cure, Ch 273-4
vieilles vignes 34

Vieux St-Sorlin, Dom du 124-5, 130
Vignoble la Grande Borie 265, 277
village 88
Villaine, A & P de 110, 115
Ville-en-Bois, La 182-3
Villefranche-sur-Saône 147, 149
Villié-Morgon 142, 149
Vilmart & Cie 68, 76, 80
Vincelottes 220, 227
vin de paille 164
vin de pays 32
vin de table 32
vintage 35
Vinzelles 119
Viognier 151, 152, 153, 160-1
Viré 119, 122
Vissoux, Dom 146-7, 149
Vlissingen 283

Volnay 106
Vosne-Romanée 98
Vougeot 97-8
Voûte des Crozes, Dom de la 144, 148
Vouvray 175, 195, 198, 200, 206

Westhalten 57, 61
winemaking techniques 23-5
Wintzenheim 55

yields 34
Yquem, Ch d' 254

Zeebrugge 13, 283, 284
Zellenberg 51-2, 60
Zind-Humbrecht 41, 54-5, 59, 124

ACKNOWLEDGMENTS

The author gratefully acknowledges the assistance of: Andrew Barraclough, Nelly Blau, Christian Chabirand, Sam Gordon Clark, Brigitte Coquard, Michel Deflache, Roselyne Delaunay, Monique Denoune, Anne Dewe, Claire Duchene, Michael Edwards, Tony Farrell, Elizabeth Gabay, Caroline Gestin, Martine Greslom, John P Harris, Didier Krieg, Dominique Lambry, Christopher Laming, Pat Lapins, Sophie Legrus, Anne Mathon, Sandrine Perroud, Elizabeth Powell, Nick Stevens, Kate Teesdale, Nicolas Thienpont, Sophie Vallejo, Véronique Vallenot, Christine Whaite, Dave Wilson, Edward Wright, and Joyce Wright.